WHEN IT'S LAUGHTER YOU'RE AFTER

WHEN IT'S LAUGHTER YOU'RE AFTER

by Stewart Harral

University of Oklahoma Press: *Norman*

BOOKS BY STEWART HARRAL

When It's Laughter You're After (Norman, 1962)
The Feature Writer's Handbook (Norman, 1959)
Profitable Public Relations for Newspapers (Ann Arbor, 1957)
Keys to Successful Interviewing (Norman, 1954)
Patterns of Publicity Copy (Norman, 1950)
Tested Public Relations for Schools (Norman, 1953)
Profitable Public Relations for Cosmetologists (National Association of Cosmetology Schools, New York, 1956)
Successful Letters for Churches (New York and Nashville, 1946)
Public Relations for Churches (New York and Nashville, 1945)
Public Relations for Higher Education (Norman, 1942)
Publicity Problems (editor) (American College Public Relations Association, Washington, 1940)
Pathways to Public Favor (Oklahoma City, 1962)

STANDARD BOOK NUMBER: 8061-0532-1

LIBRARY OF CONGRESS CATALOG CARD NUMBER: 62-16472

Copyright 1962 by the University of Oklahoma Press, Publishing Division of the University. Manufactured in the U.S.A. First edition, August, 1962. Second printing, February, 1963. Third printing, January, 1965. Fourth printing, October, 1969.

Gratefully Dedicated to George Lynn Cross

Acknowledgments

THOUSANDS OF PEOPLE—both great and small—have helped write this book. It was sparked by people—people who often remarked wistfully, "I wish I could get laughs when *I* talk." And it came into being largely because many wonderful masters of mirth were kind enough to share some of their fun-producing secrets.

This guidebook and manual represents years of research in the psychology of humor, backed by my own personal experiences, some of them not so funny—with the more than three thousand audiences I've faced in forty-two states and Canada.

Ever since Mr. Caveman scraped some cartoons on the wall of his abode, men have recorded their humorous ideas. But my publishers have emphasized that if I tried to give proper credit to everyone whose idea I've used, there wouldn't be room for anything else but the index.

I want to thank particularly Dwight Swain for his expert help in editing the manuscript, and Martha Garrett for typing assistance. I am especially indebted to Ron Carver who granted permission to use devices, forms, and approaches to comedy from the *Manual on Humor* which he wrote for writers and designers at Hallmark Cards, Incorporated. Writings of Leonard Hole on the psychology of humor proved most valuable.

Finally, I'd like to thank the countless unknown and anonymous people who first thought up the thousands of jokes used in this book. They made me laugh before you had this chance to read them!

STEWART HARRAL

Norman, Oklahoma

What This Book Will Do for You

GET A LAUGH and you've got an audience!

Yes, you'll get a thrill, a never ending thrill, when audiences respond in waves of laughter as your material, your timing, your personality—everything that makes you unique—are tuned to a high professional degree.

Easy to do? "The business of making people laugh is the toughest in the world," declares George Q. Lewis. The "life of the party" jokester whom you admire is a lonely and solitary toiler. He works in solitude, without counsel or advice. Catch him at his typewriter as he slaves to turn out a quip, and he looks about as hilarious as a morgue keeper. As soon as he's worked out some jokes for his next speech, he begins to wonder: "Could I have picked newer gags?" "Is this the right slant?" "Could the blending be done more smoothly?" "What about those punch lines?" "Why didn't I give more attention to the theme?" Doubts assail him like ants attacking a picnic cake, and by the time he has a few notes ready he envisages the audience as a many-headed monster. He fears the terrible silence when a gag falls flat—a silence so profound you'd be able to hear it for blocks.

"What did you think of the program?" I heard one man ask another one night after one of my talks. His friend's answer was a classic: "Never has anyone gone so far on so little." In Dallas a dear woman gushed, "You know, Mr. Harral, I'm so nervous and jittery. But when you talk you seem so unconscious."

Once in Louisville I arose to speak and noticed something wrong with the audience—it wasn't there. So I turned to a meek-looking little man who'd wandered up onto the platform with me and said, "Let's go."

He looked even sicker than I felt. "I'm sorry, Mr. Harral, I can't do that."

"Why not?"

"I'm the next speaker."

Once you get out on the circuit, you'll meet masters of ceremonies who can drag out enough whiskered gags to fill a half-hour television comedy in introducing each person on the program. And at banquets you'll be served celery sticks so weak that they have splints on them.

Now from all this you might imagine that a humorist's life is brief, that he falls prey to some fatal illness. And you'd be correct except for the fact that no germ could possibly stand the hours a funnyman keeps or the food he eats. He keeps going by taking out time to get his ulcers retreaded. And he often cries himself to sleep worrying over what's funny—to you.

In brief, then, this business of making people laugh is a mighty grim one. Which is why this book isn't written in a jovial tone even though you'll find jokes and wisecracks aplenty used as illustrations. The psychology of humor is too complex and tricky for anyone to laugh about. It involves too many variables, too many subtle factors that go to create that unique quality of feeling which is humor: the inner awareness of a specialized bodily response to special situations.

Still, there are valuable, specific secrets you can learn. For at root, good humorous speaking is two things: (1) wise use of techniques and psychological devices, plus (2) a speaker's flair for humor—his creative ability. Mix these two ingredients in the right proportion, and the result is a socko performance.

That's why your speaking can't help but improve when you make use of this "how to" book, a collection of tested ideas, devices, and strategies used by noted comics, after-dinner speakers, comedy writers, humorous lecturers, master of ceremonies, television personalities, and other funnymen who have learned the secret of making audiences chuckle.

Here are things like: how big-name humorists break down audience resistance; tested ways of blending jokes into situations; tips for making smooth transitions from the ridiculous to the sublime; sources of fresh and usable humor; ways to gain rapport with your audience; pointers for pretesting humor; and specific ways of writing your own material.

Armed with these keys, you can learn to look at everyday situations and turn them into laugh-provoking ideas. You'll develop a humorous change of pace so that you can face audiences with complete confidence in your ability to win acceptance and approval, and get laughs.

Above all, the special treasury of more than 4,000 laugh-getters, "For Laughing Out Loud," contains a wide variety of ready-to-use items—jokes, gags, definitions, one-liners, boners, cartoon quips, illustrative stories, proverbs, epigrams—which you can profitably use in scores of speech situations.

Your reward for your perseverance? For one thing, you'll get a kick out of the fact that you replace fear with faith in this beatnik, bored, bearded generation—a generation that needs to keep alive its sense of humor and direction. What keeps Red Skelton working so feverishly in such a grueling business? "If I can make people smile," he says, "then I have served my purpose for God." Like the noted redhead, you'll probably get the deep feeling that comes from your mission of mirth.

So, have at it; whether you are an amateur or a veteran, it will send your skill zooming. This is a "how to" book, not a book of theory. Rightly used it will show you laugh-producing techniques that are powerful and effective because they are psychologically sound. But only if you do your part. You must be willing to work at the job—to go up, over, and beyond. Keep going and you'll keep your funny bone growing. Have fun, and may all your audiences leave you laughing!

Contents

WHEN IT'S LAUGHTER YOU'RE AFTER

CHAPTER 1

What's Funny and Why

WHAT IS IT that actually makes you laugh? Have you ever asked yourself just why you giggle, chuckle, or roar happily and continuously at one humorist and turn away irritably from another one?

Just what causes a person to laugh is something of a mystery. One night, after a speaking engagement in St. Louis, I was riding in a taxi with another passenger who kept chuckling to himself.

I asked, "Excuse me, but what are you laughing at?"

"You'd really like to know?" he answered.

"Yes, I would."

"It's like this," he explained. "I was just telling myself some jokes and I just told myself one I'd never heard before."

Analysts have had their go at humor, and you can read their findings without being greatly instructed. "Humor can be dissected like a frog," someone remarked, "but the thing dies in the process and the innards are discouraging to any but the purely scientific mind." Or in seeking humor's inside workings we may be like the little boy who tore up the bellows to see where the wind came from.

Hazlitt observed that man is the only animal that laughs and weeps, for he is the only animal that is stuck with the difference between what things are and what they ought to be.

Goethe said that there is no more significant index of a man's character than the things he finds laughable. One man's prize jest is another's abhorrence. For some a smashing, well-played pun is the height of humor. For others to think that a jest is worth its salt it must involve some delightfully devilish reference to sex or wrongdoing. Other individuals prefer the merry tale that visualizes the dignified gentleman taking a sudden fall. Some like the slapstick; some like the burlesque; some the sophisticated.

Even Aristotle Had a Theory

Many philosophers have given us all-embracing definitions of humor, but none is entirely satisfactory. Aristotle defined the ridiculous as that which is incongruous but represents neither danger or pain. His definition came to be known as the Disappointment Theory, or the Frustrated Expectation. He also discussed another theory, borrowed in part from Plato, which states that the pleasure we derive in laughing is an enjoyment of the misfortunes of others, due to a momentary feeling of superiority or gratified vanity that we ourselves are not in the predicament observed.

And you'll recall that Shakespeare said in *Love's Labour's Lost*, "A jest's prosperity lies in the ear of him who hears it. Never in the tongue of him who makes it."

Basically, much of our humor comes from a playful sense of those contrasts we call incongruities. An incongruity is something out of proportion, out of its true relations. In his *Influencing Human Behavior*, H. A. Overstreet reminds us that "Life is full of incongruities. People are constantly exaggerating their own importance; saying one thing and doing another; making mountains out of molehills. Most of us solemnly note these incongruities; get irritated at them; condemn them; scoff at them. The humorist, on the other hand, gives a flip of exaggeration; and the irritating situation is transformed into laughter."

Immanuel Kant defined the cause of laughter as "The sudden transformation of a strained expectation into nothing"—or in other words, as reaching after something and finding it is not there.

Actually, the definitions of Aristotle and Kant are not too different. They merely describe the two ways in which things can be unpleasant. They can be unpleasant because they offend our sensibilities (Aristotle) or because they frustrate our impulses (Kant).

Will Rogers Wasn't Sure

"I don't know what humor is," Will Rogers said. "Anything that's funny—tragedy or anything, it don't make no difference so you happen to hit it just right. But there's one thing I'm proud of—I ain't got it in for anybody. I don't like to make jokes that hurt anybody."

"All I know about humor," Fred Allen said in Maurice Zolotow's *No People Like Show People*, "is that I don't know anything about it. Some bright boy over at NBC once told me there were only thirty-two basic jokes. Another bright boy reduced it to eleven. Somebody else has it down to two—comparison and exaggeration. Whatever it is, it never changes."

You may laugh today at a wisecrack or joke which brought guffaws from your grandfather many years ago, but each of you saw it in a slightly different form. Ancient wheezes are often kept up-to-date by a process known as switching. Here's how it works: You take one of the old stand-bys like, "He worships the ground she walks on." A gagman works it over and presto, Red Skelton says, "I worship the ground she walks on and I don't mind that property she owns on the other side of town, either."

Another example of switching may be found in the remodeling of a joke quite unjustifiably popular during public excitement over an imported French painting. The original went like this:

"Give me a September Morn sandwich."

"What kind of sandwich is that?"

"Chicken, without dressing."

This little item was resurrected for television a few months ago.

5

There was a bold stroke of switching involved. The comedian said, "Give me a Marilyn Monroe sandwich." The rest of the joke was the same.

Groucho Marx, a superb creative comedian, says there are all kinds of humor—"some derisive, some sympathetic, some merely whimsical, and that is what makes comedy so much harder to create than serious drama, for people laugh in many ways, but they cry in only one."

Some say the wisecrack is a new form of humor. But is it? "How would you like to have your hair cut?" the loquacious barber inquired. And the man in the chair replied, "In silence." And who was the man in the chair the first time to hear this gag? A king of Macedonia. When? The fifth century B.C.

Things Must Be "In Fun"

"The first law of humor is that things can be funny only when we are in fun," Max Eastman points out in his book, *Enjoyment of Laughter*. Furthermore, he says that when we are "in fun" a peculiar shift of values takes place. Pleasant things are still pleasant, but disagreeable things may acquire a pleasant emotional flavor and provoke a laugh.

Humor has a certain fragility. For instance, jokes about William Jennings Bryan were considered very funny indeed at the turn of the century, when it is estimated that there were at least ten thousand of them in general circulation. They aren't funny now. Oldsters remember the endless and extravagant anecdotes about the Ford motor car which once convulsed the nation. They aren't funny now.

Dig into the old copies of *Abe Martin Almanacs*, the musings of Artemus Ward, and the newspaper columns of Will Rogers, and you will see how certain types of humor fade in a few years.

There's another side to the story. In the words of one gagman, "If a thing was funny, it is still funny now."

That sweeping statement contains a lot of truth. Shakespeare discovered the comic possibilities of the stooge long before Ted

6

Healy, Joe Cook, or others thought about it. The stooge, as Broadway understands him, is a humble and dull character who is on the receiving end of rude and unkind remarks. Bottom, in *Midsummer Night's Dream,* was one of the first stooges in dramatic literature and remains, after more than three hundred years, perhaps the funniest stooge of all.

Humor detectives tell us that the mother-in-law joke is almost as old as time; it goes back to the taboos of primitive peoples. As recently as three thousand years ago Greek warriors pledged everlasting friendship with the toast: "And may thy mother-in-law burst."

You've no doubt heard the probably apocryphal anecdote of Lincoln and Grant. According to legend, after the triumphs of the Army of Tennessee, critics of Grant reported to Lincoln that the General was habitually drunk. "If you can find out the brand of whisky he used," President Lincoln is supposed to have said, "I'll send a barrel to all my generals." Then there's the story credited to George II of England. Enemies of General Wolfe, who subsequently died storming Quebec, told the king that Wolfe was mad and should be confined. "Mad? Mad?" said George. "I only hope he will bite some of my other generals." It seems to be the same yarn.

What about "Basic" Lists?

And how often have you heard that there are only seven basic jokes? You've seen some of the lists—marriage, seasickness, old maids, whiskers, cute kiddy sayings, brides, fat men, and other topics. Actually, these "basic" jokes are not jokes at all but only classifications of subject matter. It is not correct, therefore, to say that an absent-minded-professor joke is one of the basic jokes, for the reason that it is possible to make a hundred individual jokes about an absent-minded professor.

Let's look at four witticisms:

1. "His dog sleeps in the same bed with him. It isn't healthy, of course, but the dog has gotten used to it."

2. "The poor pup is an Einstein pup—no one can explain his relativity."

3. Mrs. Newly Rich: "Does this dog have a good pedigree?"

Kennel owner: "Pedigree? Why, madam, if this dog could talk, he wouldn't speak to either one of us."

4. Teacher: "Your theme on 'Our Dog' is identical to that of your brother's."

Kid: "Yes'm, I know—it's the same dog."

These jokes are about dogs, but it is apparent that they are four separate jokes. So you see that the number of jokes is limited only by the number of things there are in the world for man to discuss.

And you ask, "If there isn't any such thing as a list of 'basic jokes,' are certain situations always sure-fire to get laughs?" Not really. A joke, let's remind ourselves, is more than words—it is an intricate structure. It may contain all kinds of attitudes, perceptions, thoughts, and feelings, and these may differ vastly in the different individuals who laugh at it.

Sudden Twist Can Be Funny

The unexpected can be humorous. There is a sudden twist, mishap, or shock that startles us in a funny way, as when Jack Paar recently came out in favor of shorter taxicabs. "When they knock you down," he explained, "they don't stay on you so long."

Other examples: A nervous passenger on an elevator asked the operator, "What would happen if the cable broke? Would we go up or down?" and the exasperated operator replied, "That, madam, depends on the life you've led."

The little Texan rushed up to his mother and said he needed a set of holsters, pistols, and gun belt for kindergarten, and his mother asked, "What for?" "Cause," said the lad, "Teacher's goin' to teach us to draw."

A golfer told his partner, "I'm anxious to make this shot." He explained, "That's my mother-in-law up on the clubhouse porch," and his friend implored, "Don't be a fool. It's two hundred yards. You can't hit her from here."

When a man asks a saleswoman in a department store, "Do you keep stationery?" we are already on our way toward an object—an answer, namely, "Yes, indeed," "All the newest varieties," or "Oh, yes, what kind did you have in mind?" And if the saleswoman replies, "Well, up to a certain point and then I just go all to pieces," we are "pulled back" from that object abruptly and hopelessly. We will never get there, never in this world. And that is funny. But we have got somewhere else, and somewhere that we find it fun to be.

When Our Inhibitions Are Down

Another thing that strikes many people funny, Leonard Hole points out in *How to Write Television Comedy*,[1] is when the proprieties take a beating. Folks say to themselves, "I'd like to do that, but I wouldn't dare." You remember the fellow who was asked what his secret ambition was and he replied, "I've always wanted to throw an egg into an electric fan."

Hole points out that "you see this release of inhibitions on a physical level in the wild cavortings of Jerry Lewis. And you see it in the slap-happy clowning of Red Skelton as he bobs for an apple and comes up with a fish in his teeth."

Then on the verbal level, Hole continues, "many of us enjoy bursting through the bonds of propriety in the genial impudence of Groucho Marx or the deadly insults of Charlie McCarthy." You can usually get a laugh from an insult. When Noel Coward and Mary Martin did a ninety-minute show, Noel remarked to Mary. "You always hoot when you go over E flat."

"I haven't hooted in years," Mary replied defensively.

"Well," he retorted, "you haven't been over E flat in years!"

Have you ever become amused at an insignificant happening in church (it probably wouldn't amuse you in another situation) and you started to giggle? "How dreadful that I'm laughing in church," you say to yourself. And just because you aren't sup-

[1] Irving Settel (ed.) (Boston, The Writer, Inc., 1958), 14–18.

posed to giggle, you may continue to do so under such circumstances. Why do you laugh? It is the element of repression.

Some of the greatest comedians, Hole maintains, "have made us laugh by acting out playfully our own baser impulses, which we somehow manage to keep concealed, or at least controlled. How did Amos and Andy keep the nation in stitches for years? Probably we found Andy more amusing than Amos because Andy had a large streak of larceny in his heart. He always yearned for the easy dollar—just like we do!"

Say what you will, but I don't believe in using a joke that oversteps the bounds of good taste. "But they laugh louder at off-color jokes," you insist; and some audiences do laugh louder at this sort of thing. Why the big laughter? The story may really be witty. But so often it's because the subject is taboo—again it involves a repression. You really have finesse as a humorist if you can take a story which might offend and make it palatable.

Trouble Gets Laughs

Most of us, oddly enough, laugh at trouble. And as Mr. Eastman reminded us, these situations must be "in fun." Look, for example, at the type of scary comedy used successfully by Abbott and Costello. (They are caught in predicaments and we laugh at them because we're safe and they aren't.)

Here are some joke situations of people in trouble:

Scientist: "Call the doctor. Our son just swallowed my slide rule."
Wife: "What are you going to do in the meantime?"
Scientist: "Use logarithmic tables."

Hunter: "Are you sure we're not lost? I was told you were the best guide in the state of Maine."
Guide: "I am, only I think we're in Canada now."

Man on telephone: "Doctor, my wife has just dislocated her jaw. If you're out this way next week or the week after, you might drop in."

Did you hear about the first-grade teacher who sent her morning attendance report to the principal marked, "Help! They're all here."

Warden: "What would you like for your last dinner?"
Condemned: "Steak and mushrooms. Before this, I've always been afraid to eat mushrooms."

Mirth Demands a Mood

What will amuse your listeners often hinges on this fact: they differ so much in what they will and will not take playfully. In your remarks you often arouse feelings toward a person, idea, or institution, but you must not arouse feelings that are too strong or deep.

Night after night a joke which pertains to a heart attack always got a tremendous laugh for Ezio Pinza in *Fanny*. But for several days after President Eisenhower's heart attack in 1955 it was met with complete silence, Steve Allen relates in *The Funny Men*. So as humorists we must not crack jokes on subjects about which people feel too intensely to be playful.

Max Eastman feels that every joke is composed of unpleasant experiences playfully enjoyed, combined in various orders, degrees, and proportions with pleasant experiences. In his *Enjoyment of Laughter* he says that "Anything whatever that might be unpleasant if taken seriously, combined with anything that might for any reason be accepted as pleasant, may turn out to constitute the point of a joke."

Your listeners must experience a playfulness as they laugh. Pity the humorless soul (you'll never get him to admit it) who hears or sees something which amuses others, and says, "I don't see anything funny about that." He can't get away from his centeredness, his concentration that "life is real and life is earnest." He does not know how to break into play. He cannot let himself go in sheer fun, in joyous expansiveness.

Laughter, then, is the outward manifestation of a sudden inner state of mind. Your listeners won't laugh at the most amusing joke in the world if they're not "in the mood." So you see that in any analysis of humor we must always remember this: A joke is a process, not a thing.

Pathos Borders on Humor

Strangely enough, there also seems to be a close relationship between humor and pathos. "Every comedian I talked to," Leonard Hole revealed in studying the psychology of humor for an article in the *American Magazine*, "mentioned this surprising fact." One of our early American humorists, Abraham Lincoln, was criticized for telling so many jokes during the darkest days of the Civil War. His explanation: "I laugh because I must not cry."

Don Herold recognized this close kinship of fun and sadness when he said, "A humorist is a man who feels bad but who feels good about it. The nearer humor is to pain, the longer it is apt to last." And somewhat in the same vein, W. C. Fields observed that people "laugh often with tears in their eyes."

Jonathan Winters, who skyrocketed to big time from the staff of a radio station, has found that certain kinds of pain make many of us laugh. He believes the way a person gets hurt is what makes the situation because they see them as dilemmas they themselves might be in. But remember: if they think you're really hurt, they'll stop laughing immediately.

Some of the choicest humor exaggerates our everyday experiences. Sid Caesar holds up a fun-house mirror to our behavior and shows how funny we are. He finds humor, for instance, in the way we squabble in planning our family vacations. As Sid says, "The truer it is, the funnier it is." Both Sam Levenson and George Gobel amuse millions by reference to the commonplace.

Almost any joke which pokes fun at human pretensions is sure to get laughs. Pretensions of grandeur, false family pride, snobbishness, or conceit annoy us, so we enjoy destroying them with the sharp weapon of irreverence.

We all remember the irreverent way in which Dean Briggs handled the social respectables of Boston:

I dwell in the city of Boston
The home of the bean and the cod;
Where the Cabots talk only to Lowells.
And the Lowells talk only to God.

In doing an army show in Chicago, George Gobel got his biggest laugh from the story about his meeting an officer who demanded, "Young man, I'll have you know I'm the commanding officer of this post."

"Well," George replied, "you've got a good job here, so don't get drunk and louse it up."

No wonder thousands of servicemen howled with glee: Gobel had punctured a pomposity.

Do Men and Women Enjoy the Same Fun?

As you face an audience, maybe you'll wonder if Mrs. J. Pluvius Didgit and her husband Jeffrey will laugh at the same jokes. Do women have a different sense of humor than men? "Women listen more attentively than men," comedian Henny Youngman declares. "I like to have women in the audience because they are better laughers. Women laugh at themselves more than men. Women have ninety problems a day, and it's wonderful that they still have their sense of humor. My jokes are plain picture jokes. I try to make everything count so there isn't much thinking to be done."

On the other hand, comedienne Nancy Walker points out that "it's very hard to make a woman laugh—especially if you're a woman, too. Women have a fantastically good sense of humor," she explains. "But they don't like to see another woman make a clown of herself. Women want to be comfortable with their comedy. They want to identify themselves with the jokes and they want the comedienne to be human."

Women have a better sense of humor than men but they hate to show it. That's the belief of Billy Glason, a former vaudeville star who has made the comic sense his business. "Hands down, women win," he declares. "Tell them a joke and they catch on

13

quicker and laugh longer. What's more, they remember the joke and they're eager to pass it along."

"I have seen women laughing hysterically," he continues, "while the men just grunt and light their cigars; and the men are so busy trying to think up their own jokes to top the one they heard that they usually miss the point anyway."

After crisscrossing the nation and addressing countless audiences I am convinced that what people will laugh at is almost entirely determined by their conditioning—how "they got that way." You can't assume that what wowed a convention of brain surgeons will bring explosive laughter from a luncheon meeting of book publishers. Golfers always enjoy this wisecrack: "By the time you can afford to lose a golf ball, you can't hit it that far." Nongolfers rarely get the point, and it's understandable, because they have not been conditioned to do so.

How can you know what will amuse an audience? Will they chuckle at the preposterous? The surprise? The insult? The ludicrous? The absurd? The more you search for the secrets of laughter, the more puzzled you may become. For every rule explaining the psychology of laughter there are countless exceptions. But remember that you have company because no two humorists have the same ideas on the ingredients of a comic situation. As you see, humor is elusive, delicate, difficult to pin down. Keep studying and experimenting with humor. Be alert to funny things in life. Then you can develop a sense of humor—the ability to see the funny side of things and to use them in convulsing audiences.

For a summary, let's listen to Bob Hope, the all-round champion in all fields: "You have to get over to the audience that there's a game of wits going on and if they don't stay awake they'll miss something—like missing the baseball someone has lobbed at them. What I'm really doing is asking, 'Let's see if you can hit this one.' That's my whole comedy technique." Strengthen yourself in this technique and you'll not only know what's funny and why—but the response from your audience will prove it.

CHAPTER

2

Gags and Quips: 14 Sure-Fire Sources

"WHERE CAN I FIND humorous material for speeches?"

Good question. Let's remember one thing: hardly any humorous statement is wholly original. Your audience realizes this, too. One night after speaking in New Orleans a stiff old lady came up and remarked, "Your jokes are familiar but I can't place the face."

Let's face this big fact in collecting, writing, and using humor: you must work out your own salvation. There is no magic formula.

And you'll discover this sooner or later: you must go below the surface appreciation of humor to understand it and appreciate it. Unless you work, observe, study, practice, file, and experiment you simply cannot tell if something is funny or not.

A successful humorist has developed a built-in feeling for funny material. He doesn't have to stop and classify the humor as (1) exaggeration, (2) satire, (3) reverse, or one of the other countless types that have been applied to humor.

Can you develop a built-in "laugh meter"? To a certain extent. And it will come only after a long study of what has been done, what is being done, and by actually doing it yourself.

When Max Eastman was doing research for his book, *Enjoyment of Laughter*, Groucho Marx told him that if he could provide a test by which a good joke could be distinguished from a bad one without trying them out on the public, Eastman would soon be the richest man in Hollywood.

Take hope! Humorous speakers use a variety of methods in gathering material for their addresses. Many of them will work for you. Here they are:

1. *Tune in on others:*

Late one afternoon in a supermarket I heard a woman tell another, "I'm going to have a bust made of my daughter's head." The woman who made the remark is a skid-talker. Even after you've heard this sort of thing you wonder if you really did. And on a bus I heard a woman tell her friend, "Maybe men ain't all perfect, but they're the best opposite sex we got." Keep your ears tuned to bits of conversation. Listen for amusing things which people say. Then jot them down while they're fresh in your mind.

2. *Enjoy the signboards:*

You'll enjoy signs when you discover that a zany one often pops up. Some are clever. Some are mixed up. Bennett Cerf tells of seeing the following one in an apparel shop in Lima, Ohio: "Our clothes not only make girls look slim; they make men look 'round." One of our friends saw this sign in the waiting room of a clinic: "Ladies in the Waiting Room Will Please Not Exchange Symptoms. It Gets the Doctors Hopelessly Confused." In Los Angeles, I once saw this sign on an apartment window: "Saxophone for Sale." And in the adjoining apartment window was this one: "Thank God." And maybe you've seen the one in the run-down restaurant in Louisville: "Duncan Hines Wept Here." Keep an eye peeled for any sign which may cause merriment.

3. *Television and radio:*

One of your best sources of humor is through the medium of television, where you can see and hear some of the world's best comics. Best of all, you can study their timing and techniques. So keep a pad and pencil handy when you are listening to a radio or television comic. Here are a few quips from the air waves: Morey Amsterdam said he was so corny that when he died they wouldn't bury him. They'd just shuck him . . . . Henny Youngman reported a bad accident in his family—his grandmother broke her arm when she slipped off the $2.00 window at Jamaica . . . . Joey Adams told friends, "I have a habit of writing my jokes on the cuff. Was I surprised to see our laundryman doing my act at Loew's State!" Milton Berle told his orchestra leader, "Listen, if you're a conductor I want a transfer." Beginning today, watch all channels for chuckle ideas.

4. *Personal experiences:*

Late one afternoon I answered the front doorbell and found a little kid who asked, "Do you have any old whisky bottles I could sell?" Chagrined, I asked, "Does my face look like I'm the kind of fellow who would?" He looked at my face for some time and asked, "Well, do you have any old vinegar bottles?"

If you find yourself laughing uproariously and wholeheartedly at a humorous experience, set the story down while the details are clear in your mind. Then look at the story for (1) appeal, (2) timeliness, and (3) reaction. What's more, ask yourself, "Does it afford listeners a swift insight into human nature? Am I the butt of the story? If so, good! Does it throw light on some characteristic—perhaps a weakness or foible—which is common to all of us? Would listeners break into a sympathetic grin or chuckle because it points up a familiar dilemma?"

5. *Other speakers:*

We are all story swipers. Listen to the speaker at your club dinner tonight and he'll probably be using a wisecrack which you heard another speaker use last month. When you hear a good story jot it down. Be sure you get the details, and especially the punch line. See that it fits your style of delivery. Then before you trot it out at the Rotary luncheon on Tuesday remember that if it's making the rounds, others have probably heard it. And it may not suit the occasion. Instead, keep it ready for a later occasion when it can be geared to a specific idea.

6. *Boners:*

Unless you keep a close watch on the sources of humor, you'd be surprised how many funny situations spring from boners in speech, action, dress. Many people start their conversation in this fashion: "Boy, oh boy, did old Charlie Jerkins pull a boo-boo today?" and then tell of Charlie's boner. You and I pull so many boners that we get a comfortable feeling when we hear of the mistakes of others. Letters and quizzes often yield humorous sentences.

From school exams:

"On Washington's trip across the Delaware two men were frozen to death, but they reached the other side in safety."

"Two French explorers of the Mississippi were Romeo and Juliet."

"Salt Lake City is a place where the Morons settled."

"Priscilla, Miles Standish loveress, was a very sweet girl dressed in simple Dutch costume consisting of a white cap and apron."

"Maple syrup is made by sterilizing sap."

From letters:

"We have a large, well-lighted room for two persons with steam heat and southern exposure."

"We have been authorized to make monthly advances to Miss Elizabeth Johnson."

"If you buy a suit from us, you will soon want one of our topcoats to wear over it."

18

"This sum will be paid you in a single amount at the time of your death, which we understand is the way you prefer."

7. *Newspapers:*

"LOCAL MAN WINS EGG-LAYING CONTEST." That headline from a Kansas weekly newspaper shows just one way of using the newspaper as a source of witticisms. You've noticed mixed-up ideas like the following: "During the storm on Saturday, Mrs. Raymond Driskill slipped on the ice and hurt her somewhat."

Here are a few other howlers from the nation's press:

The fire caused damage estimated at $25,000. It was partially caused by insurance.

A check at a local swimming pool revealed some startling figures.

Senator Taft's speech was interrupted 39 times by applesauce.

Miss Rogers was winking for the third time when the life guard seized her and dragged her ashore.

The bride's going-away outfit consisted of a dark-green gabardine suit with coat to match. Both are well known locally.

He has been pledged to a fraternity and will study wild life.

The pastor will preach and there will be special sinning by the congregation.

For the second year, Miss Abbey won Honorable Mention for her colorful marigolds and lush poses.

Miss Preston and Mr. Hodges will liven up the gymnasium with a series of dances and stumbling exhibitions.

ATTORNEY GENERAL URGES CLOSER LOOK AT NUD-IST COLONY

—headline

DOCTOR COMPILES LIST OF POISONS CHILDREN MAY DRINK AT HOME

—headline

You can also use newspapers as a source of topics for humorous comments. Al Hirschfeld, in an article in the New York *Times,* tells how the late Fred Allen scanned newspapers for topics:

"Fred's day is spent in readin' and writin'. Apart from his correspondence he reads nine newspapers daily and manages to squeeze in a novel or two a week. The New York *Times* and the *Herald Tribune* are his main sources. A stranger watching him read a paper would be convinced that he was merely tearing it up to make an imitation lace tablecloth. In reality he is clipping source material. He showed me his clippings for next week's show. There were over a hundred items collected during the three previous days."

Beginning today, watch your newspaper for foibles of the human race—stories and anecdotes which provide an inexhaustible source of merriment. And also read them for current happenings which will provide pegs for humorous comments.

8. *Cartoon quips:*

Be on the lookout for cartoon quips which you can use in speeches. It's usually better to make them into brief anecdotes—giving enough details on which to build the story—than to rely on the quip line alone to get the story across. Before using a cartoon gag, be sure that it will strike home with your audience. Here are some typical quips which you might work into your speech.

Young stenographer to boss: "Well, if you can't give me a raise, how about the same pay oftener?"

—Chicago *Tribune*

· Husband answering telephone: "She's out. Who shall I say was going to listen?"

—Chicago *Tribune*–New York *News* Syndicate

Wife to husband: "This Christmas let's give each other sensible gifts like ties and fur coats."

—*The Saturday Evening Post*

Wife, leaving on trip, to husband: "Seventy-six per cent the human body is water. Try keeping it that way while I'm gone."

—*Gourmet*

Husband to wife studying new jacket on small son in clothing store: "Better make up your mind before he outgrows it."

—*Look*

Woman driver to friend: "The part about parking I don't like is the noisy crash."

—*True*

Man to psychiatrist: "My wife has developed an inferiority complex—what can I do to keep her that way?"

—*The Saturday Evening Post*

Man at party, turning to wife: "That reminds me of a very funny story—will you take it from there, dear?"

—*This Week*

Take a second look at clever cartoons, and then clip the good ones for possible use. But remember, you must take the punch line and build backward into an anecdote. Then slant it toward your specific audience.

9. *Experiment with humor:*

You can unflex your humor abilities by experimenting. Dan Bennett, who has written comedy for radio and television stars, gives us this advice: "Take some famous old proverbs and try to twist them around to come up with something funny or philosophical. Take some old clichés, some well known expressions, some wisecracks and play around with the wording. Add some new words, substitute other words, shorten or lengthen. Practice! Study! Write!"[1]

[1] For specific ways of writing humor, see Chapter 5 in this book.

So often you hear the expression, "Money isn't everything." It's a well-known phrase. How can you give it a humorous twist? What else is there besides money? We've thought it over and come up with something like this:

Money isn't everything and don't let anybody tell you it is. There are other things such as stocks, bonds, letters of credit, cashier's checks, money orders, traveler's checks, and drafts.

You've heard the age-old question, "What happens when an irresistible force meets an immovable object?" Does that apply to people? If so, what kinds of people? Whom do you know who has those characteristics? After experimenting we fashion this quip:

When an irresistible force meets an immovable object it serves you right for introducing your wife to the boss.

10. *Contact convention-goers:*

You can obtain quips and jokes from faraway places without getting away from your desk. How? It's easy: pick out some of your convention-going friends—particularly those who attend national meetings—and ask that they jot down some of the best jokes they heard. A friend returned from a meeting and relayed this one to me: The hypochondriac visited his psychiatrist and the doctor asked him, "What's wrong with you today?" and the man said, "What's new?" Here's another which came my way through a friend: Even the dogs are having conventions now. What's more, like humans, they have set up panel discussions. At a recent canine gathering, the first topic which came up for discussion was, "If we ever caught a car, what would we do with it?" Ask your friends to help—they'll add to your supply of humor.

11. *Books, magazines, and proceedings:*

Obtain copies of joke books—old and new—so that you can see many rib-ticklers. Then do something else: learn to dip into all kinds of books which may contain a funny story. A biography may give an amusing anecdote or two about a famous personage. Like this:

Rossini, the Italian composer, discovered that some wealthy admirers in France were planning to erect a statue in his honor.

"How much will it cost?" the composer asked.

"About ten million francs," was the answer.

"Ten million francs," gasped Rossini. "For five million francs I will stand on the pedestal myself."

On rare occasions you may find a good joke or two by reading the annual proceedings published by an organization. Obviously, you aren't likely to find many chuckles in the printed proceedings of the International Society for the Prevention of International Societies. You can waste a lot of time as you dig. Do this: when you look at a copy of proceedings, (1) see if the complete speech of everyone on the program is given—with any opening jokes, and (2) check the printed address of the person giving the speech at the dinner and see if he used any humorous observations in his introduction or in his speech.

Here's an example: Harold O. McLain, president of the Railways Ice Company, Chicago, responded to an introduction as follows:

"That is a very pleasant introduction and commentary your chairman has accorded me. You know someone has said that the three hardest things in the world to do are to climb a fence leaning toward you, to kiss a pretty girl leaning away from you, and to acknowledge with proper humility a flattering introduction. In spite of many failures, I've had some success with the first two, but the last one has me licked."

What about general magazines? One thing is certain: millions of persons read the popular weekly and monthly magazines, so you can be sure that their jokes and quips are widely read and circulated. Clip and file material from them, to be sure, but allow a lapse of time before using them.

What other magazines yield jokes? You might be amazed to know that humorous material is published regularly in thousands of professional, trade and industrial magazines. And they're available to you. Ask your friend the automobile dealer if his magazine carries jokes. Maybe your neighbor-dentist receives a magazine with wisecracks. And don't overlook a salesman-friend who may receive a selling bulletin which contains a monthly chuckle page. Ask your friends about their business and professional publications, and you'll probably discover new sources of humorous material. And when you find a specialized magazine, it will have a big advantage: its humorous stories will be fresh to people outside of its particular reading audience.

Editors will be the first to admit that they run nothing new on their joke pages. Actually, most of them clip the best anecdotes which they see in other publications. But by scanning enough magazines you will discover a few which will register a little higher than the average on the audience's "laugh meter." Here are a few rib-ticklers from a variety of publications:

A couple of bebop characters were walking through a Florida swamp. One yelled, "Help, help, an alligator bit off my leg."

"Which one?" cried his friend.

"I don't know," he answered. "All these alligators look alike."

—*Frontier*, Prudential Life Insurance Company of America

Flo: "By the year 2,000 we Americans will work only an hour a day."

Josey: "Oh, my goodness—that means the end of our coffee break!"

—*Parts Pups*, Genuine Parts Company

A man took his dog to the veterinarian. "My dog is always chasing sports cars," he explained.

"Well, that's not uncommon," said the vet.

"Yes, but he catches them and buries them in the back yard."

—*Philnews*, Phillips Petroleum Company

The inveterate golfer finally arrived home for dinner, and during the meal his wife remarked, "Willie tells me he caddied for you today."

"So that's it," said Willie's father. "I knew I'd seen that kid before."

—News and Views, General Motors Corporation

12. *Shows and movies:*

Keep your notebook near by when you watch a movie, a musical comedy, or night-club act. Some of the funniest things you hear are tied to a situation, but you will hear one-liners and other types of jokes which you can adapt to your speeches. Examples: In Nunnally Johnson's film, *Woman in the Window*, a Boy Scout said, "If I get the reward I will send my younger brother to some good college and I will go to Harvard." In a recent movie the hero told a girl, "I know a fellow who always wanted to meet a girl who already had a fur coat and her appendix out." Oscar Levant, on a program, said, "I have no enemies, but all my friends hate me." Jack Donnelly told about "the woman who had her face lifted so many times she was talking through her eyes." "A wolf," said Hal Block, "may be defined as a big dame hunter." So—take a long listen when you see a show and you'll probably get some needed laughing stock.

13. *Comic records:*

"If it hadn't been for Thomas A. Edison people would be watching television by candlelight." That's the observation of "Brother" Dave Gardner on his record, *Kick Thine Own Self* (RCA Victor), which suggests another source of humorous ideas.

Comic records aren't new. Ask any American who is pushing forty or beyond, and he will recall the molasses mutterings of Moran and Mack, the two black crows. Recently Mort Sahl, with his staccato attack on political follies, appealed to a rebellious generation and brought a new revival of funny talk on discs.

You'll pick up some funny stuff by listening to albums made by Bob Newhart, Shelley Berman, Jonathan Winters, Bill Dana, Peter Sellers, Pat Harrington, Jr., Buddy Hackett, Stanley Holloway, Dave Barry, Lenny Bruce, Tom Lehrer, and others. Just be sure that the ideas you adapt are geared to your own personality and style.

14. *Comedy writers:*

Advertisements of individuals and companies which sell gag lines and comedy material appear in *Variety, Billboard,* and other publications. If possible, check on the type and quality of material before ordering. Some of it is good but much of it is far from funny.

Now that you've gathered material follow the advice of many of Hollywood's comedy writers: keep a file. What kind of material? This might include epigrams, jokes, anecdotes, light verse, magazine cartoons, comic strips, amusing essays, collections of jokes and gags, funny true experiences, and old magazines and books containing humor items.

What's the best way of filing? Type of humor? Topic? Formula? Process? That's up to you. Many speakers file by topics for two reasons: (1) it isn't as complicated as classifying by device or process, and (2) it enables you to find what you need quicker. As a start, perhaps you can use the subtopics listed in the back of this book and build from those.

So often a joke or wisecrack can be classified in several ways. How would you classify this remark by Bob Hope: "I was teaching my girl to swim but the life guard came along and made us both get into the water." "Swimming?" "Girl friend?" "Misunderstanding?" Actually, the method doesn't matter as long as you classify it so that you can find it and use it.

A word of caution: While you are digging for jokes, remember you are looking for jokes that are funny when *spoken.* Many wisecracks "read funny" but try to switch them from print to spoken words and they fall flat.

So-o-o—how do you go about gathering humorous material? If I had a foolproof blueprint, I'd either keep it to myself or sell it and keep my earnings hidden in a private Fort Knox. First of all, keep your mental antenna operating so that it registers the slightest humor wave. Read! Read! Read! Look at every experience—every situation—for humor possibilities. What's more, always jot down every idea when it hits you. And one of these days you'll make the great discovery that fun is where you find it.

CHAPTER 3

18 Ways to Test your Jests

CAN YOU PRETEST your funny stuff?

How can you polish a witticism before it is delivered?

How can you find the type of delivery which is best suited to your personality?

What are some of the pitfalls when poking fun?

Try these 18 tools:

1. *Are you overbuilding your story?*

When you say, "Here is one of the funniest stories you have ever heard" your praise may be too lavish. The story may flop. Perhaps members of your audience have heard it. They may not understand it. Let the listeners judge the merit of your story.

2. *Is your story below par?*

Just an anecdote won't bring laughter. It must sparkle—it must be tailor-made to the audience. How do you find a good one? Dig. Read. Give a new twist to yesterday's gags. Pick out the one most likely to click. (See Chapter 4 in this book.)

3. *Will bad timing cause sad results?*

Like a smart quarterback, you must be ready to alter your planned attack on a moment's notice. Timing for a humorous speaker is difficult to define, but basically it is a close feeling for the audience's mood and reactions so that you know what to do —and what not to do.

Timing is a lot of things. Like knowing when to speak a line, how quickly to speak it, when to cut it short, when to wait for a laugh, when to speed up the tempo of your delivery, or when to alter your humor so that it is geared to audience feelings.

"Timing," says Jack Benny, "is not so much knowing when to speak, but when to pause. Timing is pauses. The closest to the idea of timing is hitting a golf ball, where your swing has to be perfect, otherwise you will hook or slice the ball, or miss it."

Maurice Zolotow, who quotes those comments from Benny in his book, *No People like Show People*, points out that "The sense of timing can only arise when a performer has a close integration with his audience. Although timing is almost the very foundation of the comedian's art, the mastery of timing is part of the arsenal of every actor. Any actor will tell you that even when he is playing in a long run his performance is never exactly the same twice, because audiences are never exactly the same. . . . Although timing may arise from a performer's need to feel close to human beings in the mass it can only be tempered and polished by years of practice. It is one of the hardest things to learn and it cannot be taught. It must be learned by a long process of trial and error."

So no matter how good your material, always remember that whether the audience laughs or not doesn't depend as much on the merits of your jokes as on your timing.

4. *Are you concise and clever?*

Noted humorists of bygone days often told long stories. For one thing, that was the custom. But the tempo has been speeded up today. And you may ask, "Shall I ever use a long story?" Sometimes. If it's a little longer than the usual length, keep it as short as possible. Eliminate all unnecessary words. "Don't elaborate and stretch your story," Edward Frank Allen reminds us in *Mod-*

ern Humor for Effective Speaking. And then he says, "Even a bad joke can be forgiven if it is mercifully short." Just be sure that it is sufficiently complete for the listener to understand it.

5. *Are you using pointless stories?*[1]

No matter how funny your story is, if it is yanked in and doesn't quite fit the situation, then it won't bring results. Members of the Middletown Garden Club aren't likely to chuckle or even smile at the story of a scientist whose miscalculation on the thrust of a rocket brought strange results. Gear your story to an idea.

6. *Does the story strike listener interest?*

Think you know how to select a joke which strikes listener interest? Below are four jokes. Mark with an X the ones which you would use at a dinner of your state medical society:

A. A doctor in Louisville sought an allergy as the basis for the patient's nervousness.

"Oh, doctor, I'm always so high-strung," she moaned. "I can't even take my shoes off before going to bed."

With this clue, he discovered that her grandfather had been hanged by vigilantes. He had died with his boots on. They were so tight he couldn't get them off.

B. "Would you like to see where I was vaccinated?" she asked him as they were driving along.

"You said it, babe."

"It's that second building from the corner—Dr. Ayer's office."

C. A doctor told a woman she had a fibroid tumor and he would operate immediately. Then she asked, "How can you be so positive everything will be all right when 14 per cent die under that operation?"

"My dear lady," explained the surgeon, "my 14 per cent have already died."

[1] For specific ways of linking a joke to an idea, see Chapter 4 in this book.

D. The doctor called the student nurse aside. "One of the primary requisites of your calling, Miss Morey, is a cheerful attitude."

"Oh, doctor, did I do something wrong?"

"In a way, yes. Here we're trying to keep up the patient's courage; giving him an incentive to live. Then you walk in with a magazine and you say to him 'If I were you I wouldn't start any serial stories.' "

What's your score? Here's how I would rate them: (A) strained—impossible, (B) old, (C) pokes fun at medicos—would be better for lay group, and (D) switch from old joke but would get a laugh if told right.

Unless you are very careful, you may be tempted to use a story which Uncle Bert told you last night. Maybe it's good, timely, applicable to your speech situation. Just be sure.

7. Do you avoid off-color stories?

Oh, sure, you are often tempted to tell anecdotes which are off-color or of double meaning. And psychologists remind us that risqué jokes sometimes produce more laughter than other types because they contain the element of a mild shock. Some night-club comedians use racy stories because they know their audiences will usually laugh louder at this sort of thing.

Speakers who lean toward the erotic story remind one of the lines in William Cowper's translation of the *Iliad*: "Might he but set the rabble in a roar; He cared not with what jest." Obviously, your reputation suffers when you resort to questionable anecdotes. So just forget them. Instead, use interesting, sparkling, clean stories.

8. Can you really handle dialect?

You read or hear an amusing story in dialect. And you say to yourself, "That's a dandy! I must use that in my next talk." But before you decide to use it, remember that much of its force depends on the use of dialect. Nothing is quite as ineffective as

WHEN IT'S LAUGHTER YOU'RE AFTER

some speaker trying desperately to use a dialect which is beyond him. Never use dialect unless you are good.

9. *Have you rehearsed your story?*

Try your quip on a miniature "audience." This group may be your office associates, your family, your golfing buddies. You'll discover this: your "guinea pig" audience may like it, even if you don't. What if they don't laugh? Sometimes a joke is just no good. Analyze the joke, your manner of presentation, the audience, and yourself. If you are fairly certain that you have a potentially funny idea, then alter it so that it may get a laugh.

Should you explain to members of a group that you'd like to test a joke on them? Ed Hegarty in his book, *Showmanship in Public Speaking*, says, "I find that it is best to try the story on a group, without saying, 'I am testing it for a speech.' If you explain this beforehand, the listeners will try to criticize, and they won't be thinking of the story merely as a funny story. All you want to know is whether a group of ordinary Joes will laugh at it."

You'll profit in two ways from giving your joke a test run to different small groups. First, you gain facility in doing it. And just as important, you may wish to revise the word choice so that it is easy to say. Study the reactions of listeners in your workouts and then study to upgrade your presentation.

Organize your presentation so that the listener gets (1) the first few words, (2) the situation, and (3) the ending. This means that you must consider the length, the tempo, and the exact second to give your punch line.

10. *Will your story offend anyone?*

Oh, yes, I know you are sometimes tempted to tell a story on those of another race, color, or belief. They seem funny to you because they probably make you feel superior. But we must remember that most people are sensitive (just like ourselves) in these areas. Some stories on others are relatively harmless and

32

you can use them, but beware of any with a dangerous potential. Try instead to find a story which bolsters your audience, a story which makes them proud to be members of a certain group.

11. *Do you portray the wise guy?*

What's the secret of Jack Benny's staying power as a comedian? Just this: Most of his material is aimed dead-center at the universal tendency to howl at the self-confident man who makes a fool of himself. Jack isn't the wise guy who tells all the jokes on his show nor the bright one who has all the funny lines. He's on the other end of the gun. He is the target of most of the jokes, most of the comic situations. You laugh at him, but you also sympathize with him because, almost inevitably, his best-laid plans blow up in his face.

"The real wit tells jokes to make others feel superior," Elmer Wheeler reminds us, "while the half-wit tells them to make others feel small." Be extremely careful when you personalize a joke and the other person bears the brunt of the fun. He laughs, yes, but it is a mighty weak laugh. "We love a joke that hands us a pat on the back while it kicks the other fellow downstairs," says C. L. Edson, who points out the danger behind a joke that is misdirected. Tell jokes on yourself. Let people laugh at you. They will love you for it.

12. *Do you know when to stop?*

"The secret of making one's self tiresome, is not to know when to stop," claimed Voltaire who knew something about human reactions. Anything that is too much or too frequent loses impact. Make 'em want more! That's the secret of professional humorists. Learn to know how many jokes to use, what timing to follow—each closely tied to audience interests—and they'll applaud you, and want more!

13. *Can you get across to your audience?*

You receive the usual skeptical applause as you are introduced. Now you've got to work hard to produce honest laughter and loud applause when you sit down. How? It's a mixture of many variables, but Joey Bishop believes that something called "attitude" is the most important thing in comedy. He explains: "Attitude means projecting. I try to project."[2] Small, thin-faced, and as cold-eyed as a cougar, he uses his sad, almost expressionless face to suggest many things: imperturbability, patience with the world, a wistful feeling that he is inadequate. Like Joey, you must get through to your audience to get laughter with your lines. You must project. What is projection? Just this: it's the ability to talk to an individual instead of an audience. It helps to tell yourself just before you are introduced, "I am going to like this audience." It depends mainly on one thing: your attitude.

14. *Do you ever hold a post-mortem?*

Sooner or later this will happen to you: You have chosen what you know will be a clever story. You tell it. But nothing happens. What can you do? First, don't get flustered. And don't back up and rehash the story. Instead, try something like this to get out of the predicament: "Well, the first time I heard that one I didn't understand it, either," or "Remind me not to use that again," or "Well, I had to try it out on someone."

Steve Allen, television star, says that "You must know how to recover from the shock of getting no laugh where one was expected, and how to turn the momentary defeat into a greater triumph."

Some comedians want a protection line, Ace Goodman, gag writer, revealed to Maurice Zolotow in his article, "King of Gag Men," in *The Saturday Evening Post*. "A protection line," Goodman said, "is a joke they can use in case the original joke doesn't get a laugh. It might be a line like, 'I know you're out there—I can hear you breathing.' I once wrote for a comedian so neurotic he wanted a protection line for the protection line—in case the first protection line didn't get a laugh."

[2] "A Dead-Pan Comic's Lively Wit," *TV Guide* (Dec. 17, 1960).

Above all, never repeat part of the story to get a response. Do not waste time trying to explain or salvage the anecdote which died. Have a protection line ready. Then be ready to move ahead rapidly to your next point.

15. *Does your delivery fit your personality?*

Actually, there is no one way to tell a story. Some humorists use the "deadpan" most successfully. Others add to the contagion with their own laughter.

Artemus Ward was seen to laugh uproariously when writing his lectures, but in delivery—to quote Charles Reade—"the refined, delicate, intellectual countenance, the sweet, grave mouth, from which one might have expected philosophic lectures, retained their seriousness while listeners were convulsed."

Josh Billings advised comic lecturers, "when they lay a warm joke, not to act as a hen doth when she has uttered an egg, but look sorry and let someone else do the cackling."

"I always try to appear as happy as possible while I am lecturing," Stephen Leacock declared. "I take this to be a part of the trade of anybody labeled as a humorist and paid as such. I have no sympathy whatever with the idea that the humorist ought to be a lugubrious person with a face stamped with melancholy. This is a cheap and elementary effect belonging to the level of a circus clown. The image of 'laughter shaking both his sides' is a truer picture of comedy . . . . Therefore, I say, I always try to appear cheerful at my lectures and even to laugh at my own jokes."

"Don't laugh in the middle of your story," advises "Senator" Ed Ford, one of the three humorists who starred on the radio show, "Can You Top This?" Instead, he says, "Always be surprised when your audience laughs—make them think they've discovered the joke."

Will Rogers would talk with a certain quizzical look and when the audience laughed he would suddenly look up as though the laughter surprised him.

Bob Hope often laughs as he talks but he is usually laughing at someone in the audience. A woman may be tittering as he talks. He may laugh a little, stop his patter, and then ask her, "Madam, which one are you working on?"

What can you do? Experiment with various types of material in different situations. Observe the techniques of humorous speakers. See which delivery—deadpan or laughter—suits your personality.

16. *Do you know how to slip in a story?*

You've found a good story to illustrate a point in your speech. Good! But just how do you plan to introduce it? Amateurs are likely to say, "That reminds me of a funny story," "It seems that there were two musicians," or "Golly, I heard a lulu at the lodge dinner last night." Never use any of those approaches. Instead, try to launch your stories with just the right casual touch.

What do you do? Just this: drift into your story as quietly as you can. You're good if you can get into the story before your listeners realize that you are relating an anecdote. One way of giving your story a more authentic ring is to tie it to some individual out of your own experience or some character whom you may invent.

Instead of saying, "You'll get the biggest kick out of the funniest thing that happened to me one night when I was speaking in Kentucky." Do it this way: "My speech tonight is a mind-reading stunt—you are wondering what I am going to say next—and so am I. My remarks are entirely extemporaneous. One night in Chicago I read my speech and afterwards I asked the chairman what he thought of it. 'Well, I have three criticisms to make of it,' he said. 'First, you read it; secondly, you read it poorly; and thirdly, it wasn't worth reading.'" You see that there was no announcement, no intimation of a forthcoming story.

Practice different ways of getting into your story. Try some of the techniques discussed in Chapter 4 in this book. Listen to professionals and you'll pick up some ideas. And by working on it you'll soon learn the art of making a smooth glide into your stories.

17. *Do you admit your shortcomings?*

Here's a little story which always gets a chuckle when I am addressing a writers' conference: "Are you often disgusted with the quality of your articles? You think they're pretty weak? Why, listen, the first stories I wrote when I was a newspaper cub were so terrible that they had to be edited before they were thrown in the wastebasket."

Why does this story always register? That's simple: the audience likes anything which shows your stupidity, ignorance, or anything in which you are the butt of the story. No wonder E. B. White once observed that although we all have troubles, the humorist is unique in that he fattens on trouble. So tell your troubles your mix-ups, and situations which boomeranged on you. Your listeners will like you all the more because of your honest confession.

Let's look at another example: "Most of us today are seeking a sense of direction. All of us need help and inspiration. One night I took Mrs. Harral and our sons, Larry and Don, with me when I spoke at a church. On the way home Larry asked, 'Daddy, why did you bow your head in silence before you started talking?' and I replied, 'I was asking that the Lord guide me and help me,' and after a short silence, he asked, 'Why didn't he?' "

Notice how Eddie Cantor uses that same device: He tells of visiting a veteran's hospital where he worked extra hard to make the boys laugh. He wound up the show with a jaunty good-by, and said, "Hope you're better soon, fellows." And the veterans shouted, "Same to you!"

Why will your audience warm up to you when you frankly tell them about your foibles and failures? They think of their own, of course. But above all, it gives them a comfortable feeling to know that you are human.

18. *Have you learned to pause before your punch line?*

Before you tell a joke, consider where to pause—just briefly. Why? You must give your hearers a chance to visualize the picture so clearly that when you introduce the unexpected or ludicrous "punch" the effect will cause laughter.

You can do it in two ways. One, you can actually pause. Or, you can use some unimportant interjection, such as, "Well then" or "And do you know what." Some comedians giggle a minute, or waggle a cigar, or slap someone's back. In each the purpose is the same: to let the audience grasp the situation.

Let's look at this one for a moment:

A man had a terrible time getting a long-distance call through from his hotel room. Finally he went down to the office and gave the operator a large bouquet of red carnations. She thanked him very much, adding "I consider this a great compliment."

"Compliment nothing," he said (repeating the key phrase with slight pause), "I thought you were dead."

Remember that humor—in its many forms and shades—is a refreshing and powerful device when it is pretested, tamed, tuned to perfection, and performed with timing and taste.

Now go back and read those tips again and you'll get a better idea of how to give your presentation a professional touch. Above all, try to pretest every element in each speaking situation. By evaluating every ingredient of your talk you can learn to bring merriment and mirth to your audiences.

38

CHAPTER 4

Link Your Laughs to an Idea

ON A ONE-NIGHT STAND in Flint, Michigan, Victor Borge was not daunted by the fact that the house was less than half filled.

Looking at the slim audience, he said, "Flint must be an extremely wealthy town. I see that each of you bought two or three seats."

Everyone chuckled. The noted entertainer had broken the ice. In one brief phrase he had won his audience. With real professional know-how, he had adapted a humorous remark to a local situation.

In a speech, you can make your point stick when you use a funny story or a witty expression with which to illustrate it. It's like this: You are stressing the importance of follow-through—personal supervision—to a group of business executives. You want to emphasize that to get the best results each executive must accept a personal responsibility and not try to run several departments by proxy. You can make the point stick by quoting the old Negro who said, "When I prays for De Lawd to sen' me a turkey, nuffin happens. But when I prays for De Lawd to sen' me after a turkey, den de Lawd gits results." So remember, know your audience.

You are called on unexpectedly, and you might say, "I'm like the drunk who fell from a two-story window and hit the pavement with a terrific impact. A crowd gathered and as the drunk

39

staggered to his feet someone grabbed him by the arm and asked, 'What happened?' and he replied, 'I dunno; I just got here.' Now that's the way I feel today when you ask me to speak."

Not long ago I spoke at a national convention and heard a speaker use a good story to make a point stick. His point: the difficulty of knowing which solution to follow in solving a problem. His story: A couple visited the doctor who checked the husband and then said to the wife, "Your husband must have absolute quiet and rest. Here are some sleeping pills." The wife answered, "Thank you, doctor, when shall I give them to him?" and the doctor replied, "You don't give them to him. You take them yourself."

How to Build a Situation

Read those stories again and you'll see that each illustrates one basic idea. Each one is complete in itself. You will use this one-idea anecdote often. But you should learn the art of stringing together a number of jokes on the same subject. It's like this: Outline quickly a basic situation. Then it's easier for the audience to follow you through the laugh-provoking complications that develop out of that situation.

Jack Benny, for example, gets into his rattletrap Maxwell and sets the situation so adroitly that he is no longer a comedian in front of a microphone with gags. He is a guy named Jack Benny, a real person, engaged in a real struggle with a specific, tangible, worn-out, broken-down 1918 Maxwell automobile. It becomes a reality, not make-believe.

What follows: Jack tries to sell his Maxwell, a car that nobody in the world could possibly want. He not only tries to sell the Maxwell, but he demands a fantastic price for it. He not only demands a fantastic price, but he flatly refuses to consider less. As you see, he starts with an idea that is basically comic, and then he gets his laughs by hanging additional embellishments onto his original idea.

Even without building a situation, you can learn the art of

blending jokes into a smooth presentation. Here's the thing you must master: you must build your sequences so that you can tie up all of the jokes in each without abrupt jumps.

Milton Berle shows the vital importance of this point in an interview with Art Buchwald of the *Los Angeles Times*:

"For example, this is the wrong way to do it: 'I was up this morning . . . crack of my knuckles, took a brisk walk to my teeth, back in bed at 6:05—and speaking of taxes—they have a plan now, you pay as you go . . . but where are you going after you pay? Boy can my wife argue . . . .'

"You see, that's bad integration. You should stick to your subject. You must relate your subjects. Tell three or four jokes about each subject.

"Suppose you're talking about a restaurant. You say: 'They had three waiters at each table—one to give you your check and the other two to pick you up. There was a sign in the restaurant, 'Watch Your Hat and Coat.' While I was watching them someone stole my soup. They were independent waiters—they took orders from no one.

"Now you want to get into hotel jokes, so in order to marry the two you say: 'But the service at my hotel was better than the service at the restaurant.' Then you go into the hotel jokes. It comes naturally."

How can you establish something of a situation—some idea or topic around which you can blend some jokes? First, select one which possesses audience appeal, and then select some gags and jokes which will carry the thread of the story. Let's see how it works as a war veteran recalls his training-camp experiences:

"Was our camp big? It was so large we had to take a five-mile walk to get a place to start. When I first went to camp they issued us lots of soap and bath towels, which would have been fine if they had had time to build some showers. What barracks we had—when the wind blew hard the termites had to hold hands to keep the buildings from falling down. And were they small—why, our barracks were so small that even the rats were hunchbacked. And crowded—the guy on my left hand talked in his sleep and the guy on my right answered him!"

Easy to do? Not at first. But you can learn the art of keeping your jokes and topics connected and marching by planning, practice, and persistence.

Tests for a Usable Story

How can you make an anecdote usable?

For one thing, it should harmonize with your type of presentation. It's pretty hard to get guffaws from a rube joke if you're wearing a tuxedo and speaking with a British accent. What's more, you'll get faster audience identification if they feel that what you're telling really happened to you—that it was in the realm of your experience. Then it has the ring of truth.

But here's the main thing in blending a joke with a speech idea: it must fit the idea, the audience, and the occasion. Experiment with several "lead-ins" on a joke. Try to inject several laugh lines into one situation. Revise them. Actually, it depends to a great degree on your own ingenuity in adding a special point, a ludicrous twist, or recalling an amusing incident.

You will note that a suggested application is given at the conclusion of each anecdote in this chapter. Few can be used verbatim. Rather you might get an idea from the suggested tie-in. Or better still, try building a comic situation from one of them. But always remember that any story can be strengthened when you add your own characteristic touches—touches which enhance its mirth or moral.

How do you tie an anecdote to a situation? These examples will show you possible ways:

Meanings:

A man said to his friend, "You know, when I was a boy, I used to think Sodom and Gomorrah were man and wife." And his friend answered, "You've got nothing on me. I thought the Epistles were the wives of the Apostles."

("So many new words have been added to our vocabulary that it's hard to understand them. It's like two of my friends who were discussing religion and one of them said . . . .")

Changing Conditions:

A man called up a doctor in the middle of the night and said, "Doctor, come over here quick! My wife is awfully sick. I think she will need an operation for appendicitis." And the doctor replied, "Man! You're crazy! Your wife couldn't have appendicitis. I took out her appendix myself six or seven years ago. Did you ever hear of a woman having a second appendix?" And the fellow replied, "No, Doc, but didn't you ever hear of a man with a second wife?"

("Things are going to keep changing and we have got to be flexible in our thinking. It's like my neighbor who called up the doctor . . . .")

Promises:

A doctor was quizzing a man at the end of a first-aid course. "Suppose," he asked, "you saw a car accident and you found a man bleeding profusely in the arm. What would you do?"

"I'd give him some brandy," answered the man.

The doctor, wishing to give him a second chance, said, "And what if you hadn't any?"

The man thought a moment. "Then I'd promise him some."

(You might suggest that promises motivate people but we should fulfill those we make.)

Compromise:

My wife wanted a fur coat and I wanted a car. So we composed a compromise: got a fur coat and keep it in the garage.
("All of us want certain things in life. But often we have to 'give in' a little. It's like my wife and me . . . .")

43

Inadequacy:

A Kentucky hillbilly, severely injured in an automobile accident, was rushed to a hospital. His worried wife watched the doctor prepare to operate.

"What's that stuff you're getting ready?" the wife asked.

"An anesthetic," explained the surgeon. "Once he sniffs this he won't know a thing."

"Save your time," exclaimed the wife. "He don't know nothing nohow."

(One way of expressing an inadequacy in a subject you have been asked to discuss. "My present situation is like that of the Kentucky mountaineer, severely injured in an automobile accident . . . .")

Divided Opinions:

A Negro gentleman had been a preacher for some time and someone asked him, "Uncle Amos, how many members have you got in your church?"

And he replied, "I got sixteen."

"Are they all active?"

And the old preacher answered, "Yes, eight of them fur me and eight of them agin me."

("We have divided opinions on our subject. What's more, people are actively supporting each side . . . .")

Among experts:

A man was walking down the street early one morning wearing a barrel. He was stopped by a policeman who asked, "Are you a poker player?" And the man answered, "No, but I just left four fellows who are."

(You might use this to admit that you are speaking to experts.)

Observation:

The beautiful blonde lay on the hospital bed outside the operating room covered only by a sheet. Every now and then a white-

44

clad figure came along, gave her a cursory examination, and walked on. When the fourth one came along, she asked, "Doctor, when will they operate?"

"Don't know, lady," the man replied, "we're only painters working on this floor."

("Sharp observation not only brings us new facts but it becomes a fascinating habit. A doctor friend told me the case of the beautiful blonde . . . .")

Service:

A man who had been married for ten years consulted a marriage counselor. "When I first married," he said, "I was very happy. I'd come home from a hard day down at the shop. My little dog would race around barking and my wife would bring me my slippers. Now after all these years, everything's changed. When I come home, my dog brings me my slippers and my wife barks at me!"

"I don't know what you're complaining about," said the marriage counselor, "you're still getting the same service."

(Illustrating the point that merely giving the same service isn't enough. You must be sincerely interested in your customers, clients, friends.)

Problems:

Little Susie finished her Christmas drawing with two camels approaching the inn, over which was painted a huge star. The third camel and rider were going directly away from it.

"Why is the third man going in a different direction?" her mother asked.

Susie replied, "Oh, he's looking for a place to park."

("Many of today's problems are actually centuries old. A neighbor tells the story of his little daughter . . . .")

Personal Worth:

A customer inquired about the service-station manager's slow-moving inefficient helper and learned he'd been fired.

45

"Do you have anyone in mind to fill the vacancy?" asked the customer.

"Nope," replied the manager. "He didn't leave any vacancy." (Illustrating the point that we must do something unique—more than required—to make ourselves remembered.)

Producing under Pressure:

Did you hear about the glass blower with a bad case of hiccups? Before they could stop him he had blown 87 percolator tops.
(A useful story showing how anyone can produce more when under pressure.)

Accepting Troublesome Situations:

The selectee went by the draft-board office to protest his call to service. "They can't make me fight!" he yelled to a member of the board.

"Maybe not," the member said, "but they can take you where the fighting is and let you use your own judgment."
(We are thrown into situations over which we have no control. Let's accept some situations—unpleasant as they seem—and make the most of them.)

Same Old Tune:

A friend of mine plays the cello—in a kind of queer fashion. He clamps his fingers on one spot and saws away, and he never moves that left hand. One tone is all he ever produces. Finally his wife said to him, "Other people don't play the cello the way you play it. They move their left hand up and down. They don't just leave their fingers in one spot the way you are doing."

"Oh," he replied disgustedly, "they are just hunting for the place to play, but me, I've found it."
(Too many of us are satisfied to do the same thing in the same way. You must dare to be different. In fact, today you must dramatize everything to gain and hold public attention!)

Looking on the Run:

Sam Levenson told of his father towing six or seven Levensons, chained, hand to hand, through a museum. Suddenly, in irritation at the slowness of their progress through the halls, the father said, "Look, kids, if you're gonna stop and look at everything, you ain't gonna see nothin'."
(What we see and what we remember are important.)

The Right Language:

The farmer had driven his team of mules to town and was late returning. "What took so long?" his wife asked.
"On the way back," he explained, "I picked up the parson and from then on them mules didn't understand a thing I said."
(Illustrating the point that you must speak the language of those to whom you are appealing.)

Predicaments:

A woman explained to her psychiatrist, "I dreamed I was walking down the street with nothing on but a hat."
"Were you embarrassed?" asked the psychiatrist.
"Terribly," the woman answered, "it was my last year's hat."
("Sooner or later every person is caught in an embarrassing situation. We can feel a certain kinship to the woman who explained . . . .")

Tough Situations:

A woman, entertaining a friend's small son, asked, after watching his struggle: "Are you sure you can cut your meat?"
"Oh, yes," he replied, "we often have it as tough as this at home."
(The truthfulness of the chairman, or of someone giving a committee report, reminds me of one of our friends who was entertaining . . . .")

Far from Dead:

A young mother had just returned from the hospital. The doctor advised her to rest often.

While she was resting on the davenport, her five-year-old son was given the job of answering the bell.

One afternoon a florist with a large container of flowers rang the doorbell. Imagine the mother's surprise when she heard the son say: "Take them back. She isn't dead yet."

(You can emphasize that the organization is far from dead and that it isn't the time to sit back and wait for bouquets.)

Sharing Worries:

The young bride noticed that her husband was depressed. "George, dear," she whispered, "please tell me what is bothering you. Your worries are not your worries now—they are our worries."

"Oh, very well," said George. "We just had a letter from a girl in Detroit, and she is suing us for breach of promise."

("Only as we know and understand all of our problems can we strengthen our internal public relations. Sometimes we are as surprised as the young bride . . . .")

Commanding Speaker:

One day in New Mexico an Indian was transmitting smoke signals to other Indians on a distant hill. All at once there was a big explosion and he jumped between two rocks. It was the atomic-bomb experiment. As he arose he saw a tower of smoke billow toward the sky. He watched in awe-stricken silence for a moment and then murmured, "I wish I had said that."

(Here is an excellent story which you may use to commend the preceding speaker or the chairman. Like the Indian you may find yourself wishing you had said some of the witticisms, proverbs, or inspirational lifts given by Mr. Speaker.)

Peculiar Problems:

The traffic officer became highly enraged at an elderly woman who, after he'd flagged her to stay on the sidewalk, strolled calmly out into the street. "Lady," roared the officer, "don't you know what it means when I hold up my hand?"

"I ought to," she snapped. "For the past twenty-five years I've been a schoolteacher!"
(You may confess that you are intimately acquainted with some of the problems and worries of the particular group which you are addressing.)

Spilling the Bones:

A family had been enjoying the big steak dinner in their favorite restaurant, but they weren't able to finish it all. The father signaled the waiter. "May we have a bag for the leavings, please? We'll take them home to the dog."

"Oh, boy," piped up the young son, "are we going to get a dog?"
(We should take people into our confidence. Only then can we avoid misunderstanding and trouble.)

Sense of Humor:

John Barrymore's frequent sieges of illness in his final years greatly restricted his activities. The actor was permitted to eat, drink, and do very little. Once, after serving the starved Barrymore his usual crumb of dinner, his nurse asked: "Is there anything else you would like?"

"Why, yes," he replied, "could you get me a postage stamp? I believe I'll do a little reading."
(Illustrates value of a sense of humor—a gift which gives us power in problem situations.)

What's the first step in gearing a gag to a situation? Find out all you can about your audience—what motivates it—what it sees as humorous. Then blend jokes with the basic ideas of your talk. Never, never, drag in jokes simply because they are funny—make them fit the event. First learn to weld a single wisecrack to an idea. Next, try to build a comic situation of several jokes. Personalize and localize. Then you'll hear chuckles because you have learned the art of linking laughs to ideas.

CHAPTER 5

How to Make Your Own Mirth

SAM LEVENSON MAKES US LAUGH by holding up a mirror to life.

We chuckle at Jack Benny because the jokes are "on" him, on his personality traits—stinginess, conceit, impatience.

Milton Berle gets laughs because he has perfected the art of buffoonery.

Sid Caesar combines pantomime, timing, and hilarious phrases so that you are amused and actually live in the world which he creates.

George Gobel blends the ridiculous with the sublime truth, and, combining a fresh approach and a unique delivery, he perceives what is comical and translates it so that we chuckle.

Groucho Marx, as an impromptu jester, combines a sharp wit and a smooth delivery to amuse audiences.

Each is a unique humorist. But just as important: these humorists and especially their writers are masters in the use of certain formulas in creating and presenting humor. You should know some of these patterns because by practice, work, and study, you can create jokes.

How can you start to make your own mirth?

By mastering five basic principles:

1. Gather and analyze raw material.

51

2. Learn to identify vital formulas and devices in humor patterns.

3. Develop a comic point of view.

4. Apply the formulas until you find the best way of getting humor from a situation.

5. Write! Experiment! Revise! Work!

First of all, read all the jokes you can—old jokes, new jokes. You may gradually tire of this because you won't smile at one in a thousand. But you'll begin to see the structure and also understand some of the devices used in mirth-making. And, as an added benefit, this study will strengthen your comic point of view.

"Good enough," you say, "but tell me exactly how I can manufacture my own jokes." Very well. Let's take a swing around and look at some of the processes, strategies, and devices which will produce jokes.

Files Generate Many Ideas

Every humorous speaker should keep a file of comic material —not just to use in speeches but as a springboard for new ideas. One successful speaker saves humor from magazines, and when he gets enough clippings, he has them bound in a hard cover with a label showing contents.

File examples any way you wish. Categories might include puns, anecdotes, jokes, amusing essays, funny true experiences, published epigrams, comic strips, light verse, cartoons, collections of jokes and gags, or old books or magazines containing humor items.

In using this idea file you'll find it invaluable in analyzing types and techniques of humor written in the past. This is important: classify your material in such a way that you can use it best.

Let's suppose you run across this joke in your files:

Doctor: "How old did you say you were?"
Woman: "I never mention my age, but as a matter of fact, I've just reached twenty-one."

Doctor: "Indeed. What detained you?"

As you analyze this you see that it is based on an old topic: a woman's fear of revealing her age. Secondly, note the choice of the two characters chosen to express the idea. We see that the writer decided that dialogue would be the best form of getting across the idea. Could the dialogue be improved? Is the setting logical? These and other questions and comments occur to you as you dig to see what makes the example click. Best of all, you can experiment with this basic characteristic of women and perhaps you'll come up with a new anecdote which you can use.

Extend Other Quips

As you read and devour joke books you'll find that others' quips will frequently furnish the starting point for your own. Many modern witticisms, as you know, are merely treatments of common expressions, adages, familiar sayings, and clichés. So you take something a bit old and clever and try to give it a new twist—something unexpected.

All your life you've heard that "Cleanliness is next to godliness." Someone took this observation, stretched it out a little farther, and emerged with "Cleanliness is next to godliness, but in children it's next to impossible." Another writer took the phrase "Reap as you sow," gave it an extra phrase, and made it into "Every man reaps what he sows, except the amateur gardener." James A. Sanaker took an oldie, gave it a different twist, and wrote: "He who hesitates will hear horns tooting."

Share Typical Experiences

Watch life about you and you'll find a lot of chuckles in the commonplace. When you give a typical experience a touch of fun you'll have a ready-made audience. For when a person hears something familiar, he is already along the road to laughter.

Take, for example, the husband who is dressed and ready to go to the party and who impatiently waits on his wife. Or, here's the man whose hat blows off and who scrambles to retrieve it. Then there's the kid who is homesick at his first summer camp.

It's like this: Every day things are happening to you that are happening to other people. Your hair is gradually falling out, your waistline is expanding, and your teen-age daughter continues to monopolize the family telephone. Each of these can provide the take-off for scores of jokes.

In developing this shared experience as one of your sources of humor, you do not tell about it too directly, too plainly. Rather, use indirection. "Let him 'get it,'" John Bailey, former humor editor of *The Saturday Evening Post*, advises. "This will give him pleasure, and he will sometimes laugh just at "getting it."

How many customers in a supermarket lift and perhaps pinch each head of lettuce before buying? Practically every adult has shared that experience (or knows someone who has the habit). I use this by telling that I was shopping and was "testing" the lettuce. I took each head, lifted it, and felt it for firmness. Actually, I had no idea how long I stood there. Finally, just as I had picked out a large, firm head and placed it in my shopping basket, an old lady (whom I did not know was near by) asked, "Could you please tell me which is the second-best head?"

Try Switching the Setting

Often the impact of a joke is determined by switching something out of its natural order or setting. In this device you take a person, place, or thing out of its natural setting and put it into another which is abnormal or unexpected.

Here a modern situation in a primitive setting:
Cannibal chief's remark as he holds burning stake over white man: "But first, our national anthem."

Modern sales situation in old-time background:
Nattily dressed young man—cutaway coat, striped trousers, boutonniere—to Indian woman in native dress making vases outside tipi: "O.K., Mother, you can knock off for lunch."

Reversing situation:
Huge bartender with both arms encircled around neck of little man at bar: "Now let me tell *you* about *my* troubles."

Mother rabbit to small one: "A magician pulled you out of a hat, so stop asking questions."

Papa flea, after a hard day at the circus: "Shall we walk or take a dog?"

Words of an intellectual uttered by a hobo:
Red Skelton, dressed sloppily as Freddie the Freeloader, tells a policeman: "How dare you impugn the veracity of my statements by casting aspersions on my character?"

Here's the key in using this process: Pick up the normal and lift it into the abnormal.

How to Invent Topicals

Chances are that if you read a Bob Hope script of even a year ago you won't find it too amusing. Why? It's simply because Bob is a master of the topical joke, a quip based on today's headlines. He did not invent topical humor, but he has carried it to its greatest heights.

Unlike Will Rogers, who also tied in his humor with happenings of the moment, Bob's quips are not based on any philosophical or satirical content. Rather, he reels off snappy jokes based on headlines—headlines screaming the big news of the day.

Examples of topicals? Here you are:

Everybody's worried—even the psychiatrists are going to psychiatrists.

"Nikita Khrushchev was very flattered at going to the luncheon at 20th Century–Fox. He thought the studio was named after him."

—Bob Hope

55

Bing Crosby bought a secondhand rowing machine to help him lose weight. He got it for a ridiculous figure.

A baby sardine was frightened when the "Nautilus" submarine came into sight. But his mother calmed him when she said, "Don't be afraid. It's just a can of people."

Inflation is just a drop in the buck.

A resident of Cape Canaveral, Florida, saw the Washington Monument for the first time and remarked, "They'll never get it off the ground."

In America we have more experts on marriage than any other country in the world—and more divorces.

Now you're asking, "How can I produce topicals?" First, pick something in the headlines—something people are discussing. It can be a personality, a movement, invention, a contest—practically anything. Watch for news reports for comments and predictions made by speakers. Suppose you see the headline, "Psychologist Says Too Many Gifts Spoil Children." Think of how parents often tell their children what they had to do without when they were growing up. And then you might come up with this: "What on earth will today's younger generation be able to tell their children they had to do without?"

It's Smart to Use Dumb Jokes

Audiences love stories which make them feel superior. You can use this element of humor in "dumb" jokes—jokes in which your listeners feel superior to the characters therein. "Dumb" jokes will get laughs because they involve the ego motive of your listeners.

Let's look at some examples:

Girl to boy: "Ah, the moon is out. There's romance in the air. Look at all those parked cars in this shady lane. Doesn't that mean anything to you?"

Boy: "Yeah, let's get out and steal some hubcaps."

Mrs. Newly Rich, showing living room of the new mansion to country cousin: "Do you realize that this particular pattern is extinct?"
Cousin: "It sure does."

Stooge: "I just played some checkers with my dog."
Comic: "He's a pretty smart dog."
Stooge: "I wouldn't say that—I beat him three out of four games."

Judge: "What's the charge against this man?"
Cop: "Bigotry, your honor. He's got three wives."
Judge: "You dumbbell! That's not bigotry. That's trigonometry."

Boss: "Why are you carrying only one board when the other men are carrying two?"
Laborer: "Maybe they're too lazy to make a second trip."

Try these suggestions in creating "dumb" jokes:
1. Beware of poking fun at someone whom your audience respects.
2. Size up your audience and then think of something—or somebody—on which you can build this type of joke (businessmen will laugh at dumb qualities of their competitors, motorists at traffic cops, etc.)
3. Jot down every idea that pops into your mind in connection with the subject. Then find some trait around which you can build a ridiculous subject.
4. Reduce your joke to the fewest possible words. Polish it. Be sure the surprise comes at the end.

Right Association Is Funny

One form of humor is to find and exaggerate the similarities and differences between any two objects. How do you start? You jot down every possible idea which is connected with an idea, person, event, place, or whatever you are working with. Ordinarily, the more ideas you have, the better your chances of emerging with something funny. Let's suppose you are going to compare a glamorous movie star with a football coach. Think of all the possible characteristics of each and write in separate columns. Like this:

A. Football coach
strict disciplinarian
formations
defensive plays
offensive plays
officials
players
worrier

B. Movie star
photogenic
hard worker
dazzling beauty
on guard against wolves
temperamental
publicity seeker

Here's the situation: The Hollywood star is asked to speak briefly as guest of honor at a football coaches' luncheon. We try different combinations from each of the above lists. Finally, we associate "defensive plays" from the coach list with "on guard against wolves" from the starlet list and come up with this line for the star: "I probably have devised more defensive plays than all of you put together."

Give Definitions a Whirl

Experiment in devising new definitions. A humorous definition, Ron Carver, expert on humor, points out, "can be whimsical, but usually has more reality than whimsy." The next time you watch Bob Hope on television, pay special attention to the masterful way in which he uses clever definitions to get laughter. Something like this: "Went down today to get my automobile plates. Plates—in California, that's a license to hunt with a car."

Sometimes you can create a definition by association (meteorologists—forecasts, highs, lows, storms, weather) and punning. Like this: a meteorologist is a man who can look into a girl's eyes and tell whether.

Study the ingredients in the following:

Hollywood is where, if a guy's wife looks like a new woman, she probably is.

He's at that awkward age—too tall for keyholes, too short for transoms.

A popular song is one that makes us all think we can sing.
—*Brick Bits*

Adolescence is that period in a child's life when his parents become more difficult.
—*Mad*

At the party, we played "Pony Express." Pony Express. That's like "Post Office" but with more horsing around.

Politics is a game in which some men are self-made but most are machine-made.
—Rochester (N. Y.) *Democrat & Chronicle*

Flattery is something said to your face that wouldn't be said behind your back.

Poise: the ability to continue talking while the other fellow picks up the check.

A caddy is a boy who stands behind you and didn't see where it went, either.

A pretzel is a drinking man's filter.

Keep Your Verse Terse

Do you have a knack of turning a phrase or two into light verse? Can you create humor in verse? Good! Then by all means step up this skill so that you can use some of your original material in humorous addresses.

59

This form of writing differs from poetry in that it takes the form of ridicule and absurdity. What about forms? "Light verse emphasizes rollicking meters, odd and unexpected rhymes, novel arrangements of lines and stanzas, along with word play and double meaning," it is explained by Richard Armour, a past master in creating this type of humor, in *Writing and Selling Fillers and Short Humor* (edited by A. S. Burack).

Let's look at some examples:

No wonder the little duckling
Wears on his face a frown:
For he just discovered
His first pair of pants is down!

IT'S ASTRONOMICAL

Twinkle, twinkle, little star,
I don't wonder what you are:
I surmised your spot in space
When you left your missile base.

Any wondering I do
Centers on the price of you,
And I shudder when I think
What you're costing us per twink.
　　　　—William W. Pratt in *The Wall Street Journal*

Don't tell your friends about your indigestion:
"How are you!" is a greeting, not a question.
　　　　—Arthur Guiterman

MY PASTOR'S EYES

My pastor's eyes I've never seen
Though the light in them may shine:
For when he prays, he closes his,
And when he preaches, mine.

NOT A CLOUD IN THE SKY

The Indians chant and dance about
To break a crop-destroying drought,
But I've a simpler means by far:
I only have to wash my car.

—Richard Armour

Obviously, your light verse, like most other forms of humor, should have a little surprise at the end. Read the foregoing examples again and note the climactic twist at the end of each.

Here are some things to keep in mind in writing light verse: (1) keep each as brief as possible, (2) stick to commonplace experiences, (3) keep hooking the listener through originality of thought, humorous touch, expectation of what is to come, or keeping him curious to see what word you can possibly find to rhyme with the word at the end of the line he has just heard.

If you are really an avid "versifier" you will always be on the lookout for words that sound alike and bring to mind an entertaining idea, John Fellon reminds us in *Writer's Digest*. And then he asks, "Who can deny that 'awakening' and 'egg-and-baconing' were meant for each other?"

How can you write amusing verse? Be alert to human foibles, bits of conversation, news items, experiences—all of these can produce ideas. Study the works of Richard Armour, Arthur Guiterman, Dorothy Parker, Margaret Fishback, David McCord, Morris Bishop, Phyllis McGinley, and others. Experiment with rhyming. And take each piece you turn out and rewrite and polish it until it finally can be given naturally and easily.

Exaggerate for Fun

For some reason or other, when you exaggerate things enough, it makes people laugh. The word exaggerate is defined in *Webster's New Collegiate Dictionary* as: "to extend beyond bounds or the truth; to overstate the truth concerning . . . to enlarge or increase beyond the normal." As you delve into the fun factors of jokes you'll be surprised to see how many are based on some form of exaggeration.

Ron Carver points out that there are three types of exaggeration. They are (1) idea type, (2) image type, and (3) the wacky-zany variety. Let's look at examples of the first two and then take a longer look at the third type:

1. *Idea type:*

"My girl friend is so shy. In school she won't even do improper fractions."

"Music is so terrible in the new cafe that when the waiter dropped a tray of dishes last night, everyone got up and started dancing."

"I wouldn't say the steak was tough, but I tried to get the waiter to take it back and he refused. He accused me of bending it."

2. *Image type:*

"He was so fat that when he got a shine he just had to take the shine boy's word for it."

"Is he ugly? Well! He goes on right after the monkey act and the audience thinks it's an encore."

"She had so many chins I didn't know which one she was going to talk out of next."

"There's a guy in Toronto who has so many gold teeth he has to sleep with his head in a safe."

"He plays the pinball machine so much that every time he swallows his face lights up."

How can you create jokes with this device? Obviously, decide first what you want to exaggerate. This can be a quality, a situation, a characteristic, a trait, an emotion—anything distinctive which applies to something.

Let's suppose, for example, that you want to exaggerate the age of an automobile. Here are some things that might come to mind:

motor ("It's so old the rubber bands keep coming off.")
fuel
lights ("So dim they look like a couple of lightning bugs.")
tires
noisy
durability ("It's really strong—it was struck by lightning and the lightning was hauled away for repairs.")

Now let's see how Ed Wynn exaggerated his car's age when he gave it to James Melton for his antique-car museum: "It's so old the insurance covers fire, theft, and Indian raids."

3. *Wacky-zany type:*

Don't overlook wacky witticisms. We've seen that some jokes are based on reality—things that can happen or do happen. Now on the other extreme we have gags based on the wacky-zany formula. They combine exaggeration with a touch of whimsy. they are never rooted in reality. "These gags," Sidney Reznick reminds us, "are completely irrational and fantastically ridiculous."

Here are examples:

First dog: "I feel so poorly lately—tired all the time."
Second dog: "Have you thought of going to a psychiatrist?"
First dog: "Heavens, no! You know I'm not allowed on couches."

One ghost asked another, "Do you believe in people?"

"I caught a fish so big that when I pulled it out the tide went out."

"A sailor got so thin that the battleship he had tattooed on his chest shrunk to a rowboat."

A pink elephant, a green rat, and a yellow snake entered the cocktail lounge and sat down at the bar. The bartender gazed at them, looked up at the clock, and said, "You're a little early, boys —he ain't come in yet."

Depositor: "I want to see the person in charge of my account."
Banker: "See the Vice-President in charge of sinking funds."
Depositor: "Where is he?"
Banker: "Near the sink. He's probably tap happy."

"Here's an autograph of Mark Twain."
"All I see is an X."
"Well, that's his Mark."
"Where's the Twain?"
"Down at the station."

I know there are plenty of fish in the seas—but who wants to park in the dark with a shark?

In writing this "it can't happen here" type, you must take a topic and extend your imagination into ridiculous possibilities. Keep bouncing your ideas around. Do plenty of freewheeling. Example: Let's imagine that a midget falls into a bowl of soup. Let's say it's alphabet soup. How can he save himself? Swimming to shore? Yelling for help? Floating on the surface until someone rescues him? After trying many possibilities, we might decide on the following: "Then there's the one about the midget who fell into a bowl of alphabet soup. He saved himself by throwing out an SOS."

Word Play Brings Witticisms

One night on a television show George S. Kaufman got himself mired in the word "euphemism." After playing with it for a few seconds he turned to his fellow panelist Sam Levenson and declared, "Euphemism and I'm for youse'm," and closed the discussion.

Experts on the same quiz show were asked to identify a certain Middle Eastern potentate. John Gunther confidently supplied the correct answer.

"Are you Shah?" Clifton Fadiman, the emcee, asked.

"Sultanly," Gunther replied.

You recognize that these are puns which constitute one type of humor (some people groan when they hear them) in the broad area of word play. Fadiman, who relates both in *Any Number Can Play*, says that "To a great practitioner a pun is language on vacation, but to the nonpractitioner it may seem more like language in agony."

How does a pun play a trick on the mind? Mainly because each word carries a meaning—and we expect a meaning. So when one does collapse or our expectation comes to nothing—or to something altogether different—we know that it has fooled us.

As a speaker you can give comments on the news and add lightness by using a few good puns (they are so rare!). Here are some collected by Gurney Williams of *Look*, with the comment set off in parenthesis:

In Denver, Colorado, a hen flew into the tax collector's office and laid an egg. (The ordinary taxpayer does this only when he is called on to try to explain a deduction.)

Two airmen demolished their light plane near Lupin Lodge, California, after skimming the treetops of a nudist camp. (Contrary to the accepted flying procedure, it's obvious they should have been less attentive to the take-off and avoided the strip altogether.)

The National Macaroni Institute estimates that every American ate an average of 25,000 inches of spaghetti last year. (This obviously does not include yardage lost by incomplete passes.)

Here are some other types of humor which come from a play on words:

Secondary meaning:

From a Classified ad: Woman wanted as housekeeper. No clothing.

From a News story: The pastor will preach his farewell address. The choir will sing "Break Forth into Joy."

From a Theater column: "Flo Burton was picked for one of the leading roles in *Pajama Game*. (And to show how talented she is, she got the part without pulling any strings.)

King Arthur: "I hear you've been misbehaving."
Sir Galahad: "In what manor, sir?"

Wife: "I thought you were going to the lodge meeting tonight."
Husband: "I was, but the wife of the Grand Exalted Invincible Supreme Potentate won't let him out."

Dialogue type (double meaning):

Personnel interviewer to pretty young applicant: "Have you had any experience?"
Girl: "Now that you mention it, I had a funny one last night."

Dear Dr. Whoosit: Our baby looks healthy and we are not going to take your advice and take him to a pediatrician as there is nothing wrong with his feet.

—Mrs. J. P. Cogginschmell

Policeman (producing notebook): "What's your name?"
Speeding motorist: "Aloysius Chysianczjichas."
Policeman (putting away notebook): "Don't let me catch you speeding again."

The boss, who was born in Europe, still had a struggle with the English language. Welcoming a new employee into his organization, he said warmly, "We are very happy to have you with us. As you know, we're a little underhanded around here."

"Psychic" slip (often creates a truth):

Bob Hope's gag of last winter at a Miami Beach hotel: "I've never seen so many millionaires in one place. And I don't mean the guests—the waiters!"

Return to the literal:

Pawnbroker's sign: "See Me at Your Earliest Inconvenience."

From a Petersburg, Virginia, paper: "The doctor felt the patient's purse, and admitted that there was nothing he could do."

Substitution (intentional):

Where there's smoke, there's toast.

One touch of scandal makes the whole world chin.

Men often make passes at girls who drain glasses.

Parody (follows form of original but changes its sense to nonsense):

The kind of girl who likes to eat her cake and have yours, too.

Early to bed, early to rise, and you never meet the regular guys.

Laugh and the world laughs with you—cry and you end up on "Queen for a Day."

You know that people often laugh because it gives them a feeling of superiority. Remember this principle as you use word play in the jokes which you write. It can work like this: Wife, to her dragged-in husband at opera: "Hasn't that soprano a large repertoire?" and he replies, "Yes, and that dress she is wearing makes it look worse."

You can often create a joke by putting the wrong word (but one which sounds similar) into the mouth of a child:

Kid: "My sister's getting married tomorrow."
Second Kid: "Bet she's busy right now."
First Kid: "Sure is. She's in her room getting her torso ready."

As you see from these examples, some of them are verbal tricks. They are the old trick of starting you off in the figurative and landing you in the literal spot—or vice versa. And yet the humor of some of the lines does not lie in that trick alone. Artemus Ward's best joke, in the opinion of Josh Billings, was his remark when talking of Brigham Young and the Mormons that "the pretty girls in Utah mostly marry Young." Ward mixed mischievous exaggeration with a pun, and the result is comical.

How can you create fun with words? Study the types and examples given here, and then start freewheeling on your own. Be sensitive to words and their meanings. Experiment with words which sound alike or similar. Think of others which have a double meaning. Be alert to the mispronunciation of certain words.

Watch, too, to see that many of the witticisms in this area of humor are not plays upon words only, but upon imagination and emotional atmosphere.

Summing up: a play on words can be atrocious and pointless; but where you create a verbalness with its point keen and clear, then you can bring joy to your audience.

Don't be Afraid of Insults

Ever notice how Groucho Marx insults contestants on his program? Some viewers think he is very rude. What they don't know is this: contestants are chosen many days in advance of the filming of the show, and their interviews are prepared by a staff of comedy writers. Men and women are not dragged from the audience to cower before Groucho's wit. He does not see the contestants before the show, but he works some in advance from an outline which gives a few facts about each person.

Of all comedians, he is undoubtedly the master in using the insult-quip.

Humorous speakers use two kinds of insults. One is the self-insult (often stated unconsciously), plus truth regarding oneself. Example: "Anybody who takes me for a fool makes no mistake!" The other type involves two persons, with one receiving the insult. For instance, two men meet at a party and one says, "This sure is a dull party. Think I'll leave," and his friend answers, "That should help some."

Here are others:

He: "Why won't you marry me? Is there someone else?"
She: "There must be."

"Did your mother have any children that lived?"

"I've got a splinter in my finger."
"Been scratching your head?"

"He's a born wit—and lost ground ever since."

"He worked with a name band. You should have heard the names they called it."

"For a moment I didn't recognize you—and believe me, I never spent a more enjoyable moment."

Your audience will be delighted with an insult or two. How can you be a bit brash and bold at times? Why the popularity of this type of humor? Milton Berle explains that "The insult is popular because it always boosts an audience's feeling of superiority over the object of the gag."

How can you create insult humor? Suppose that the master of ceremonies has mentioned the fact that your coming reminded him of the days when you were in college together. He emphasizes the fact that you were an outstanding student, well known. And then he adds, "He attained that remarkable distinction of being a four-letter man—Y.M.C.A." And the audience chuckles.

Now comes your turn. How can you create a barbed witticism which you can relate to your college days together? How can you deflate him? Would you like to show his low grades? His failures as a campus Romeo? How many years he attended? Let's take the last idea and see what happens. Suppose you say: "Mr. Big-dome was certainly well-known on the campus—everybody knew Percy Bigdome. Of course they should (slight pause) because he was a sophomore five years!"

Your listeners will always laugh at the self-insult—when the joke is on you. But before you "attack" suddenly; or "treat with insolence" another person or group, be sure of your audience. Through experience you will learn to use certain types of bold effrontery. Indeed, you'll learn to get away with some brazen flippancy when your listeners know that it's "all in fun."

Misunderstanding Causes Merry Mix-ups

Many a joke is a trick played on the mind—"playful disappointment of a momentary expectation." You hear the beginning of a joke, and your mind starts organizing the elements into a structural whole. And just as you expect a certain ending—pow!—something collapses.

You've often laughed at situations around you in which there is confusion and misinterpretation of viewpoints. One reason, of course, why you are amused is that you see both sides in the situation. Jokes based on misunderstandings follow this pattern.

You may use either the dumb or the deliberate approach in writing jokes with this device. Be sure that your listeners see both sides. Here are examples of both types:

Husband, answering the phone: "I don't know—call the weather bureau."
Wife: "Who was that?"
Husband: "Oh, some jerk asking if the the coast was clear."

Cop: "Don't you know you can't turn around in the middle of the block?"
Lady: "Oh, officer, I think I can."

Small boy: "Grandpa, were you on the ark?"
Grandpa: "Of course not!"
Boy: "Then how come you weren't drowned?"

"Do you believe in clubs for women?"
"I certainly do, but only when kindness fails."

Let's fashion a joke on the dumb approach combined with misunderstanding. Suppose we take Mr. Gotrocks, newly rich, but with all of his money not too bright. We want to indicate that he tries to throw his weight around with his wealth because he thinks money will buy everything. His wife needs an operation. So we fashion this scene: "The doctor asks Mr. Gotrocks, "Shall I give your wife a local anesthetic?" and he replies, "No, I'm rich. Give her the best—something imported."

In using this pattern, set up a situation where the listener experiences what Max Eastman termed "the suddenness of disappointment and the immediacy of reward." In other words, you must lead the listener with entire plausibility right up to a certain point and then make a rapid shift. Summing up: Success of this device depends largely on the dexterity with which the trick is played.

Too Little Often Is Ludicrous

Just as too much of something can often be funny, so too little of anything can bring laughter. Good example: Abraham Lincoln's story of a dog who swallowed a bomb with the fuse attached. "Rover was a good dog," his owner said, "but as a dog I am afraid his days of usefulness are over."

Another classic is the famous trapeze joke published in the *New Yorker* years ago. A trapezist, swinging high in the air by his feet, fails to catch a fellow trapezist who swings from another direction. The one high above yells to his mate as he hurtles downward, "Oops—sorry."

Why are these things humorous? "What really is to be learned from such jokes is the magic power possessed by a playful un-

71

derstatement," Max Eastman says in his *Enjoyment of Laughter*. "We all know it is not funny . . . for a flying trapeze artist to plunge to the earth in a circus. Such things are too wrenchingly terrible to be comic. But this little trick of the not-enough can make us laugh no less."

Here's another:

Comic: "There I was, hunting in Africa when suddenly a tribe of natives surrounded me! They beat me over the head, smashed every bone in my body, and ran their spears through me!"

Stooge: "It must have been painful."

Comic: "Only when I laughed."

Now let's see how we can use understatement in writing a joke. Suppose we start with a conflict—a woman and her husband with domestic trouble. Then we'll imagine a friend telling the woman the rumors she has heard about her and her husband. Now it looks like this:

"People are saying that you and your husband are not getting on very well together."

"Nonsense, we did have some words and I shot him, but that's as far as it went."

Plan Your Mispronunciation

Watch your favorite television comedian tonight. He may mispronounce a word (that gets a laugh) and then cover up with an ad lib (and that also gets a laugh). Both are planned. He may tell of his recent reunion with his fellow servicemen and say: "I saw my old buddies . . . brave men who left their families to fight in the South Pacific. As I mingled with these bottle-scarred (laughter)—I mean battle-scared. . . ." And then he covers the fluff: "I can't trust these store-bought teeth" (laughter).

This is known as the break-up formula, and when well-constructed it will bring two waves of laughter. Why? Your listeners enjoy your blooper. Well done, it contains a strong element of surprise. And if you do it realistically—with an all-over show of embarrassment—you'll get two laughs.

72

In working with this formula, try to find a word or phrase which sounds similar to the thing the audience expects you to say. Be sure that it could happen. Then when you find that, you must devise some remark to cover the fluff. Hard to do? Yes, indeed, but keep experimenting with some of your material until you have added the break-up formula to your creative repertoire. Then you can use it for a double payoff!

Letters Are Often Laughable

Humorists of several generations have used letters as laugh producers. Charley Weaver, the sage of Mount Idy and a veteran of the golden days of radio, made a big comeback with his letters from mama. He gets laughs with news items like the following:

"Birdie Rodd is pretty upset. Saturday night somebody broke into her house and stole her bathtub. She says whoever did it can keep the washrag, soap, and the tub, but she would like them to return her mother."

In his format he reads his mother's comments on funny happenings in the old home town. You will note that each joke revolves around a person whose name is given (jokes about persons are always funnier than jokes about things).

Another type of letter is a shorter one in which the joke is on the humorist. Its effect depends on a surprise ending. Like this:

DEAR MR. HARRAL:
Your humorous talks are terrific! They will be remembered long after Mark Twain, Will Rogers, Robert Benchley, Abe Martin, and Groucho Marx are forgotten—but not before.
Sincerely yours,
ELMER BOTTLEBAUM

If you'd like to use an occasional message, you can get ideas by reading collections of humorous letters. In writing one of comments, see that you (1) stay in character, (2) comment on things which could happen to the particular person writing it, and (3) blend your jokes and stories together so that they "read" like a letter. In writing a letter in which the joke is on you, work for a big build-up and a quick letdown.

"Sight Laughs" Get Hilarious Results

You'll get extra dividends in audience response when you show something which ties in with a joke. You may say, "The chairman asked me to say a few words," and you start unrolling a large roll of paper (supposedly containing your notes) across the podium. Or, you may start your talk like this: "Ladies and gentlemen, a few nights ago in Chicago I had the very great pleasure of addressing the Executives' Club dinner at hotel—hotel—what was the name of that hotel? Just a moment, I have it right here (and you reach in your inside coat pocket, pull out a silver spoon and read)—it was Hotel Congress." Do two things in combining sight and sound in a joke: (1) try to use something which is clever and unexpected, and (2) be sure that every person in the audience can see the gimmick you use.

Try Names for Fun

As a practicing jokesmith, you should know some of the many ways of using names with humorous results. One way: you can step up the fun impact of a story by tagging the character with a humorous name. Examples: Effie Klinker, Folfinger J. Undercuffer, and Mortimer Snerd (Edgar Bergen); Gomar Cool, Clara Kimball Moots, and Elsie Crack (Charley Weaver); Van Creighton van Eppess, Ivan Popnikoff, and Drizzle Puss (brother of Chief Rain-in-the-Face) (Harry Hershfield); and Oscar Fozzengoggle, Heminway Screble, and Elmer Smudgegunk ("Senator" Ed Ford).

Another way to use names in creating humor is to give a big build-up followed by a sudden comedown. Like this: "In the words of a noted child psychologist, Nancy Marie Jensen, our teen-age baby sitter . . . . Another: "We are reminded by Tennyson—that's my brother Tobias Tennyson, who drives a city dump truck . . . ."

At times you may do a take-off on some notable. Example: "You've heard of Hopalong Cassidy. Well, I'd like to present limpalong . . . ." Another: "And now we present one of Ziegfeld's greatest follies . . . ."

Occasionally, you can toss a brief insult by calling the recipient by a well-known person's name. Be sure that you select the strongest trait of the notable in using this "name-calling" device. Examples: When someone gives advice on marriage—"Now just a minute, Mickey Rooney (or Tommy Manville)." Or if someone becomes domineering—"Look here, now, Jimmy Hoffa."

In some situations you can give the characteristics of the celebrity without actually using his name. In a Bob Hope show a comedienne appearing with walrus-mustached Jerry Colonna called him "Beaver Puss" and later addressed him as "Shrub Mug."

Tagging a bald-headed man "Curly" or a human beanpole "Shorty" (reversal device) is a technique as old as mankind. We have a classic example in the writings of Tertullian: *"Cornelius Tacitus, sane ille mendaciorum loquacissimus"* ("Silent Cornelius, the most talkative liar of them all").

Here are other possibilities of using names in fun:

Pun:

A professor of Greek tore his suit and took it to a tailor named Acidopolus, from Athens. Mr. Acidopolus examined the suit, and asked, "Euripides?"

"Yes," said the professor. "Eumenides?"

Epitaph:

Walter Winchell: Here lies Walter Winchell in the dirt he loved so well.

Review of play:

"Tallulah Bankhead barged down the Nile last night as Cleopatra—and sank."

—John Mason Brown in the New York *Times*

75

Combination:

A short-story manuscript submitted to Whit Burnett at *Story Magazine* was a startling mélange of Hemingway, Dos Passos, Faulkner, Cain, and Saroyan. "Tell me," asked Burnett in his letter of rejection, "was your father an anthology?"

"Ego-Twist":

Oscar Levant, after listening to the late George Gershwin's monologue about himself, inquired: "George, if you had it to do over, would you fall in love with yourself again?"

Garbling:

Walter Pidgeon, the actor, had just given a talk before a group of clubwomen. As he was leaving, a flustered matron waylaid him, "Oh, my dear Mr. Privilege," she gushed. "This occasion has certainly been a pigeon!"

Wrong address:

The editor of a Vermont weekly sent to one Hiram Jones a notice that his subscription had expired. The notice came back with the laconic scrawl: "So's Hiram."

Odd combination:

Time reported a Montana marriage. Names of the wedded couple? Owen Smells and Mary Knows.

Diplomacy:

Little Mary's mother and father both fancied themselves as violinists. In front of both of them a visitor asked Mary, "Who do you think plays better your mother or your father?"

Mary, who will probably end up in the diplomatic corps, answered, "Heifetz."

Wrong association:

A parson was introduced to a Mrs. Hummock, and he tried to fix her name in his mind by rhyming it with stomach. He repeated it over and over—just to be sure. The next day he met her and yoohooed, "How do you do, Mrs. Kelly."

Good Build-ups Are Always Mirthful

You can add to your original fun files by learning to write build-ups. Here's how it's done: Take a line or a thought and build it into a certain pattern—always in a logical fashion. In this way you establish a dominant idea. Then you suddenly say the punch line or phrase, which gives a contrast.

Analyze these examples:

"I am delighted to have the privilege of visiting in your wonderful city—Briarwood Heights—deep in history, deep in tradition—and deep in debt."

First hunter: "Just met a big bear in the woods!"
Second: "Good! Did you give him both barrels?"
First: "Both barrels, hell! I gave him the whole gun."

Robber: "This is a stick up! Everybody reach!"
Woman: "Reach for what?"
Robber: "Don't confuse me. I'm a new man."

"Do you own your own boat?"
"No, but my dad has a schooner."
"How big is it?"
"It holds three quarts."

"Washington was a great man—
First in war
First in peace
—but he married a widow."

Boy describing girl friend: "Ah, those eyes, those lips, those chin."

"Teacher keeps me after school every day."
"Because you don't know the answers."
"Nope. Because I do."

"Is your husband bothered by evil thoughts?"
"Bothered? Why, he enjoys every one of them."

Bob Hope: "Colonna, I hear you know all about riding."
Colonna: "Of course, Hope. I've been riding sidesaddle since I was two."
Hope: "Colonna! Riding sidesaddle? That's a sissy way."
Colonna: "On an elephant?"

I'll never forget our old teacher, Mrs. Duffy, and she never forgets her former students. Occasionally she drops us a note and always addresses each in terms of his scholastic average—like Hundred Per Cent Harry, Ninety Per Cent Norman. I had a letter from her today—it began "Dear Zero."

It's Funny If You Write It Right

As you analyze devices and structures of humor you will note this: Each joke is based on certain words—words which build up to the punch line. Each word in a joke must contribute to the smash ending. What to do: make sure that each joke you write or use is tightened and polished into its best form. By making a few changes in wording and phrasing, improvements can often be made.

Brevity is usually the soul of wit; but another element is just as important: holding the surprise until the end. Note this: the joke that people don't really see coming is the most powerful of all. For example, take the following witticism, in its first and then in its improved form:

(First draft):

Lawyer, reading will of the deceased: "I leave my sun lamp to my brother-in-law, George, who always maintained that health was more important than wealth."

(Second draft):

"And to my brother-in-law, George, who always maintained that health was more important than wealth, I leave my sun lamp."

Notice that the phrase "my sun lamp"—which gives the joke its kick—is placed in its proper end position in the second draft.

Word choice and order determines whether your jokes click or clank. Should you avoid the choice of certain words? Is the specific more effective than the general? In *How to Write Jokes*, Sidney Reznick gives these helpful suggestions:

(1) Keep the language in the comedian's (or speaker's) character and keep it simple.

(2) Avoid odd or tricky sentence structure.

(3) Don't clutter up a joke with words that distract and are not necessary to your joke.

(4) Try to get the key word or words in your punch line as close to the end of the gag as you possibly can.

(5) Equally as injurious to a gag as overwriting is underwriting (by trimming too many words you rush the joke, kill its fundamental rhythm, present an inadequate exposition of the key points, and sacrifice clarity).

(6) Replace neutral words with more colorful ones where they help add zing to your gag (use an exact name rather than mention of a product itself; say "Once when I was visiting in Chicago," not "in a big city"; say "our Cocker Spaniel," rather than "our dog.")

(7) Substitute neutral words for certain "emotional" words which may evoke serious, unpleasant thoughts in the minds of your listeners (avoid saying "physically handicapped," "incurable disease"—any words or phrases which evoke negative reactions).

Strengthen Your Flair for Fun

By now you have seen some of the main devices and formulas

which the expert jokesmiths use. Some of them are actually over-simplifications. You have seen that this business of "being funny" is not the simple thing that it might have seemed on first inspection. Rather, you see that you must understand the basic humor patterns and learn to fashion jokes from them.

One thing is clear: creation of humor is much more than following a set of rules. Humor involves a point of view. "To write effective humor," Robert Orben in *Comedy Technique* reminds us, "you have to think funny. When you think funny enough the comedy bursts out in all directions and your only remaining job is to write it down. That's all there is to it. If you approach comedy with a sober face and a book full of rules, you're foredoomed to failure. There isn't a comedy writer today who uses mechanical means to create his humor. They just sit down at a typewriter, think funny and type."

By working hard enough you can dream up gags and jokes through sheer inspiration (which usually strikes when you are working hardest), or you can take the essence from old wisecracks and dress them up in new clothes. Let's be frank: writing humor is hard work, and there's nothing amusing about rewriting one line for four hours before you come up with a funny one.

Yet there is something beneath the process. It can be called "savvy" or "know-how" or a flair for humor. If you can say or do funny things—if you want to work hard in a complex but fascinating area—then you can follow the tips revealed in this chapter and gradually you'll discover the thrill and satisfaction of manufacturing your own mirth!

6

The Finer Points of Funny Talks

WHEN CALVIN COOLIDGE was serving as president of the Massachusetts Senate, one senator, in the heat of argument, advised another to go to hell.

"Mr. President," shouted the offended senator, "did you hear what my colleague said to me? I demand action!"

"I heard," Coolidge replied. "I've already looked up the law, and you don't have to go."

Wise "Cal" took a serious situation, kidded it a bit, smoothed over a rough place, and everyone was happy.

To be successful in amusing people, you must keep your sense of humor operating under all conditions. Comedian Ernie Kovacs once spent fifteen months in the hospital. His illness was critical, but he never lost his manic sense of humor.

One doctor recalls the day they brought Ernie to the X-ray laboratory on a stretcher, draped in a sheet: "When we looked at him through the fluoroscope we were startled to see a sign that read OUT TO LUNCH." Ernie had cut it out of aluminum foil and pasted it on his stomach.

As a practicing humorist, you will discover that the whole world—its fun and frustrations—can provide situations for amusing comments and stories. With hard work and practice, you can twist these into funny gags and jokes. You can become more amusing. You can put more punch into your delivery. Let's get down to business and look at some of the qualities that will give you secret power as a jester.

Watch for Chuckles in the Commonplace

Sam Levenson is a master in the art of making humorous comments about contemporary things: television, dieting, child psychology, taxes. "Basically," he explains, "I seek the common denominator, the emotion, the fact, the memory, the experience that brings men closer together, and very often I find the denominator in the 'little things,'" How does he do it? He focuses on the commonplace, exaggerates a bit, and the results are strong humorous impressions.

Look how other humorists comment on the current scene:

Those new compact cars are great: you can now squeeze twice as many cars into the traffic jam.

—Earl Wilson

You know why drive-in banks were established, don't you? So the cars could see their real owners.

—Thomas J. Mullen

Many of the newest hairdos look not quite done.

—Indianapolis *News*

Income taxes often transform nest eggs into goose eggs.

—Shannon Fife

Spend your vacation right in your own back yard and your friends will know the kind of person you are—sensible, imaginative, home-loving, and broke.

—Bill Vaughan

Science has been taking great strides forward. Now it's only fifty years behind the comic book.

HUMOR IS PUTTING WORDS TOGETHER AFTER
YOU'VE LEARNED HOW PEOPLE AND LIFE ARE PUT TOGETHER.

Concentrate on the Actual

Once when I went to a high school to give the commencement address the valedictorian, speaking with dead earnestness, got one of his lines mixed up. Peering over the footlights, with his right hand placed across his brow, he was giving his stirring oration. Still in the position of a man looking into the distance, he said, "As he skinned the damn horizon" (instead of "as he scanned the dim horizon"). Titters. Giggles. And then the whole audience broke into a roar.

The incident points up this fact: there's no substitute for the strength of the actual in humor. You must remember this as you gather material and whip your speech into shape. Oh, yes, we laugh at jokes we hear on the radio and TV and the sketches we see enacted at the theater. But your listeners will be more likely to double up with laughter if you relate amusing incidents in which they have become involved. Sam Levenson charms us with his wonderful stories—stories which we associate with ourselves in the most personal of ways. It is the laughter of recognition.

At a convention of pharmacists I told this story: A druggist became so deeply in debt with his business that he was summoned by his banker. After quite a long talk the druggist asked hopelessly, "Have you ever been in the drugstore business?" and the banker answered, "No." To which the druggist replied, "Well you're in it now."

My listeners broke into laughter. They recognized the actual in the situation.

Look and use the actual in your stories. Instead of telling a story about a man, tell it about a particular man. Don't say you were visiting a city—make it Louisville, Denver, or Omaha. By every possible means create the illusion of reality, because your listeners' enjoyment of your story increases in direct ratio to the completeness with which they are able to throw themselves into it and to believe it.

A JOKE MUST LIVE BEFORE
IT HITS PEOPLE WHERE THEY LIVE.

Picking Your Subject

"What can I discuss from a humorous point of view?" you ask. Try to pick a topic that is timely and appropriate for your audience. Obviously, your subject should be one that you know something about. For example, think of the many books and magazine articles which urge that we relax, let ourselves go.

Note carefully how Corey Ford takes this topic and amuses us in *Reader's Digest* (May, 1960):

"Who says I'm tense? I'm perfectly calm, I tell you. I'm as cool as a cubercum. I mean cucumber. I can lift a cup of coffee without spilling it, provided I hold onto my wrist with the other hand, and when I go to bed I sleep like a top. (Sometimes I spin all night.) I've been reading a book on how to relax, and I'm completely cucumbered, I mean cured.

"It's this undo-it-yourself fad that's sweeping the country these days. We're all wound up tight, the doctors warn. The accelerated pace of modern living and the effects of war (all those sergeants yelling 'Tension!') are causing people's nerves to snap like garters. The way to get hold of yourself is to let yourself go. Don't worry about being worried. Be loose.

"The trouble is that the looser I try to be, the tighter I get. I've taken all the doctors' cures to give me peace of mind, and now I'd like to give them a piece of my own. It isn't the tension that makes people tense. It's this effort to relax that's tying us all in knots."

YOU'LL GET MORE LAUGHS WHEN YOU TIME
AND TUNE YOUR SUBJECT TO THE PUBLIC PULSE.

Get a Balance in Your Buffoonery

Too many jokes can spoil the flavor of any subject. For instance, you may tell a few on your mother-in-law ("she looks like John L. Lewis in a housecoat"), but nobody could laugh at that one target of humor for too long.

It's like this: unless you are extremely careful you can overdo any subject, person, event, idea. And when you do the idea becomes repetitious. Furthermore, your presentation becomes one-sided and partial.

Note Bob Hope's impartiality in his comments about candidates in the 1960 presidential election. "I've always tried to keep it down the middle of the road," he said in an interview published in the Washington *Post.*[1]

"If I made a joke about one candidate, I'd balance it with one about the other. For example, I'd tell the one about Kennedy's mother asking him, 'Son, do you want to go to camp this summer or do you want to go to the White House?'

"I'd follow with one like 'Whittier was so sure Nixon was going to be elected, they built the log cabin in which he was born.' "

This tip is worth remembering because almost any audience is composed of persons of various beliefs, doctrines, attitudes, and feelings. They often like a balance in their humor—not just jokes about the "other side" but a few wisecracks about each of the opposing forces or ideologies.

PLAY UP BOTH SIDES AND YOU'LL WIN

THE BATTLE OF WITS.

Learn to Break down Audience Resistance

I'll never forget what a big-league baseball player told me. "There are times," he confided, "when I can't hit a pop fly to infield." You'll experience the same thing as a humorous speaker.

You work hard to get audience laughter. But it simply doesn't come. Oh, a few ripples but not a contagious laughter that tells you that everything is all right. You think to yourself, "This is supposed to be a live show, but the audience is dead." What is wrong? How can you break down audience resistance?

That's tough to answer because each situation contains so many variables. Why doesn't Mr. Elmer Magoo laugh? Maybe he wants to give the impression that he's been around—he's heard it all. He may listen briefly and think that the jokes aren't

[1] Army Archerd, "How Bob Hope Escapes Censorship," *TV Channels*, Washington *Post Magazine* (November 13, 1960), 6–7.

up to his intellectual level. Perhaps he was dragged, very much against his will, by his wife to attend the meeting so he is determined not to be amused by anything. Maybe he's the reserved type who cannot enter into the spirit of playfulness which is basic to a sense of humor.

How can you surmount audience apathy? For some of the best ways let's listen to a master writer and teacher of comedy, Ron Carver. Here are his suggestions:[2]

1. *Spirit of fun.* This emanates not only from the material, but also from the personality of the performer as well. It is not easy to write into the script.

2. *Superiority.* The performer's objective is to allow the viewer or listener to feel superior. The basic way to do this is to establish the character as inferior, scatterbrained, or to make him the butt of jokes. Red Skelton, Jack Benny, and Gracie Allen use this method.

3. *Identification.* This is a special kind of audience participation—empathy. The performer attempts to provide a reasonable symbol of the viewer or listener, as he is now or was in past situations.

4. *Surprise or shock.* Almost any form of these can cause laughter if they are not preceded by an extreme state of anxiety (if the person merely laughs at himself and his anxiety, there has been no real entertainment value). During the last war I used this line in a routine: "Now, folks, if a bomb does drop—please—try not to go to pieces!" I had to take it out; it was in poor taste; it played on their anxieties.

5. *Respect.* This is a potent force which can crack the spell of resistance. Any legitimate display of talent will create respect, and the audience will have less resistance to comedy which may follow. Often a dance team or anyone who comes back after a performance can do one joke, and the audience will roar, because there is no wall of resistance. Another thing which creates respect is a display of spontaneous wit, as in a genuine ad lib.

[2] Nancy Vogel, "Writing TV Humor," *Writer's Digest,* Vol. XL, No. 4 (April, 1960), 42–47.

Prestige, too, can create respect and crack that wall; if a performer is sufficiently popular through reputation, or only publicity, the audience will feel he is worth watching and listening to.

Read the pointers over again. This time test yourself on each suggestion. Then evaluate a humorous speech which you plan to give on the basis of these five points. Be completely honest with yourself. Next rebuild your presentation so that you and your jokes will penetrate the apathy barrier.

YOU CAN BREAK DOWN THE WALL OF INDIFFERENCE
WHEN YOU USE METHODS AND MATERIALS THAT MAKE A DIFFERENCE.

Plan Smooth Transitions

Would-be humorists keep popping this question, "In planning my speech how can I bridge the gap between a joke and the serious part of the speech?" And I always advise them to practice ways of gliding from one type of presentation to the other without calling attention to the act. Never, never say, "And now to resume the serious part of my talk." Instead, change the inflection in your voice, slow down the rate of delivery, pause, tell a dramatic story, change your expression.

"When you swing back into the serious part of your speech," Richard C. Borden tells us in *Public Speaking as Listeners Like It*, "don't use such phrases as 'to become serious again,' or 'let's get back to the point.' The last sentence of your story and the first sentence of your resumed speech context should mesh with easy naturalness."

So telling jokes isn't enough. You must know how to weave them into your talk. Actually, no audience wants to laugh all the time. Too much mirth can be monotonous. Your listeners like a mixture of the ridiculous and the sublime. Watch your favorite comedian and you'll notice that he often ends on a serious note—and this gives his presentation variety.

BRIDGE THE GAPS FOR YOUR LISTENER AND
HE'LL MOVE ALONG WITH YOU.

Develop a Unique Style

You'll move up the humorist's ladder more quickly if you develop an individual style—a uniqueness or method which is partly your own. No funnyman is wholly original. Most humorists have been influenced by others. Herb Shriner was influenced by Will Rogers, and Rogers by Mark Twain. Jackie Gleason must have learned a trick or two from Jack Oakie and Harry Langdon. Jerry Lewis demonstrates some of the methods once used by Harry Ritz.

Dynamic Phil Silvers gets laughs with his brash confidence and boasting. Jerry Lewis is awfully funny to many because he is a complete buffoon, not a joke teller, but this is the secret of his appeal. George Gobel, by personalizing his humor (he is often the victim of his stories) and giving it as a monologue, has created a personal trade-mark.

Tennessee Ernie Ford, "the pea-picking Plato of the country music field," has created a strong image with his homespun expressions. He uses phrases like "Contented as a swarm of June bugs in a barrel of mash," "I'm as eager as an octopus at a milkin' contest," "I'm as tired as a two-pound hen that's laid a three-pound egg," and "hotter than a bucket of red ants."

Call it what you will—personality, style, manner—but you should work on an individual one by which you are remembered. How? One way is to find the types of presentation at which you excel and polish them.

IF YOU'LL MIND YOUR UNIQUENESS AND
STRENGTHEN IT, YOU'LL BE REMEMBERED IN THE PUBLIC MIND.

Keep Them Laughing and Learning

"Keep them laughing and learning!" That's what one of the nation's outstanding after-dinner speakers told me when I asked how he captivates his audience. "Your listeners want to laugh," he explained, "but they also want to hear something informative, something useful."

Dick Borden stressed much the same idea when he said, "After-dinner listeners want a worthwhile message—but they want that message brightened." Obviously, this tip applies to all types of humorous talks.

If you really want to learn the art of humorous speaking, you must enjoy storytelling. As a narrator you must enter whole-heartedly into the spirit of funny stories and tell them with a certain joyous abandon. "Unless you have a good time," Maxwell Droke reminds us, "your audience is likely to be pretty well bored."

To succeed as a funnyman, you must be more than a humorous storyteller. "It isn't enough to walk on the stage and make faces and repeat jokes, as any bank clerk who has ever tried to entertain can attest," Steve Allen, television star, reminds us in his book, *The Funny Men*.

"You must know at precisely which fraction of a second a grimace will add to the power of a joke and not weaken it. You must know exactly what to do with your hands, how to stand, how loudly to speak, how to spar with an audience." What's more, you must use illustrative material.

Here's your problem as a humorous speaker: You must know how to select and present jokes and quips to get the desired laughs, but just as important you must know the finer points of public speaking—you must know how to win and hold an audience. (For tested tips from professionals, see pages 94–106 in this volume.)

YOU CAN BE FUNNY—AND BE ENTERTAINING—
AND STILL SAY NOTHING. CONTENT COUNTS!

Give Your Best

Art Linkletter, as a little-known performer, was invited to join Jack Benny, George Burns, Gracie Allen, and several other stars in a glittering Community Chest benefit show in Hollywood. At showtime, when he was given the cue to open the program, he went out front and was stunned to see exactly fourteen people in a playhouse with three thousand seats.

"I stood there, appalled by the emptiness, and decided not to exert myself," he tells us in *The Saturday Evening Post*. "I made a few perfunctory remarks and introduced Jack Benny."

Jack gave him a puzzled look as he brushed past him, and then went on the stage for his act. "He'll be right back," Linkletter told himself. But he didn't come right back. He worked his heart out for thirty-five minutes in one of the finest performances of his career, and those lucky ones in the audience will never forget it.

Later Jack took Art aside and said gently, "You know, Art, when a customer leaves his home and buys a ticket to see you, he's entitled to the best you've got, even if he's the only one in the house." And that night Art made a vow that he would never again fail those who came to watch him perform.

YOU CAN CLIMB HIGHER AS A HUMOROUS
SPEAKER WHEN YOU GIVE YOUR LEVEL BEST.

Let's repeat: being a humorous speaker is demanding. And after all is said and done there's just one sure test for a humorous speech: how many laughs did you get? If your audience broke into guffaws and chuckles, then your speech was a success. If it didn't, it was a failure. Nothing is quite as pitiful as a speaker who is the only person in the room who thinks his jokes are funny. (Have you ever seen one?) So if you want to make humorous talks, you must first be sure that you have mastered some techniques of polished performers.

Summing up: Whether your audience roars with laughter or remains silent is triggered by many variables. Some you can control. Others you cannot. Basically, audience reaction is a matter of mass psychology. The appreciation of humor is at its heart an emotional matter. Your listeners won't laugh at the most amusing joke in the world if they aren't "in the mood."

You might think a joke in the hands of any smooth professional would stand or fall largely on its own merits. But such is not the case. Actually, its effect is determined by timing, choice of topic, manner of presentation, personality of the speaker, adaptability of material, audience conditioning, and other factors. One thing is certain: take the tips of top funnymen revealed in this chapter, put them to work for you, and you'll make your listeners laugh!

CHAPTER 7

How Experts Get Laughs

WHAT ARE THE DIFFERENCES between the top-flight humorous speaker and the amateur? After all is said and done, it is the know-how—the specific techniques plus the ability to get desired reactions—that you find in the polished performer. By some peculiar magic, he can deliver humorous material in such a way that he gets plenty of chuckles.

Sheer comic genius, you see, consists of a lot of answers all put together—answers you will get from reading, analyzing, planning, practicing, evaluating, and improving—and from watching the experts in action.

Maybe you're asking, "What should I look for when I watch a funnyman in action?" Two main things: methods and material. Let's take Milton Berle, for example. Part of his talent is his energy, his enthusiasm. His timing is superb. Oh, yes, he is a ham. But he gets the laughter. Berle can take lines you have heard and make you laugh at them again. He has a prodigious memory (he is a walking gag file of ten thousand jokes) and this is vital in his success. Study his monologue technique in which he seems to be engaged in a sort of running battle with his audience. Stock lines like, "What is this, an audience or a jury?" are his specialty. A woman in the audience laughs and he asks, "Are you laughing longer or am I telling 'em better?"

Notice how Bob Hope links his humor with today's events and

personalities. He is a master of topical humor. Why this type? "For my money, the No. 1 joke of them all is the topical joke, a quip based on today's headlines," he says in his autobiography, *Have Tux, Will Travel.* And it works because, as he explains, "When you use one everybody is with you as soon as you tee off."

As you study the expert performers and evaluate your own experience you will realize that "being funny" isn't just telling jokes. Audience reaction is largely a matter of mass psychology.

As a matter of fact, any person who seeks laughter from his listeners must realize the many variables—some of them unpredictable—in a speaking situation. How do my listeners feel toward me? Will a heavy meal, plus too warm a temperature in the room, make my listeners drowsy even before I start? Can I establish a quick empathy between myself and the audience? As you see, your situation is complex. It may not consist, for example, of doing the "right" thing in the "right" way.

That's why you must study yourself—your own needs, your own capabilities, your own approach. But you may say, "Some directional road signs would help. Some pretested ideas can replace the high cost of trial and error." And that is exactly what you will find in this chapter: specific suggestions from many of the best-known humorists and after-dinner speakers.

What peculiar magic do big-time humorists possess? How can you size up an audience situation and make the most of it? To what extent does the occasion determine audience reactions? How can you put a story across? What determines the type of humor which might appeal to your listeners? Should you use personal incidents as basic structures in entertaining an audience?

For answers, let's visit with some veteran humorists who have brought laughter to hundreds of audiences. You'll hear the professional secrets of men who have received praise for their mirth-provoking talks—talks that bring such spirited responses that most of them are kept busy filling return engagements.

Proof? One of these has delivered nearly seven thousand talks in thirty years in forty-six states and five foreign countries. And he has entertained audiences at one thousand national conven-

tions. *The Saturday Evening Post* characterized another as "sharp
. . . a natural showman . . . recognized as a practitioner of the
world's toughest profession—a humorist." And the London *Free
Press* of Ontario praised another by stating, "Over 400 guests
rose to their feet to applaud an hour-long talk laced with wit and
popping with anecdotes." All of them generate a magnetic mirth
that has kept audiences in stitches at meetings ranging in size
from national conventions to village civic clubs.

Let's listen as they reveal some of their secrets in giving humorous addresses:

"Timing is everything"
—Tom Collins

There are two types of storytellers. One can pad the telling
and get by on sheer ability to use dialect or to act. Then there
are those like me, who use a parable technique and try to tell
a gag short and to get to the point quickly with intent that the
story's point should illustrate the point of the theme.

To put over a story, you should be glib and never repetitious.
It must fit your personality. It must be apropos. It must be told
with some enthusiasm and not delivered in a monotone. The
snapper or end must be quick and make sense (this is the platform speech). Timing is everything—without that no story can
be successful.

Material is everywhere—newspapers and magazines, old and
new, collections of jokes. It's no trouble finding material; the big
job is adapting it, learning to use it. Old stories can be rebuilt
with a new twist that will make them useful. I get very few from
people telling them to me. Not one in a hundred jokes told me
is new.

Don't drag your story in by the heels. Make it serve your purpose of nailing down a point. I believe dialogue is difficult to use
without giving offense or being obscure. For example, in the
Middle West we don't understand many Jewish words which
are current and well known in the East. Same way with Cajun
Indian gags—they are wasted on people out of Louisiana.

Never tell a story detrimental to a race, religion, business profession. Any story needing a victim had better be told against the teller—never any member of the audience.

You've got to establish empathy. So as a humorist, you must get the agreement of your listeners. If people don't like you, they won't laugh at anything you say. If they feel superior to you (Dale Carnegie's point) they'll like you and laugh.

"Use some of the best punches in the first few words"
—Cecil M. Hunter

1. You're off to a good start with a good introduction. Be very dynamic and use some of your best punches on the first few words so that you awake and shock an audience into alertness. If you are to be funny, make it real funny—some of your best lines. If you are to be serious, make it serious on the first few words.

2. Once you get your audience in your grip, run at a speed just barely ahead of them so they are getting it but will have to pay attention to keep up with you. Slow down and speed up with your talk and line of thought to keep them off balance just like you would in boxing. Don't let them know what you are going to say or do next, but make them extremely curious. Surprise them on every turn with what you say and how you say it. Have several transitions throughout your speech so you will not get into a rut and your listeners will not be lulled to sleep. Do something fairly dramatic every few minutes in your performance. Build to climax separately each phase of your speech. This will give you rising and falling action, change of pace, and it keeps any subject from becoming stale or boring.

3. Manufacture as many wisecracks and anecdotes as you can, and fit them into your subject matter. "Tailor-made" stories, wisecracks, or side statements give greater interest to any group. So the more you know about the group or profession to whom you are talking (how they function) the better you can treat the subject with wisecracks and anecdotes. Don't use too many canned jokes.

95

4. Speak on the audience level. If the audience is fast and intelligent, make your package quick and concise. If the group is unaccustomed to entertainment and slow to interpret gags, use a longer build-up and a more simple approach and lighter jokes.

5. Your listeners will laugh when you have surprised them with a sudden or funny ending. It is like throwing the whip to make it crack or pop. Quick and surprise endings will cause your listeners to burst out in laughter even when the point is not particularly funny.

"Use the right locale for your story"
—Edmund H. Harding

There are certain musts, and one of them is light and another is not too high a ceiling. As to where I find material, I pick it up wherever I can; but you have to be careful of using the right locale for your story. For instance, you cannot tell a story about salting meat where only frozen meat is the order of the day.

You should not pick on the minority. If you have a house full of Jewish listeners, give them a fit. If you have only two or three of them, let them alone. I use 2,500 stories currently, and when I find a better one I throw the old one away or discard it if it becomes out of date.

"People want wisdom, encouragement, inspiration . . . in comic form"
—Jeff Williams

Humorists are scarce—and, people want to laugh. Most people, that is. One must never forget that, here and there, some people look upon humor with condescension—they look upon humor as a Duchess does upon bugs. Yet, by and large, here and there—and everywhere—clean, wholesome, hearty, healthy laughter constitutes the best medicine for whatever ills beset mankind.

But we must never forget that humor must have a wallop—

which is to say that people don't want to be "shortchanged." They want you to impart some wisdom—some inspiration—some encouragement for the future—but, in comic form. What's more, they want to be told about the things they like to hear—and not so much about the things they ought to be told. Not many people can be saved—nor can the course of history be changed—in an after-dinner speech. So—MAKE 'EM LAUGH and now and then throw in a touch of common sense.

Many fine things have been said about humor and laughter. The old potato grower in Idaho once said, "If you can't have a little fun as you go along—why go?" Truly, humor is God's aspirin to soothe the headache of reality—humor is a pop-off valve in times of tension. These truths were known to King Solomon, King David, Abraham Lincoln, and above all, Jesus of Nazareth. And, too, you'll find that Dr. Reinhold Niebuhr in his book, *Discerning the Signs of the Times*, said: "Laughter is not only the vestibule of the Temple of Confession—but, the 'no man's land' between cynicism and contrition."

After a good many years up and down and across America it is my considered opinion that:

1. There's not much difference in people.

2. Men and women react about the same to any given speech. And that everybody loves flattery if judiciously dispensed.

3. Ideas dominate fact—and the power of suggestion is a dynamic force.

4. If a speaker pleases 99 out of 100—and offends one—he has failed.

5. Nothing can be said after 40 minutes that amounts to anything.

6. Women's groups are not as loose with their money as men's groups, but they can do one more harm—or good—once they decide.

7. Introductions are—many times—much too long, and that somebody ought to write a book entitled, "Things Not to Do at a Public Meeting."

"If you don't have a style you won't be in the humor business long"

—Cayce Moore

You need a good introduction. Write it yourself and have them get someone to read it who can read.

Seat the folks close together (the most important of all).

Keep the rest of the program short. Instruct the master of ceremonies to leave off his gags. (Use him next year as the speaker if this is what he wants.)

The wording of the punch line is very important. Often leaving out a word or adding a word will make the story funny.

If the story is long, add a few quips along the way before hitting the punch line.

You'll have to find your own jokes and tailor them to suit your style. If you don't have a style, you won't be in the humor business long.

You'll have to develop confidence in yourself and in your material. If a story doesn't go over you'll have to muster enough confidence to continue and not become rattled. Of course, you'd better have some material worthy of confidence or you will be left hanging at the mike.

"Don't make yourself the hero"

—Dr. Dan Procter

1. Your story must be appropriate for the occasion.
    (a) It must be clean and aboveboard.
    (b) It must "fit in" to the conditions and atmosphere of the occasion or into the theme of the meeting.
2. Be familiar with your story. Try it out on individuals before attempting it in a speech.
3. Your punch line must be timed. Usually a slight pause just preceding delivery, always with a twinkle in the eye and an appropriate facial expression, will get a good response.
4. Use spicy quips to illustrate points (never long, drawn-out stories).

5. When in doubt about a story—DON'T. It is poor judgment to risk offending anyone.

6. Use a majority group as brunt of your story—and avoid using the opposite sex if you are a man.

7. Develop a change of pace—just as a long-distance runner knows he must pace himself, so must the speaker in getting laughter from an audience.

8. Don't relate as a personal experience something which didn't really happen to you—the incident may be new to you but not to your audience.

9. Avoid reaching out for quips or anecdotes which illustrate nothing pertinent to the subject.

10. Don't stay over your welcome. As someone so aptly said, "The mind can't absorb more than the seat can endure." Your last story may fall flat if the hour is late. Leave your audience wanting more!

Experts Give Their Magic of Mirth

Few humorists have succeeded in all media—radio, television, movies, night clubs, theaters, dinner clubs, and the public platform. And that isn't strange because each situation has its own unique variables. But a few funnymen have shown such versatility that they function successfully in a number of situations.

How have these stars remained in public favor so long? How do they keep their popularity as humorists? What are some of their secrets in getting chuckles and guffaws? What is their philosophy of humor?

In the following pages, the experts discuss their individual methods and their application of them. By studying them carefully you will step up your abilities.

"Good joke is a work of art"

—Sam Levenson

To put a story across you should know what you are talking about. You have to be a bit of an "authority" on the subject matter. If you've never been to church you'd better stick with atheist humor.

As for the details, make it *clear*. Keep your ideas on the road. Know where you're heading. Otherwise your punch line may be a crack-up.

I don't believe in "audience interests." Make *your* interests interesting enough and they will become the audience's interests. Shakespeare didn't concern himself with his audience's interests.

An amateur must practice. You know the joke: The man on the street asking a stranger, "How do you get to Carnegie Hall?" Answer: "Practice!"

As a general principle: Tell your story with enthusiasm in your voice, authenticity in detail, dramatic build-up en route, a little suspense before you bring the curtain down. A good joke is a work of art and should be treated as such. It needs planning, composition, selectivity in detail, an inner logic, and finally a frame to put it in.

"Touch on the experience of each one in your audience."[1]
—Red Skelton

I think it is a mistake to assume that a comedian's business is simply to make people laugh. I feel that a funny man has two jobs: to present human foibles in broad enough terms for most people to recognize, and to provide an emotional experience.

Recognition is awfully important. People love to recognize themselves, or their relatives, in a comedy sketch. I've heard many a woman at ringside turn to her husband, after a bit showing the way in which a certain type of human being reacts to one of the ups and downs of life, and stay "Isn't that Uncle George all over again?"

This world is full of essentially lonely people. It gives them a warm sense of belonging, of not being alone, when they see themselves being portrayed, in general, by a comedian.

It helps to laugh at yourself with others, or to cry for yourself

[1] Nonean Conner, "Red Skelton's Magic Secret," *TV Radio Mirror*, Vol. LIII, No. 5 (April, 1960), 36.

with others. It binds humanity together, and that closeness is what we all need, consciously or unconsciously.

We must remember that each member of an audience is interested in what touches upon his own knowledge or experience. It's like a game of dominoes: everybody laughs at what makes connection with his own beliefs or background.

"Gear your humor to specific audience"

—Eddie Cantor

What type of audience are you addressing? There's a big difference between talking in a Sunday school or addressing some church group and addressing a club in Las Vegas. You must gear your humor, therefore, to a specific audience. I have made it a point, for more than forty years, to keep my stories absolutely clean. I do believe that things obscene should not be heard.

When in doubt, leave it out. My philosophy is you can't flop in the dressing room. Take no chances.

Timing? An amateur can develop it by watching, observing, listening to professionals, and seeing how it is done by the people who make a living out of storytelling.

Know when to get off. Apropos of that, for many years I have carried with me one page of printed material. Whenever it was my function to be the toastmaster for the dinner, I would gather the other speakers around me and ask, "How long is your speech going to be?" Their answers would be about twenty-five minutes, a half hour, or some only fifteen minutes. I would tell them they would have to edit their speeches if the audience would not be bored to death. This sounded insulting, and then I would bring out the page of material and have them read it. Carrying a stop watch with me, I would point out that what they read was less than two minutes. Then I would say, "You evidently know what you read." It was Lincoln's Gettysburg Address. "Now, if you think your speech will be remembered as long as the Gettysburg Address and if you cannot do it in less than twenty-five minutes or a half hour—go ahead." Invariably they would cut what they had to say to the bone.

"Don't oversell your story in advance."[2]

—Bennett Cerf

Don't make a story too long. The commonest and most fatal mistake of the amateur storyteller is to stretch his yarn beyond all reasonable limits.

Don't forget your point in the middle of the story. The most pathetic spectacle in Raconteurritory is the man who suddenly slows down in the course of his narrative, scratches his head, and announces sheepishly, "Good Lord, I've forgotten how it ends."

Don't laugh too much yourself. A hearty laugh at the end of the story, constituting yourself as sort of cheer leader, is not only permissible, but, if not carried to excess, sound strategy. While the story is in progress, however, let your audience do the laughing—if any!

Don't give the point of the story before you begin. Many a hapless amateur has killed a good anecdote by introducing it in some such fashion as "Did I tell you about the wife who directed a man inquiring for her husband to a fishing camp, suggesting that he look for a pole with a worm at each end."

Don't oversell your story. The man who prefaces a recital with "This is the funniest story you have ever heard in your life" is apt to find the burden of proof sitting too heavily on his shoulders.

Don't tell your stories at the wrong places. A quip that convulsed the boys in the club car can fall awfully flat at Mrs. Waxelbaum's tea for the bishop.

Don't tell your stories at the wrong time. The best story will fall flat if it is told at an inappropriate time. A gathering engaged in a serious discussion often will resent the introduction of unseemly levity.

Don't tell stories that depend for their humor on events or personalities never heard of by your audience. Many stories, hilarious if you know the people involved, or the circumstances that provoked the original situation, are unbelievably dull to a stranger.

[2] Adapted from *Laughter Incorporated* (Garden City Books, 1950) and used by permission of the author.

Avoid dialect stories as much as possible. Dialect stories are the hardest to tell properly. The endeavor of amateurs to impersonate Scots, Negroes, or Hebrews is often too horrible to think about.

"I like creative humor"[3]

—Dave Garroway

I enjoy humor that makes you laugh, chuckle, or smile without creating prejudice. Humor can be funny yet not be mean or discriminatory. It can be constructive, not careless, thoughtless. And it does not have to be contrived. Nothing makes me more uncomfortable than somebody's saying in effect, "Now get ready to laugh. I'm going to tell you a joke."

The kind of humor I like is creative humor. This brings about a deeper bond of communication between people, whether it's in the form of a word, a story, or a look. Actually, humor may take a thousand different forms, may rise from a thousand different sources.

But whatever its shape, it serves to give a common base to the understanding that is essential for people's liking or loving each other. More people get married because they laugh together than for any other reason.

It requires a watchful eye and a careful tongue, but I try to keep all questionable humor away from my programs. This includes stereotypes such as stuffy Englishmen; pitiful and humble Negroes, always happy and always dancing; loud-mouthed Irishmen; unwashed Italians; and so on. Untrue as well as unkind, these stereotypes always hurt the subject of the humor more than they can possibly amuse the hearers.

Once I was doing a television show on the problems of psychoanalysis and I wanted to show an analyst's couch (which thereby involved the network and its props). A network official called me to inquire whether I planned to ridicule the analyst. Of course I didn't. I have great respect for psychoanalysts and would never consider them humorous, and it pleases me that

[3] "My World at Large," *McCalls*, Vol. LXXVII, No. 10, (July, 1960), 24.

"sick jokes" are running out as the public understands the seriousness of mental-health problems.

Alcoholism, in my book, is about as unfunny as mental disease and cancer. It ultimately destroys lives, physically and morally. I believe alcoholism not only is not funny, but is a disease, partly chemical and partly emotional. The only cure is day-to-day abstinence, which is not a true cure but a lack of indulgence in the symptoms of the disease or, in one word, drinking. Thus an alcoholic is always close to being drunk or just one drink away, and the basic principle of Alcoholics Anonymous, as I understand it, is to persuade people never to take that first drink.

The person who laughs at the alcoholic may also laugh at these equally nonfunny subjects: retarded children, old maids, baldheaded men, wearers of false teeth, fat men—all of which subjects have fallen into the no man's land of bad taste.

These things are laughed at by people not in such condition, who need to cultivate within themselves an inherent feeling of superiority. The laughers are, therefore, basically insecure people trying to build themselves up at the expense of others. The well-known life of the party who indulges in this form of humor is compensating, through aggression, for his own weakness.

For instance, the vulgar and boasting man with a shock of hair (no matter what is underneath it) often loves to poke fun at balding acquaintances. Such laughter doesn't establish humor but merely breaks down the communications between men. The subject may take it with a smile, but he is not smiling inside. This is true of all the other "humorous" stereotypes.

When are you going to be funny, consider whether the joy the humor is going to give you will give even greater pain to the subject of the humor. If it will, you had better try another theme.

"Project a character that's honest"[4]

—Joey Bishop

If you've got a joke in your routine that'll cause an audience to

[4] Gilbert Millstein, "Portrait of a Well, Well, Well Comic," New York *Times Magazine* (January 1, 1961).

walk out talking about the joke instead of you, take it out. Everything I do is within the framework of a certain attitude.

You can spend twenty years entertaining the wrong people. When I started making money in this business was when I stopped thinking, "Will this line get a laugh at Lindy's?"

You've got to eliminate yourself from the run-of-the mill comic. Other guys may have funnier jokes than the fellow last week, but as far as the people are concerned, it's the same kind of comic. The best proof of it is along come guys like Mort Sahl, Shelley Berman, and Bob Newhart who approach comedy like it's never been approached before and that difference alone makes them a standout.

The next requirement is to adapt yourself in such a manner that you fit in nationally. Now, you can be this year's Catskills' Oscar winner and still not be understood by other people in the country. So, you have to ask yourself, what jokes would make you nationally known? And all of a sudden you realize it isn't a joke or routine so much as an attitude—being yourself and being honest. You're in trouble when you project a character that's not honest.

All gimmick performers fall by the wayside. When the tricks are through, they're through. Things have got to get to the point where they don't sound like jokes any more. It's *you're* serious and *they're* laughing in spite of themselves.

The next thing you realize is you're no longer just developing yourself—you're being developed by the people, by their tastes and their likes and dislikes. You can be the funniest guy in the country and still not get public acceptance. For example, there's a fear on the public's part of liking someone and then finding out they're a fraud. The funny man who walks on humbly and stays that way only until he gets an audience and then becomes aggressive—he converts himself right on the floor and he's dead. To pretend humility can't be brought off. It's like I say, a trick, and all tricks are dishonest.

My attitude is not trick. It's the way I am and it's an attitude which will always be one of gratefulness. There's nothing that can happen on a night-club floor or anywhere else that ever make me feel less grateful.

"Polish that punch line"[5]

—Jack Benny

In the interest of a lot of storytellers—and their long-suffering friends—I'd like to pass on a few pointers I have picked up in thirty years of public jesting.

1. Polish that punch line. People laugh with surprise. A perfect example of the effect is in Adlai Stevenson's great opening line to the Gridiron Club after losing the Presidential election: "A funny thing happened to me on my way to the White House."

2. Tailor your material to your audience.

"My uncle takes a drink now and then, just to steady himself. Sometimes he gets so steady he can't move."

George Gobel told that one, and the audience screamed. But how would it have gone at a temperance meeting? Remember, too, if everybody at the party is a doctor, they may enjoy jokes about quacks; but picking on the only doctor in the crowd makes him a victim and you a bully. That's not a funny situation.

3. Your humor should match the situation. Anything funny is funnier if it "fits"; if it touches on something the audience is interested in at that moment. If everybody in the room is arguing about the Cleveland Indians' chances against the Yankees, it's the wrong time for a talking-dog story. If you must tell it right then, at least try to make it a dog who can play shortstop.

There are many other tricks to the comic trade which you can learn by practice: how long to stretch out a story, how long to pause before a punch line, what gestures to use, intonation, etc. These must be shaped to your own personality, and the only way to find what fits you is by trial and error.

As you see, getting through to your listeners with humor is a complex and tricky art. At its best, it demands several abilities. A joke doesn't really have a value of its own, but its qualities as

[5] "How to Tell a Joke," *This Week Magazine* (March 26, 1961).

106

a laugh-getter rest mainly on the funnyman's ability to amuse. For every rule explaining the psychology of audience reaction to humor there are countless exceptions. So here's a suggestion: read and then reread the tips revealed by these front-line humorists. By intense study and practice you can use many of their ideas in stepping up your abilities as a humorist.

Never forget: how fast you travel toward the promised land hinges largely on your uniqueness in building comic emotions, your own ingenuity in creating a personal quality which makes you funny to others. Develop a style which has a high professional polish. And in the language of show business the results will be socko!

CHAPTER 8

What Every Humorist Should Know (Checklist)

WHAT ARE SOME TRICKS which give the professional speaker a persuasive power with his audience? What are some tested techniques which can be used in all speech situations? What are some of the conditions which you must accept and anticipate?

You'll get tips from many of America's best known humorous speakers in the suggestions which follow. Reading gives knowledge, but practice brings power!

Preparation Pointers:

a. Audience—
   Basic wants?　　Size?　　Past history?　　Objectives?
   Men and women?　　Approximate age of listeners?　　Prestige of group?
   Have you addressed this group before? If so, what was audience reaction?

b. Meeting place—
   Size of room or auditorium?　　Acoustics?　　Are seats comfortable?
   Is microphone available and in good working order? Temperature comfortable? Possible distractions (will waiters start clearing table in next dining room just as you begin)?

Distance of speaker's stand from audience (always stand as close to your audience as possible)?

Can you stand where audience can see you and hear you?

Will 300 listeners be scattered around in 1,800 seats?

c. Program—

Occasion (luncheon, dinner, breakfast, workshop, convention, clinic, etc.)?

Other speakers?   Introductions?   Announcements?

Special entertainment?   Time used in serving banquet?

Time of your speech on program (tough spots: early in morning, just before lunch, final speaker on afternoon session, or late spot on night program)?

Ability of toastmaster or presiding officer (he can give you a big boost with a lively introduction or a weak start with a matter-of-fact, lifeless introduction. You can be sure of getting off to a good start by writing your own speech of introduction—facts, not flattery—and mailing it to the chairman)?

d. Material—

What will interest your listeners (answer questions under section a)?

Can you present your ideas in their language?

Can you use specific examples which are tailor-made for the group?

What are best sources of finding examples, facts, case histories (a few: books, magazines, newspapers, interviews, questionnaires, scrapbooks, observation, travel, letters, government bulletins, public relations directors)?

e. Methods of Presentation—

How can you present these ideas in a new and different way?

1. Visual aids (slides, models, photographs, drawings, movies, etc.).

2. Demonstration.

3. Audience participation.

4. Through different characters. Think of how Red Skelton portrays Clem Cadiddlehopper, Cauliflower McPugg, the

Mean Wittle Kid, and others. Caution: Don't try it unless you can do it well. But by hard work and practice you can learn to portray different characters.

Tested Ways to Win Your Listeners:

1. Can you use anecdotes from your own experience?
George Gobel personalizes most of his humor. Like this: "My wife and I were sittin' around talkin'—the way you do when the TV set is busted."

2. Will your humorous examples be illustrative?
People are doubly pleased when a story illustrates some idea. So let your story make a point.

3. Do you have the right emotional attitude?
Your impact on an audience will be determined more by your mental attitude than by your material. If you enjoy entertaining an audience, then your listeners are more likely to enjoy you. Call it what you will—vitality, aliveness, enthusiasm—it will give you a magnetic appeal. This quality is a must for you as a humorous speaker because you must create moods of merriment. So always appear before your listeners with an attitude that seems to say you are glad to be there. Enjoy yourself and you're more likely to get an enthusiastic response. "Like begets like," Harry Overstreet says in *Influencing Human Behavior*. "If we are interested in our audience, there is likelihood that our audience will be interested in us."

4. Is your material uniquely adapted to your style of delivery?
Fred Allen functioned best as an observer, a commentator, a humorist. Sid Caesar can make a face and make almost any line seem funny. Jerry Lewis can strengthen a weak gag by mugging it.

5. Can you state your ideas so they will be remembered?
In one of my addresses on "How to Worry Successfully," I work hard to get over the idea that chronic worriers shouldn't be

too concerned about the way others feel toward them. To sum it up I say, "You wouldn't worry much about what others think of you if you knew how seldom they do." Try phrasing the main ideas of your speech so that they are clear, simple, and striking. Your listeners will remember your idea longer if you can wrap it up into an epigram, slogan, or other short statement.

6. Will you have an opportunity to test and rehearse some of your material?

Will Rogers used to prepare every night for his radio broadcasts by telling his reactions to the day's events. By the end of the week he had thought of dozens of new angles and interesting approaches.

7. Have you learned something complimentary about the group?

One of the best ways to make listeners like you is to compliment them on some service or achievement—something that they didn't think you could possibly know. Dr. Russell H. Conwell, who delivered his famous lecture, "Acres of Diamonds," over six thousand times, always spent hours in each city interviewing men and women about their accomplishments. Then during his lecture that night, he told of local men and women who had found "Acres of Diamonds" in their backyards.

It's easy to find out something about an organization. Ask the person who invites you to tell you about the accomplishments of the group. He may give the facts in a letter or send you newsletters, reports, proceedings, or a magazine.

If you've been too rushed to do any fact-finding before you arrive for your engagement, you can do as I often do: ask the chairman or presiding officer to tell you of some of the group's achievements. This is easy to do when you are seated next to the chairman at a luncheon or dinner meeting.

Why do this? Your listeners will warm right up to you when you pay them graceful compliments and do it sincerely. So whether you're addressing the Weeping Willow Unit of the Middletown Garden Club or the Society for the Prevention of

Guests' Peeping into Their Hosts' Medicine Cabinets, find out something about the achievements of the group. Then you can win friends with your opening remarks.

8. Can you end with a bang?

Aim at a specific action. Do you want your hearers to join something? Contribute to something? Change their attitudes? Put your best into your ending. You can use novelty, humor, inspiration, or examples. Be sure that the action you ask for is within the power of your audience. Here's the main thing: end on the upbeat!

9

What Makes America Laugh

"THE RITE LENGTH tu cut oph a dog's tale has never yet bin discovered, but it iz somewhere bak of his ears provided yu git the dog's consent."

This witticism went over big in this country about one hundred years ago. In those days most American wit and humor depended on two tricks in writing: crude phonetic spelling and the use of the wrong word.

The quotation is from the writings of Henry Wheeler Shaw who, in 1860, began to call himself "Josh Billings."

It seems rather difficult to read in this dizzy age, but Howard Florance in *Saturday Review* reminds us that "the folks loved it at the time. The nights were longer then, for there were few magazines to read, no radio to listen to, no television to watch. There was time to chuckle over each misspelled word."

Now let's listen to today's style of humor presented by Bob Hope as he discusses taxes: "The tax system is very simple now—they just take last year's income and then they take this year's income, that's all. You know the saying 'March comes in like a lion and goes out like a lamb'—that's because no matter how loudly you bleat, the tax collector still says, 'baaa!' I know one old fellow ninety-five years old who wouldn't pay his taxes because he said he was going to die anyway. The tax collector came around wearing a space suit, and said that 'you can't take it with you and if you try I'm going to follow.' Last year I had a wonderful guy who knew all the angles and loopholes but he can't help me this year—it seems there aren't any angles or loopholes at Alcatraz."

As you see from the remarks of two funnymen—causing audiences to laugh one hundred years apart—there is nothing static or fixed about humor. Comedy is an art. So you need to understand its history and dynamics if you're to be more than a routine joke-teller.

How has American humor changed from the bad-spelling technique which caused Grandpa to chuckle to the streamlined method of today? What has brought about the change in styles of humor from decade to decade?

For one thing, its national characteristics are plainly rooted in the conditions of American life. "The frontier spirit has been the strongest element in our national consciousness for three hundred years," Schulley Bradley reminds us.[1]

He continues: "In 1607, the frontier, for Captain John Smith, was Pocahontas in Virginia; in 1900 it was the great Northwest. But as the margin of conquest moved westward it left behind an increasing area of frontier consciousness which survives today even in eastern cities. Frontiersmen must live their lives with the mother of invention. They must be quick and cunning and strong. They must not be taken in by the appearance of things. They will come to value simple integrity of character and homely philosophy. As these attitudes grew in American thought, they were reflected in American humor, and they still persist."

The Tall Story Flourishes

Worship of strength and size which were principal requirements for survival in frontier life, triggered the element of exaggeration in humor. A frontiersman, for instance, could run down a deer. He had killed a bear so big that he could not carry the pelt. Davy Crockett told of shooting an eye through the head

[1] "Our Native Humor," *The North American Review*, Vol. CCXLII (Winter, 1936–37), 351–62.

of a weathercock across the Ohio River. Bill Merriwether lost his brother in an extraordinary manner: during a drenching rain his new deerskin breeches shrank so rapidly that he was shot high in the air and never seen again. Paul Bunyan, at the age of two, built Niagara Falls for a cold shower.

Many American humorists have used exaggeration as a fun-producing technique. To this the English have impolitely referred as the habit "of telling a lie and laughing at the person who believes it." Not too many years ago stories from American newspapers and magazines, which no American was intended to believe, and which were passed as good hoaxes at home, were reprinted in England as the solemn truth.

Who started this element of exaggeration in our native humor? Some historians think that the first settlers who ever wrote letters home began the practice. Many of them had come over against the earnest advice of family and friends, and they were anxious, above all, to make good.

Captain John Smith, as early as 1608, began his remarkable series of publications about Virginia. Today their charm as literature rests chiefly on the quaint exaggerations which render them wholly unreliable as history. In 1788, Samuel Peters, a clergyman, published *A History of Connecticut,* and he mentioned the fact that the rapids of the Connecticut River were said to be so swift that an iron crowbar would float there.

Exaggeration forms the foundation for the "tall story" which was highly regarded in early American life. Many of the yarns were printed in newspapers as a regular branch of journalism from the Jacksonian era until after the Civil War. They inspired a school of fiction which produced Simon Muggs, Major Jones, Sut Lovingood, and others. Mark Twain used this device in many anecdotes in *Roughing It, Tom Sawyer,* and other books.

"I went away from there," he writes in *Innocents Abroad* (1869), recalling in Milan his boyhood experience of discovering a corpse in his father's office, where he had taken refuge for the night. "I do not say that I went in any kind of hurry, but I simply went. That is sufficient. I went out of the window. I carried the sash along with me. I did not want the sash, but it was handier to take it than to leave it. I was not scared, but I was considerably agitated."

Listen to conversation today and you'll hear that the tall story still lives in many forms. You'll remember that Fred Allen told about the scarecrows which were so lifelike that the crows brought back the corn they had stolen the year before.

We Laugh Things Off

Most people are content to enjoy the humorists without inquiring why they are amusing. People laughed when Will Rogers told us that after they got the constitution all amended up they were going to start on the Ten Commandments, "just as soon as they can find somebody in Washington who has read them."

"Ours is a land of kidding," L .H. Robbins declares.[2] "Since the time of Dickens," he continued, "every foreign visitor has noted that we decline to take the depression or the President of the moment, the foreigner himself or any other serious thing very seriously. We laugh things off. We get square with the iniquities of reality by grinning at them, and we make prophets and privileged characters of those who assist us in grinning."

Eugene Field amused people of his day when he reported that the train bearing the Illinois legislature on a junket to New Orleans had been stopped by bandits, and that "after relieving the bandits of their watches and money the excursionists proceeded on their journey with increased enthusiasm."

A tedious evolution was necessary before we could begin to have national jesters, Robbins tells us. It was a risky thing, in 1646, for Parson Nathaniel Ward of Ipswich to publish his *Simple Cobbler of Aggawam in America*, with its flings at the manners of the time. His book was frowned upon by Puritan circles, but Europeans called his book the funniest ever.

In tracing the early history of humor, Robbins points out that the long-faced dominated the early social order. He continues:

[2] "American Humorists," New York *Times Magazine* (September 8, 1935).

116

"The solid citizens of New Jersey petitioned a facetious governor of theirs to conduct the business of the colony without joking. Benjamin Franklin was not trusted to write the Declaration of Independence, for with all his wisdom he had a weakness for wit; for he was always saying things like: 'The poor man must walk to get meat for his stomach; the rich man to get a stomach for his meat.' Washington Irving might poke broad fun at the bygone Dutch of New Amsterdam, but in his comment on his own day he had to restrain his pen in the best European fashion."

For years, the American comic spirit lived suspect, hiding in the taprooms and the crossroads store, until the start of the last century, when the Jacksonians changed all that.

The Funnymen Rush In

All of a sudden, the funnymen came in with a rush in the hundreds of newspapers that sprang up as the nation expanded west and south. "With the mind of democracy and the tongue of the hardy frontiersman they vociferated in rollicking scorn of the nice-Nellie East," Robbins says. Then he adds, "Cheerfully wild, banal and disreputable they were."

But not everyone laughed. The writings of humorists were such a blow to primness that Edmund Stedman wrote in tears to Bayard Taylor, "The whole country is flooded, deluged, swamped with a muddy tide of slang, vulgarity, impertinence, buffoonery that is not wit," and the *Encyclopaedia Britannica* advised that their eccentricities "should be universally discredited as blasphemies against the first principles of taste."

For years the Yankee ("built on hard luck and codfish") was depicted as a comic rascal, and a caricature of the stolid Dutchman was a stock amusement. Actually, both of these were European types merely transplanted to the colonies.

The peculiar humor which is characteristically American is actually Midwestern since it did not really spring forth until the Western migration spilled over the Alleghenies and peopled the plains that stretched to the Mississippi and beyond.

Why this new kind of humor? For one thing, the Midwestern frontier was something new in human experience, and it produced new responses. Whether in New York or in Virginia in 1607, the expectations of the immigrant (who had been lured to a land which flowed with milk and honey and where gold lay in lumps on the ground) were to receive a rude shock. Indians were not always friendly, trees were tough, and the gold turned out to be iron pyrites.

Here was a common experience: A family of settlers would pole a raft up the mammoth sides of the Mississippi or Missouri, past the forlorn settlements, looking for a place less muddy and unfriendly. At last, finding it all to be the same, they would choose a spot and build a log house. In three weeks of hard labor they would achieve a romantic dream of abode. Then one night, just as the new mansion was nearly completed, floods would descend, the river would change its course, and the house would become an island, if indeed, it did not float off toward the gulf.

Experiences of this kind were the common lot of our forefathers. "If you could not laugh at this or yourself in the role of the sucker," Bradley remarks, "you were doomed."

The vast discrepancy between the vision that had brought them out there and the actuality they found on arriving must have been almost unendurable to the settlers, and laughter was their only relief. Mark Twain, who as a child saw the last of the Midwestern frontier, said: "The secret source of humor is not joy but sorrow; there is no humor in Heaven."

The frontier was not heaven so you laughed or died. And since the pioneers were too tough to die, they laughed. Their laughter was often uncouth, boastful, bombastic, and irreverent. Much of the "tall talk" now seems turgid and forced, too thin a veneer over the underlying violence and desolation. But it became a great literature, and it still gives everyday living a saving sense of absurdity. "All modern men are descended from wormlike creatures," says Will Cuppy, "but it shows more on some people."

Out of these early struggles came stories like the following: First hillbilly: "Zeke, I heard yore barn was struck by a tornado

What Makes America Laugh

—was it damaged much?" and the second hillbilly: "Cain't tell—ain't found it yet.

A distinguishing characteristic of American humor is its anti-romanticism. "We love to puncture an illusion, to burst an iridescent bubble of hot air," Bradley explains. "Pretensions of grandeur, false family pride, snobbishness, or conceit annoy us, and we enjoy destroying them with the sharp weapon of irreverence."

One of our most comic figures, for example, is the sucker. He is the victim of practical jokes, the "goat." At different periods he was the tenderfoot who walked blithely into an Indian ambush, the fool who thought he could go up in a balloon, or the loon who believed a carriage would run without a horse. In other periods he was the apprentice who ran to fetch a left-handed monkey wrench or a bucket of steam, the "sucker" who bit on the leading question, or the simple soul who was taken by those odd novelties, decent or otherwise, on which American merchants thrive just before the first of April.

The Midwest Monopoly

Bergen Evans, in pointing out the influence and growth of Midwestern humor, once asked, "What part of the earth can match the Midwest's humor list—from Davy Crockett through Mark Twain, Finley Peter Dunne, George Ade, Booth Tarkington, Kin Hubbard, Damon Runyon (merely to skim the surface) to Don Marquis, Ring Lardner, Charles Morton, and James Thurber? And these are only 'literary,' a conspicuous eddy in the immense stream of talking humorists, of whom Lincoln was the greatest example and Will Rogers the best known."

What's more, in *The Saturday Review*, he emphasizes that Red Skelton, Clifton Webb, Joe E. Brown, Bobby Clark, Buster Keaton, Harold Lloyd, Jack Benny, Bob Hope, Burr Tilstrom, Herb Shriner are all Midwesterners, and that there are scores of others. "The whistle stop teems with them, begallused and belligerent, waiting expectantly for some smart-aleck Easterner upon whom to break the vials of their scorn." "We're all funny," said one of George Ade's brothers; "George just writes it down."

Evans believes it obligatory to be a wit in the prairie hamlets. "If you think before you speak," Ed Howe once complained, "the other fellow gets his joke in first."

"Most of the local humor is corny," Evans admits, "but it's shrewd, earthy, and droll, burlesquing in its extravagance the pompousness of our national esteem, deflating false pretensions, gilding hardship with a saving grace, asserting equality with an irresistible impudence."

Some observers believe that American humor is undergoing a change. "We Americans like to delude ourselves that we have a grand sense of humor," Jerome Beatty, Jr., says.[3] "It may once have been so, in the days of Lincoln's deceptively hick anecdotes, or Mark Twain's savage satires, or Charlie Chaplin and Mack Sennett, but it ain't so now.

"These days we seem to be so insecure that we can't bear to be laughed at, or to laugh at ourselves, even though, God knows, we never needed it more. Our desperate materialism and strange values today leave no room for attack, no room for a joke which might release our tensions for a moment and let us see ourselves as we are. We are going through a stage in which we suppress any healthy humor which makes us the butt of the joke."

The Revolt against Pomposity

A new school of comedians—most of whom stayed close to an essentially offbeat and imaginative style—came on the American scene in the late fifties. It's leader, Mort Sahl, young, irreverent, and trenchant, with an appeal that is hardly universal, is proclaimed by some as the freshest comedian around. "Bellylaughs he doesn't get," Earl Wilson observes, "it's more egghead chuckles."

"He does not tell jokes one by one," a sketch in *Time* stated, "but carefully builds deceptively miscellaneous structures of

[3] "Humor vs. Taboo," *The Saturday Review* (November 23, 1957).

jokes that are like verbal mobiles. He begins with a spine of the subject, then hooks thought onto thought, joke dangling onto joke, many of them totally unrelated to the main theme, till the whole structure spins but somehow balances. All the time he is building toward a final statement, which is too much part of the whole to be called a punch line, but puts that particular theme away forever."

Here are some Sahl's-eye views:

Lung-cancer tests: There is a moral question here—whether or not mice should smoke.

Missile gap: Maybe the Russians will steal our secrets. Then they'll be two years behind.

Bomb tests: Contamination without representation.

Publication of Yalta papers: They should come in a loose-leaf binder to you so you can add new betrayals as they come along.

Sahl has become the patriarch of a new group of comics. Far removed from the old stand-up, joke-book comedians, they mostly do set pieces that are almost playlets. Others dishing out a similar offbeat humor are Shelley Berman, Bob Newhart, Lenny Bruce, and Mike Nichols and Elaine May.

What's behind the new trend? Historian Arthur Schlesinger, Jr., says that it is "a mounting restlessness and discontent, an impatience with clichés and platitudes, a resentment against the materialist notion that affluence is the answer to everything, a contempt for banality and corn—in short, a revolt against pomposity."

Though much of our humor today does show a drift toward the sophisticated, the hard-boiled and the surgical, the old, genial, ingenious, home-remedy sort still wins big laughs, as Herb Shriner demonstrates: "Back home in Indiana they decided to try out these one-way streets, but it didn't work. We only had one street and folks couldn't get back into town."

The distinguishing mark of our contemporary humor, what has come to be called "New Yorker humor," is that it is of, for, and by the great bulk of our population who are engaged in interminably busy idleness, who are never at grips with their environment, but who live by delegated powers and vicarious atonements, believes Kenneth Rexroth.

"American radicalism lost its sense of humor long ago. And, of course, the 'media' chew up everything—songs, jokes, personalities—365 days times 24 hours. What is wrong with American humor is what is wrong with American life. It is commercialism. True humor is the most effective mode of courage."[4]

To what extent is a humorist conditioned by life about him? By the peculiarities of the age in which he lives? "The old-time comics were generally uneducated (although many of them were of superior intelligence), calloused by rough and tumble experience, made shrewd by poverty, and brought to worldly-wiseness by travel, a wide range of social contacts, and adventurous activity," Steve Allen observes.[5]

"Today's comedian, in the main," he continues, "is cushioned by economic, social, medical and philosophical changes and/or improvements that have taken place in our society during the past quarter of a century. The times make the man, and if the times have changed, the man will change with them."

Are We Overly Amused?

Are we deluged with humor? What does an overabundance of funny material do to the mass mind? Steve Allen observes that the world has known no other time when the mass mind was so completely humor-washed. "Traditionally comedy has been something of a rare treat, an aesthetic delicacy, and even though radio made it a relative commonplace, it remained for television —with its brain-numbing, hypnotic attraction—to offer comedy during almost every hour of the day, every day of the week.

"The result has been that the man on the street first of all spends less time than ever on the street and secondly that he has developed an over-awareness of comedy, a lack of respect for its

[4] Kenneth Rexroth, "The Decline of American Humor," *The Nation* (April 27, 1957).
[5] "The Vanishing Comedian," *The Atlantic Monthly* (December, 1957).

omnipresent practitioners, and a cynical critical attitude toward its performance."

One thing certain: we shall always need humor. As Jack Benny observed, "Gags die, humor doesn't." Humor, at its highest, is a sense of values. Whenever men get together to do a hard job, humor is bound to crop up because it restores values and relieves strain. What's more, we'll always need the sting of humorists to deflate stuffed shirts, the high hats, and others.

And yet whoever takes an interest in humor is struck by its spirit of toleration and human sympathy. A shrewd German once said, "Only he who loves mankind may smile on human weakness." No longer dependent on mere tricks and quibble of words, much of today's humor is based on deeper contrasts offered by life itself.

In a real sense, as Carlo Bos reminds us, "Humor is blended with pathos until the two are one, and represent, as they have in every age, the mingling heritage of tears and laughter that is our lot on earth."

As you see from this kaleidoscopic rundown of humor through the years, it does not follow a fixed formula. Rather, it is an art, fluid and flexible, attuning itself to the tempo of the times.

Maybe you can play it by ear and develop new stylings of your own. How? By experimenting. Look for the ludicrous in the new experiences through which we are living—stereophonic sound, beatniks, jet planes, frozen food, electronic computers, and others. Then, create witticisms about them. Or, watch for chuckles in the commonplace. As James Thurber observed, "There is always a laugh in the utterly familiar." At its highest, humor is more than repeating old stories. To succeed at it, you must understand the dynamics of fun.

Then, by observing and experimenting, you may become the innovator who conceives a new type of humor—even, heaven preserve you, tomorrow's Mort Sahl.

On the Sunny Side (Selected Readings)

1. *Humor: Its Techniques and Traditions*

Allen, Fred. *Much Ado about Me.* Boston, Little, Brown and Company, 1956.

Allen, Steve. *The Funny Men.* New York, Simon and Schuster, 1956.

Barker, Bryan. *Humor in School Papers.* New York, Columbia Scholastic Press Association, 1951.

Blair, Walter. *Horse Sense in American Humor.* University of Chicago Press, 1942.

———. *Native American Humor.* San Francisco, Howard Chandler Publishing Company, 1960.

Brashear, Minnie, and Robert M. Rodney. *The Art, Humor, and Humanity of Mark Twain.* Norman, University of Oklahoma Press, 1959.

Cerf, Bennett. *Laughter, Incorporated.* Garden City, Garden City Books, 1950.

Croy, Homer. *What Grandpa Laughed at.* New York, Duell, Sloan & Pearce, 1948.

Eastman, Max. *Enjoyment of Laughter.* New York, Simon and Schuster, 1936.

———. *The Sense of Humor.* New York, C. Scribner's Sons, 1921.

Fadiman, Clifton. *Any Number Can Play.* Cleveland, World Publishing Company, 1953.

Froschels, Émil. *Philosophy in Wit.* New York, Philosophical Library, 1948.

Fujimura, Thomas H. *The Restoration Comedy of Wit.* Princeton, N. J., Princeton University Press, 1952.

Gaver, Jack, and Dave Stanley. *There's Laughter in the Air.* New York, Greenberg, 1945.

Godsey, Townsend. "The American Newspaper Humor Column, Its Rise and Decline." Norman, University of Oklahoma Graduate College (unpublished thesis), 1961.

Grotjahn, Martin. *Beyond Laughter.* New York, Blakinston Division, 1957.

Hasty, Jack. *Done with Mirrors.* New York, Ives Washburn, Inc., 1943.

Hazlitt, William C. *Studies in Jocular Literature.* London, E. Stock, 1890.

Herzberg, Max John. *Humor of America.* New York, Appleton-Century Company, Inc., 1945.

Hoig, Stan. *The Humor of the American Cowboy.* Caldwell, Idaho, Caxton Printers, 1958.

Holliday, Carl. *The Wit and Humor of Colonial Days.* Philadelphia, J. B. Lippincott, 1912.

Hope, Bob. *Have Tux, Will Travel.* New York, Simon and Schuster, 1954.

Hudson, Arthur Palmer. *Humor of the Old South.* New York, The Macmillan Company, 1936.

Hughes, Leo. *A Century of English Farce.* Princeton, N. J., Princeton University Press, 1956.

Kronenberger, Louis. *Cavalcade of Comedy.* New York, Simon and Schuster, 1953.

———. *The Thread of Laughter.* New York, Alfred A. Knopf, 1952.

Lawrence, Jerome (ed.). *Off-Mike.* New York, Duell, Sloan & Pearce (Essential Books), 1944.

Leacock, Stephen B. *Here Are My Lectures.* New York, Dodd, Mead, and Company, 1937.

———. *Humor: Its Theory and Technique.* New York, Dodd, Mead, and Company, 1935.

Loflin, Z. L. *Just for Fun.* Lafayette, Louisiana, Southwestern Louisiana Institute, 1948.

Lynn, Kenneth. *The Comic Tradition in America.* Garden City, New York, Doubleday and Co., 1958.

Mahoney, Patrick. *Barbed Wit and Malicious Humor.* New York, Citadel Press, 1956.

Masson, Thomas L. *Our American Humorists.* New York, Moffat, Yard and Company, 1922.

Meier, George Friedrich. *Thoughts on Jesting.* Austin, University of Texas Press, 1947.

126

Overstreet, H. A. *Influencing Human Behavior.* New York, W. W. Norton and Company, 1925.
Rapp, Albert. *The Origins of Wit and Humor.* New York, Dutton, 1951.
Repplier, Agnes. *In Pursuit of Laughter.* Boston and New York, Houghton Mifflin Company, 1936.
Rourke, Constance. *American Humor: A Study of the National Character.* New York, Harcourt, Brace and Company, 1931.
Sawyer, Newell W. *The Comedy of Manners.* Philadelphia, University of Pennsylvania, 1931.
Seyler, Athene, and Stephen Haggard. *The Craft of Comedy.* New York, Theatre Arts, Inc., 1946.
Untermeyer, Louis, and Ralph E. Shikes. (eds.). *The Best Humor Annual.* New York, Henry Holt and Company, 1951.
Wells, Carolyn. *An Outline of Humor.* New York, G. P. Putnam's Sons, 1923.
White, E. B., and White, Katharine. *A Subtreasury of American Humor.* New York, Coward-McCann, Inc., 1941.
Wilson, Earl. *The NBC Book of Stars.* New York, Pocket Books, Inc., 1957.
Wolfenstein, Martha. *Children's Humor, A Psychological Analysis.* Glencoe, Illinois, Free Press, 1954.
Wright, Milton. *What's Funny and Why.* New York, Whittlesey House, 1939.
Zolotow, Maurice. *No People Like Show People.* New York, Bantam Books, 1952.

2. Getting Ideas Across (Public Speaking)

Allen, Edward Frank (ed.). *Modern Humor for Effective Speaking.* New York, Citadel Press, 1945.
Borden, Richard. *Public Speaking as Listeners Like It.* New York, Harper and Brothers, 1935.
Brings, Lawrence M. *Clever Introductions for Chairmen.* Minneapolis, T. S. Denison and Company, 1954.
Carnegie, Dale. *Public Speaking and Influencing Men in Business.* New York, Association Press, 1955.
Droke, Maxwell. *The Speaker's Handbook of Humor.* New York, Harper and Brothers, 1956.
Hegarty, Ed. *Showmanship in Public Speaking.* New York, McGraw-Hill Book Company, 1952.
Lee, Josh. *How to Hold an Audience without a Rope.* Chicago, Ziff Davis Company, 1947.

Monroe, Alan. *Principles and Types of Speech.* New York, Scott-Foresman, 1955.

Powers, David Guy. *How to Say a Few Words.* Garden City, New York, Doubleday and Company, 1953.

Prochnow, Herbert V. *1001 Ways to Improve Your Conversation and Speeches.* New York, Harper and Brothers, 1952.

———. *The Speaker's Treasury of Stories for All Occasions.* New York, Prentice-Hall, Inc., 1953.

———. *The Successful Speaker's Handbook.* New York, Prentice-Hall, Inc., 1951.

Sandford, W. P., and W. H. Yeager. *Practical Business Speaking.* New York, McGraw-Hill Book Company, 1937.

Wheeler, Elmer. *How to Sell Yourself to Others.* New York, Prentice-Hall, Inc., 1947.

Whiting, Percy H. *How to Speak and Write with Humor.* New York, McGraw-Hill Book Company, 1959.

Yeager, Willard H. *Effective Speaking.* New York, Prentice-Hall, Inc., 1954.

3. *Putting Fun into Words*

Bergson, Henri. *Laughter.* In George Meredith, *Essays on Comedy.* Doubleday Anchor Books, 1956.

Burack, A. S. (ed.). *Writing and Selling Fillers and Short Humor.* Boston, The Writer, Inc., 1959.

Esar, Evan. *Humor of Humor.* Horizon Press, 1952.

Kanigher, Robert. *How to Make Money Writing for Comic Magazines.* New York, Cambridge House, 1943.

Leacock, Stephen B. *How to Write.* New York, Dodd, Mead and Company, 1943.

Margolis, Sidney K. *Turn Your Humor into Money: How to Create Humor that Sells.* New York, The House of Little Books, 1938.

Orben, Robert. *Comedy Technique.* New York, Louis Tannen, 1951.

Reznick, Sidney. *How to Write Jokes.* New York, Townley Company, 1954.

Seldes, Gilbert. *Writing for Television.* Garden City, New York, Doubleday and Co., 1952.

Settel, Irving (ed.). *How to Write Television Comedy.* Boston, The Writer, Inc., 1958.

Thomson, Arthur A. M. *Written Humor.* London, A. and C. Black, Ltd., 1936.

Yoakem, Lola Goelet (ed.). *TV and Screen Writing.* Berkeley, University of California Press, 1958.

For Laughing Out Loud

For Laughing Out Loud

ABILITY

Ability is the power to do some special thing, like speaking several languages or keeping your mouth shut in one.

The one thing that most men can do better than anybody else is to read their own writing.

ABSENCE

Absence: It makes the heart grow fonder, except when it's the absence of your mother-in-law.

ACCIDENTS

Man at factory was asked what caused the explosion and he said, "The boiler was empty and the engineer was full."

What some people don't know about accidents would fill a hospital.

One hospital refers to its accident cases as its bumper crop.

A woman, after a head-on collision with a man motorist, exclaimed, "You had no right to assume that I had made up my mind."

News item: "Charles Parker is at the hospital suffering from head injuries and a shock caused by coming in contact with a live wife."

Policeman to man whose car has been struck by a woman driver:

"I'd settle if I were you, sir. After all, it's just your word against thousands of hers."

A judge's definition of an accident after hearing both drivers' stories: A head-on collision between two stationary cars parked on their own side of the road.

Neighbor told woman: "I hear your husband is in the hospital. What happened?" and the other replied, "Knee trouble. I found a blonde on it."

In filling out an application for factory job, a man was puzzled for a long time over this question: "Person to notify in case of accident." Finally he wrote, "Anybody in sight."

Did you hear about the bell ringer who got tangled in his rope and tolled himself off?

ACHIEVEMENT

After all is said and done, more is said than done.

In order to make a place in the sun for yourself, T. Harry Thompson believes, you have to be a shade better than the next fellow.

It is when we forget ourselves that we do things that are remembered.

Everything comes to him who hustles as he waits.

Sooner or later, the man with pull must get out of the way of the man with push.

ACTING

Telling her child a bedtime story, a movie actress began: "There was a mama bear, a papa bear, and a baby bear by a previous marriage."

An actress, noted for her apple-polishing ability, sashayed over to critic George Jean Nathan's table and cooed: "I just can't tell you how much I enjoy your reviews," and Nathan replied, "Well, send over someone who can."

An actress, in mourning for her fourth husband, insisted on black olives in her martinis.

132

Actress telling dentist of her aching tooth: "First row, right, in the balcony."

The director was dissatisfied with the leading man's acting in the deathbed scene. "Come on," he pleaded, "put more life in your dying."

Actor: one who believes that a small role is better than a long loaf.

Ham actor: one who is egged on by ambition and egged off by the audience.

Hollywood crack: "She'd make a perfect Juliet—she can't act, but oh brother, can she lean over the balcony!"

ACTION

Be first in the office every morning, the last to leave at night, always work through the lunch hour, and one day the big boss will call you in and say, "I've been watching your work very carefully, Jones. Just what are you up to, anyhow?"

Anyone who has time to look for a four-leaf clover needs to find one.

Mankind falls into three classes: immovable, movable, and those who move.

"I told her I was a go-getter," a boy told his chum, "but she was looking for an already-gotter."

It was a beautiful morning and a man in a small town remarked to a native, "A day like this really makes a person feel like working," and the native drawled, "Well, now, I wouldn't go so far as to say that, but I will say it makes a body feel like he ought to."

You never can get much of anything done unless you go ahead and do it before you are ready.

Roadside sign in Kentucky: "Pray for a good harvest, but keep hoeing."

Getting an idea and sitting on a tack are much alike—both should make you rise and get into action.

Once, during World War I, railroad crossties were urgently needed at the front. An officer sent this wire to Charles G. Dawes who headed the General Purchasing Board: "Exigent we have crossties. Move heaven and earth to get them by Saturday." Dawes telegraphed back the same day: "Raised hell and got them today."

It's great to have your feet on the ground—but keep them moving.

We know a fellow who not only starts things he can't finish, he starts things he can't even begin.

If you are a self-starter, your boss doesn't have to be a crank.

Most things come a lot faster to those who won't wait.

One letter that you don't have to read clear through: Dear Sir, Will you report as soon as possible to the office of the Internal Revenue Department, and bring all of your records for the past three years. . . ."

Many a man who puts his shoulder to the wheel is either no mechanic or else he's stuck in the mud.

You can't make a place for yourself in the sun if you keep sitting in the shade of the family tree.

ADMIRATION

A woman admires a man who stands on his own two feet—particularly when he's on a crowded bus.

ADOLESCENCE

Adolescence is when a boy stops collecting stamps and starts playing post office.

Adolescence: when boys begin to notice that girls notice boys who notice girls.

Growth-wise, up to the age of twelve boys are about a year behind the girls; during the ages of twelve to seventeen the boys are gradually catching up; and from seventeen on it's neck and neck.

Nowadays when they speak of a girl reaching that "awkward age," it means that she's too old for teddy bears and too young for wolves.

Included among things that rise slowly: biscuits in a cold room, husband reading a newspaper, teenager from a warm bed.

As any parent will tell you, mealtime is when the kids sit down to continue their eating.

134

ADVANTAGES

Harry Ritz tells of the fellow who was born with a silver spoon in his mouth but who hasn't made much of a stir with it.

ADVERTISING

Classified ad: "Lovely kitten desires position as companion to little girl. Will also do light mouse work."

Classified ad: "Man wanted to work in dynamite factory; must be willing to travel."

Classified ad: "Girl wants board and room in private home. Non smoker, noon drinker."

A Chicago nut shop boasts: "If our peanuts were any fresher, they'd be insulting."

Samson had the right idea about advertising. He took a couple of columns and brought down the house.

A visiting Englishman, after staring at broadway's electric signs and listening to an account of the miles of wiring and hundreds of light globes, remarked: "Quite, quite, old chap—but isn't the whole thing rather conspicuous?"

Sign in store window: "This is a nonprofit organization—please help us change."

"Your ads sure bring results," a woman wrote the Arizona *Star*. "My lost dog has been returned—with four pups."

A city child, upon seeing his first rainbow in the country, asked, "What's it supposed to advertise?"

A mint is the only business that makes money without advertising.

A farmer who sent for a book on "How to Grow Tomatoes," wrote the publisher: "The man who writ the ad shoulda writ the book."

If all the vitamins advertised as breakfast foods were standing end to end, men would still hanker for the good old ham and eggs for breakfast.

Spotted in a rose catalog: "Lady Godiva—a pale pink sport."

Sign on dairy truck: "You can't beat our milk, but you can whip our cream."

From an advertisement in an Indiana newspaper: "Attractive lunging pajamas."

ADVICE

No woman ever takes another woman's advice about anything. Naturally, you don't ask any enemy how to win a war.

Mountain guide: "Be careful not to fall—it's very dangerous. But if you do fall, remember to look to the left. You get a wonderful view."

Maybe you've never thought of it, but there is a big difference between giving advice and lending a helping hand.

The reason that God made woman last was that He didn't want any advice while creating man.

"When I want your opinion," the Hollywood producer snapped to his assistant, "I'll give it to you."

Richard Armour observes that it's not necessary to take a person's advice to make him feel good—all you have to do is ask for it.

Free advice is the kind that costs you nothing unless you act upon it.

Advice is what a man gives when he is too old to set a bad example.

Group medicine: where twenty-five relatives and friends pitch in with a cure apiece for the cold in your head.

Folks wouldn't think so much about paying for a doctor's advice if they had enough sense to take it.

Most of us don't have any use for the advice of our parents until we start raising families of our own.

Advice is information given by someone who can't use it to someone who won't.

Don't fail to give out advice. It passes time and nobody will follow it anyway.

Words you aren't too likely to hear: "As your physician, I insist that you force yourself to eat more delicious, fattening foods; chocolate sundaes, lemon pies, strawberry shortcake . . . ."

And then there was the Irishman who asked, "Please don't lie on the pool table, grandmother. You're wearing off the green."

Socrates was a Greek philosopher who went around giving good advice. So they poisoned him.

From a garden-club magazine: "To have prize-winning blooms you must use Bordeaux mixture and pray regularly."

AFTER-DINNER SPEAKERS

An after-dinner speaker is one who talks in other people's sleep.

AFTERTHOUGHT

Afterthought: that mad desire to shut your mouth after you've put your foot in it.

AGE

You're getting old when the gleam in your eye is the sun hitting your bifocals.

The three R's in the school of experience: at twenty it's romance; at thirty it's rent; and at sixty it's rheumatism.

Old age: that time of life when a man flirts with girls but can't remember why.

Scientists announce that by measuring radioactivity they can find the age of any object less than a million years old. Fair warning, ladies.

"I don't think I look thirty, do you dear?" a woman asked her husband and he answered, "No, darling, not now. You used to."

Nothing makes a woman older than having friends discover when she was born.

A teacher asked her class, "How old would a person be who was born in 1920?" and a kid answered, "Man or woman?"

A man is as young as he feels—after trying to prove it.

A youthful figure is something that you get when you ask a woman her age.

Old age: that morning-after feeling without the night before.

There's no telling how long Methuselah might have lived if his appendix and tonsils had been removed, and if he had used the right brand of tooth paste and smoked filter cigarettes.

"If your wife economical?" a man was asked, and he replied: "Sometimes. She used only thirty candles on her fortieth birthday cake."

A man is as old as he feels—a woman as old as she feels like admitting.

A widow is the proof that women live longer than men.

Christopher Morley once observed that "the first proof of old age is when you think that other people aren't having the fun you had."

When asked how old he was, an old Chinese replied: "I full-bloom."

One of the pleasures of age is looking back at the people you didn't marry.

Perhaps fewer women would conceal their age if more men acted theirs.

It isn't time that tells on a woman—it's her best friends.

Sixty is the age when a man realizes that his grandfather at seventy-five wasn't so old after all.

Maurice Chevalier says that "age is bothersome only when you stop to coddle it."

Fred Houston says that the declining years are those in which a man declines almost everything.

As a man gets older he suspects that nature organized him for the benefit of doctors and dentists.

More people might live to a ripe old age if they weren't so busy providing for it.

Here's to the man who can live long enough to do everything his wife wants him to do.

Thirty is the ideal age for a woman—especially if she's forty.

The years that a woman subtracts from her age are not lost; they are added to the ages of other women.

As you grow older you can make a fool of yourself in a much more dignified manner.

138

When a man has a birthday he takes a day off. When a woman has one, she takes a year off.

An old man was asked, "To what do you attribute your old age?" and he replied, "The fact that I was born a long time ago."

Erskine Johnson says that no matter how well a woman carries her years, she's bound to drop a few sooner or later.

An actress once told Bob Hope. "I'm approaching the age of thirty," and he queried, "From which direction?"

If in the last few years you haven't discarded a major opinion or acquired a new one, investigate to see if you're not getting senile.

They now say we'll live fifteen years longer than our grandfathers, but they don't say why.

By the time a man gets old enough to watch his step, he isn't going anywhere.

Photographer told an old man, after taking a picture of him on his ninety-eighth birthday, "I hope I'll be around to take your picture when you're one hundred," and the old man replied, "Why not? You look pretty healthy."

The three ages of man are the school tablet, aspirin tablet, and stone tablet.

Thirty: when a woman's youth changes from the present tense to pretense.

Middle age: when dangerous curves become extended detours.

A woman, applying for a position, wrote nothing in the space asking for her age, and when she was asked about it she replied, "I refuse to answer because it might eliminate me."

At fifty one can be eccentric, whereas at thirty the same actions were considered rude.

Dangerous age: any time between one and ninety-one.

The President of the Over-Eighty Club was challenged for admitting two members who were only seventy-eight, and he explained, "Well, every organization needs some young blood."

An authority on aging says that men are smartest at the age of fifty—which is precisely when there is nobody around the house to listen to them.

The squire had reached his eightieth birthday, and his gardener was offering congratulations. "I never thought, sir, that I should live to be working for an octogeranium."

AGREEMENT

Samuel Goldwyn once said, "I don't want any yesmen around me. I want someone to tell me the truth—even if it costs him his job."

A wise man gives in when he is wrong—and if he's married he will give in when he's right.

Compromise: a deal in which two people get what neither of them wanted.

AIMS

Marjorie Johnson says that a lot of people consider themselves ahead of the times when they aren't even going in the same direction.

ALARM CLOCKS

There's nothing like the clanging of an alarm clock to remind you that the best part of the day is over.

One thing an alarm clock never arouses is our better nature.

ALIBIS

Dairyman was charged with selling adulterated milk. Judge asked him if he had anything to say, and he replied, "Well, your honor, the night before it was raining hard and the only cause I can give is that the cow must have got wet clear through."

Drunken driver's alibi: "I didn't know I was loaded."

An alibi is a first cousin to an excuse, and they're both mighty poor relations.

Said a woman driver arrested on a speeding charge, "The wind blew so hard it made me go faster than I really wanted to."

He who hesitates better have a good alibi when he gets home.

Asked why he didn't invent a story to tell his wife when he was going home late, a husband explained, "If my wife's asleep I won't need a story and if she's awake I won't get a chance to tell it."

The office boy, wanting to see the night ball game, went home and told his grandmother his boss had died.

ALIMONY

A female battle-ax said to her lawyer, "And you might warn my husband that if he misses a single alimony payment, I'll repossess him."

Alimony: if you don't pay in due time, you'll do time.

Alimony: giving comfort to the enemy.

Alimony: the high cost of leaving.

Martin Block points out that alimony is heart-earned money.

Bill Cullen quipped, "She told him she wouldn't marry him for all the alimony in the world."

ALLOWANCES

The average boy uses soap as if it came out of his allowance.

AMBITION

Did you hear about the fellow who lifted himself up by his boot licks?

A boy's ambition now is to graduate from college, get a good job and his own parking space at the plant.

Some men are not satisfied to be at the bottom of the ladder. They want to be lower.

Lots of people have the right aim in life but they run short of ammunition.

Our business in life is not to get ahead of others, but to get ahead of ourselves.

Maurice Seitter observes that too many people miss the silver lining because they're expecting gold.

At twenty a man thinks he can save the world; at thirty he's tickled if he can save part of his salary.

The grass may look greener on the other side of the fence, but it's just as hard to cut.

Not so long ago ambition used to be rewarded. Now it is punished with higher taxes.

AMERICA

An American is a person who shouts at the government to balance the budget, and then in a whisper borrows ten dollars until payday.

An American is a man with both feet on the ground and both hands in the air.

America: a country that was once a melting pot and is now a pressure cooker.

An American is the only fellow in the world who will pay fifty cents to park his car while he eats a twenty-five cent sandwich.

When the people aren't sure of what they want in democracy, they vote for something different from what they have.

No American ever feels he's down and out as long as he has a tankful of gas.

The American way: using instant coffee to dawdle away an hour.

American: One who knows when and where the Pilgrims landed but has no idea why.

An American is a person who isn't afraid to criticize the President but is always polite to the traffic cop.

What this country needs is a good five-second commercial.

The United States is the first country to have thought up the idea of making unemployment financially attractive.

The American way of life: one dollar down and one dollar a week.

Before you complain about America, remember it's the only place where people don't want to move to another country.

America is the proof that immigration is the sincerest form of flattery.

You get some idea of this great land of ours when you realize that about four thousand drivers a day run out of gas, not one of them in sight of a filling station.

America: the country that developed hybrid seed and the soil bank.

Lewis H. Mumford says that Americans who once expressed their love of our rocks and rills, our woods and templed hills, can now sing: "We love our expressways and parking lots, big clover leaves and traffic knots."

America is land of which one-quarter is covered by forests and the rest by mortgages.

What this country really needs is to have the ceiling price on a five-cent cigar dropped to seventeen cents.

America: the wonderful land where it's trashy to sit on the back stoop in your undershirt but gracious living if you've got nothing on but your shorts.

ANCESTORS

Ancestral pride is going forward by backing up.

He who boasts of his ancestors confesses that his family is better dead than alive.

ANGER

Blood is thicker than water—and it boils quicker.

On two occasions you should be careful to keep your mouth shut—when swimming and when angry.

Swallowing angry words is better than having to eat them.

A hothead is a person who flies off the handle because he has a screw loose.

ANIMALS

One mother kangaroo to another: "Don't you just hate these rainy days when the kids can't play outside?"

Ad in *Billboard*: "Lion tamer wants tamer lion."

A city youngster, in the country for the first time, rushed to his mother and said, "I've seen a man who makes horses. He had one nearly finished when I saw him. He was just nailing on its back feet."

Then there's the sad, sad story of the rambunctious little ram who committed suicide when he heard the song, "There'll Never Be Another You."

Inscription on a monument in France marking the grave of an army mule: In memory of Maggie, who in her time kicked 2 colonels, 4 majors, 10 captains, 24 lieutenants, 42 sergeants, 432 other ranks, and one Mills bomb.

Sign in Yellowstone National Park: "Never pat a bear until it is a rug."

Little kid was telling the teacher about his dog and she asked, "What kind is it?" and he answered, "Oh, he's a sort of cocker scandal."

Man leaving pet shop with a new puppy: "C'mon little feller, you're going to change someone's mind about wall-to-wall carpeting."

Warning sign on lawn: "Great Dane–ger!"

There was a tenderhearted lass who loved her goldfish so much she kept them in a bathtub. When asked how she managed to take a bath she explained modestly, "I blindfold them."

Paul Larmer says that a hick town is a place where you wait for a dog to cross in front of your car because he's a friend of yours.

Classified ad in North Carolina newspaper: "Will the party who picked up the black cocker spaniel puppy Friday on Lindsay road either return him or come back and get the four-year-old boy he belongs to?"

"You mustn't pull the cat's tail," a dad told his little son. And sonny replied, "I'm only holding it. The cat is pulling."

Ad in Oregon weekly: "Puppies five weeks. Mother: boxer show dog. Father: leash-law violator."

Christopher Morley called his kittens "Shall" and "Will" because so few people can tell them apart.

Alligator: an animal whose skin is fashionable for ladies' wear, especially among lady alligators.

144

Headline in St. Louis *Post Dispatch*: "Beavers Multiply . . . And That Adds up to More Dam Headaches."

Monkeys in the St. Louis zoo were recently sent to a rest home. It seems they were about to crack up, watching the anxious faces of all visitors who looked in their cages.

Elephant: an animal occurring in one of three colors, depending on whether you're on a safari, a church committee, or a weekend party.

Elinor K. Rose says that a bird, a bee, a mouse, or a flea, can do their loving noiselessly; likewise a gnat—why can't a cat?

ANSWERS

A contestant on a TV program was asked to name three ways of saying good-by and he replied: "Adieu, Adios, and Arsenic."

ANTIQUES

Antique: something so old that it is worth more than it really is.

Sign in antique shop window: "There's no present like the past."

One man's junk is another man's antique.

APARTMENTS

From Columbia, Missouri: "$10 reward for south side apartment. Large enough to keep young wife from going home to mother. Small enough to keep mother from coming here."

Apartment: a place where you start to turn off your radio and find you've been listening to your neighbor's set.

APOLOGIES

An apology is the only means of having the last word with a woman.

APPEARANCE

Our barber looked at the young man's sleek hair and asked if he wanted it cut or just the oil changed.

If, before going to town, a man spent as much time on his personal appearance as his wife does, she'd suspect he was up to no good.

Betty Dobendorf says that haircuts are what men in barbershops get that their wives don't notice unless they don't get them.

What we need is a mirror with a little more consideration for middle age.

APPLAUSE

Did you hear about the actor who turned surgeon? He took out a man's appendix in the operating theater, and was so gratified by the applause that he took out the patient's tonsils as an encore.

APPLICANTS

The personnel manager told a prospective employee: "We have our own special type of incentive plan: we fire at the drop of a hat."

In Philadelphia a woman filled out a job application at a factory, noted that she had previously worked at a nudist camp, wrote as her reason for leaving: "Change of scenery."

APPOINTMENTS

Frank Scully, a writer, had an important lunch date with Louis B. Mayer, head of M-G-M, and the former's wife asked "How did it go?" when he returned home. "Fifty-fifty," reported Frank. "I showed up and Mayer didn't."

APPRECIATION

"How can I ever show my appreciation?" gushed a woman to Clarence Darrow after he had solved her legal troubles, and he answered, "My dear woman, ever since the Phoenicians invented money there has been only one answer to that question."

ARGUMENTS

Man and his wife were engaged in the usual hassle and she said angrily: "I'm not trying to start another argument—this is the same one."

146

There would be fewer arguments if we tried to determine what's right instead of who's right.

A husband and wife were engaged in an argument and she said, "I was just as unreasonable when we were first married but you thought it cute."

"It says here that a man throttled his wife," said a woman looking up from her paper. Her husband replied, "Sounds like a practical choker."

Too many people, Dr. Samuel Johnson advised, raise their voices when they would better reinforce their argument.

A person who always butts in has an infuriating complex.

When arguing with a fool, be sure he isn't similarly engaged.

Many an argument is sound—just sound.

A wife told her husband, "I didn't say there weren't two sides to every story—I just said I wasn't listening to your side."

Woodrow Wilson, in speaking of a statesman, said, "He is more apt to contribute heat than light to a discussion."

The last word in an argument is what a wife has. Anything a husband says after that is the beginning of another argument.

The only person who listens to both sides of a family argument is the woman in the next apartment.

Argument: two people trying to get the last word first.

Woman to husband: "Are you a man or a mouse. Squeak up!"

ARMED FORCES

A GI explained his black eye: "I was hit by a guided muscle."

Disheveled girl just back from a date, to her roommate: "That's what I get for going out with a soldier—combat fatigue!"

Sign on shop near army post: "Hats altered to fit any promotion."

Jack Paar told us of the young man who tried to make a deal with his draft board to go to every other war.

A Marine sergeant caught a recruit with a single button unfastened and sneered, "Oh, sunbathing, eh?"

In an American hospital in the South Pacific a list of men to receive hypodermics was headed: "Targets For Tonight."

Sweet young thing when asked the rating of the navy man she'd been out with: "I think he was a Chief Petting Officer."

When the recruit complained of a pain in his abdomen, the medico said, "Young man, officers have abdomens, sergeants have stomachs— You have a bellyache!"

An airman, whose wife was expecting, was asked just how soon the great day would be. "Don't know," he replied, "but if it ain't soon the doc will have to bring it in on instruments."

A selectee told members of his draft board, "They can't make me fight," and one of the board replied, "Maybe not, but they can take you where fighting is and you can use your own judgment."

Over the bunk of a GI just returned from a three-day pass, his buddies hung a sign: "Temporarily Out of Ardor."

"Who the hell put those flowers on the table?" the mess sergeant yelled and an orderly said, "The captain" to which the sergeant said, "Purdy, ain't they?"

"Do you know my sergeant talks to himself?" one rookie asked another. His friend answered, "So does mine, but he thinks someone is listening."

During wartime a young lady received an envelope addressed in familiar handwriting from a far-flung army outpost, but instead of the expected letter she found a note from the censor, "Your boy friend still loves you, but he talks too much."

Army nurses who came into wards to give hypo injections often yelled, "Bottoms up." One popular nurse's patients chipped in at Christmas to buy her a present which they tagged, "To the best rear gunner in the outfit."

The platoon was drilling raggedly, and the disgusted sergeant finally brought the men to a halt. "You should be ashamed of yourselves," he growled. "I've seen better drilling by little cans of beer on my television set!"

Garry Moore asked a contestant on "I've Got a Secret" what made him decide to be a parachute jumper, and the fellow replied, "A plane with three dead engines."

148

Two sailors, asleep on a Brooklyn park bench, had this sign hung on their feet: "Don't Disturb—the Fleet's All In."

An army man stationed in Oklahoma hitchhiked home in a hurry when he stood by the road with a duffel bag in one hand and a banner tied across his chest reading: "To Mother for Christmas."

A master sergeant made a big hit with every GI in his office when he hung up a small sign beside his desk. It stated: "I am fairly stupid myself, but I have some very intelligent help."

Guess you heard about the chaplains at Fort Richardson, Alaska, organizing a bowling team and calling themselves "The Holy Rollers."

Bride whose wedding had been repeatedly postponed due to troop movements: "I've been alerted five times."

Chaplain: an army official who works to beat hell.

Comedian Red Skelton, serving at Camp Roberts during the war, went to the drinking fountain one day and boomed out, "My God! Somebody put water in the chlorine."

A youngster, quite proud of his uncle's promotion, exclaimed, "The longer he stays in the Air Force, the ranker he gets!"

A soldier ended his love letter with, "Oceans of love and a kiss on every wave."

A military expert is one who tells you what's going to happen to-morrow—then tells you why it didn't happen.

At Fort Sill there is a large, weather-beaten wooden fence. Carved on it, beside such sentiments as "John loves Susie" and "Sam loves Kathy," is "Harry loves civilian life."

Draft board: the world's largest travel agency.

Did you hear about the captain who got sore because someone sent him a letter marked "Private"?

A sergeant bawled out a rookie for not standing at attention, and the boy replied, "I am at attention. It's the uniform that's at ease."

Sweet young thing to girl friend: "I'm knitting something to make the boys in service happy," and her friend asked, "Oh, a sweater for a soldier," and the young thing replied, "No, a bathing suit for me."

Learning the phrases incidental to sentry duty proved confusing

149

to one soldier. An officer of the day was surprised when this fellow challenged him with: "Halt! Look who's here."

A Des Moines recruit was being loaded into an Army truck already jam-packed with Wacs. "Hey, sergeant," she protested, "have a heart. This bus is full." Said the tough male sergeant, "Lady, I've been getting eighteen men in these trucks and I sure as hell can get eighteen Wacs in." Wailed the squeezed Wac: "But men are broad in the shoulders."

ART

Abstract art: the proof that things aren't as bad as they are painted.

A stranger visiting the Metropolitan Museum of New York stood watching several students copying originals. Finally the visitor tiptoed over to one of the young artists and said, "Say, mister, what do they do with the old pictures when the new ones are finished?"

Modern sculptor: A man who can take a rough block of stone or wood, work on it for months, and make it look like a rough block of stone or wood.

Artist's model: a girl who works only when the boss is looking.

ASSOCIATES

A man is judged by the company he keeps, and a woman by the company she has just left.

ATHEISM

Inscription on tombstone: Here lies an atheist, all dressed up and no place to go.

ATMOSPHERE

Atmosphere: what the quaint little eating places use instead of fresh air.

ATOM

Atomic age: when two can live as deep as one.

Splitting an atom would not be too difficult for a salaried man who must divide his income between the U. S. Treasury and his family.

Atom bomb: an explosive container under which all men are cremated equal.

ATTITUDE

There is no danger of developing eyestrain from looking on the bright side of things.

AUCTIONS

Auctioneer: a man who can sell nothing for something to a buyer who is looking for something for nothing.

AUTOBIOGRAPHIES

An autobiography is the story of a man's life written by his worst enemy.

An autobiography, Philip Guedalla says, is an unrivaled vehicle for telling the truth about other people.

AUTOMATION

Automation is bringing in a new kind of fringe benefit. Workers in an automated British oil refinery see so few human beings that they have demanded "lonely money."

Things won't change much in the completely automated office. The button that gets ahead will still be the one with the most push.

AUTOMOBILES

An announcer reading a commercial on a Georgia radio station came up with: "No matter how small the matter is with your car, you can depend on Blank's Garage making a major repair."

Sign in Kentucky garage: We Take the Dents out of Accidents.

Motorist (on phone after accident): "My Jaguar just hit a pig and turned turtle," and the mechanic replied, "This is a garage, not a zoo."

Woman, explaining to friend: "You don't get into one of those foreign cars—you pull 'em on like a girdle."

Fulton Lewis, Jr., says to give the automobile manufacturers two years and you'll have to be born in an automobile to get in it at all.

Mechanic to motorist: "Let me put it this way—if your car were a horse, it would have to be shot."

When it comes to used cars, it's hard to drive a bargain.

What the average man wants out of his new car is his teen-age son.

Used car: something you buy in haste and repaint at leisure.

In this country there are three persons to every car—and they are always in front of it at crossings.

Pedestrian: a man who thought there were still a couple of gallons of gas left in the tank.

Sign outside San Francisco garage: "Car washed, $3.00. Sports cars dunked, $1.50."

Car advertisement: Room for the more abundant wife.

One nice thing about sports cars: if you flood the carburetor, you can just put the car over your shoulder and burp it.

Sign on back of sports car: HIT SOMEONE YOUR OWN SIZE.

You have to take off your hat to some of these new model cars— or get it knocked off as you enter.

Used car: a car in first-crash condition.

Husband asking wife, "What did the man say was wrong with the tire?" and she answered, "He said the air was beginning to show through."

Nothing damages a car more than attempting to trade it in.

Sign in paint and body shop: God Bless Our Women Drivers.

"Mama," a little girl asked, "what becomes of a car when it gets too old to run?" and the mother replied, "Someone sells it to your father."

His car was so old they issued it upper and lower plates.

"Yes, judge," the man told the judge, "I was going ninety miles an hour—but I had just finished washing my car and wanted to give it a quick drying."

Fewer people would be paying for their mistakes if they'd bought new cars in the first place.

Rubbing elbows with a man will reveal things about him you never before realized. The same is true of rubbing fenders.

A station wagon is a vehicle a city person buys when he moves to the country so the country people will know he's from the city.

A mechanic advised a car owner: "My advice is to keep the oil and change the car."

Sign on car with Kansas license plates: "Please drive carefully; we have lived through drought, dust storms, prohibition, and the New Deal, and we want to see what happens next."

AVERAGE MAN

Groucho Marx says: "I'm an ordinary sort of fellow—42 around the chest, 42 around the waist, 96 around the golf course, and a nuisance around the house."

BABIES

The Memphis *Commercial Appeal* reported: "A precious little bungle of love arrived at the home of Mr. and Mrs. Gordon Sauls, Wednesday morning, a nine-pound bouncing boy."

Wife to husband: "You'd better get up and see why the baby's not crying."

If the hand that rocks the cradle rules the world, a good many babies must be rocking themselves these days.

"Well then," demanded the baby stork, "who DID bring me?"

A baby's slightest whimper instantly awakens the mother. What slows things up is rousing her husband to see about it.

The proud parents of a baby daughter sent out announcements reading: "We have skirted the issue."

Triplets: twins with a spare.

153

A father, feeding a toddler, asked his wife, "She wants more strained prunes; shall I give her a second coat?"

A baby is an alimentary canal with a loud voice at one end and no responsibility at the other.

BABY SITTERS

A baby sitter, frazzled after a long tussle with the kids, told the parents when they returned: "Don't apologize—I wouldn't be in any hurry to come home, either."

Just a few days after her latest son's arrival, a young matron received a beautiful plant from her baby sitter with a card reading: "Thanks for the new business."

Baby sitter: a girl you hire to watch your television set.

Bookstore clerk to couple: "Here's a practical book on child training written by an authority—a sitter."

BACHELORS

A bachelor never quite gets over the idea that he is a thing of beauty and a boy forever.

Any bachelor can dry his girl's tears by throwing in the towel.

Bachelor: a man who has failed to embrace his opportunities.

Ed Wynn says a bachelor is a man who never makes the same mistake twice.

A bachelor, declares a writer for the Louisville *Courier-Journal,* is a guy who is footloose and fiancée-free.

The world's greatest mystery from the married man's viewpoint: what does the bachelor do with his money?

When a bachelor walks the floor with a babe, he's dancing.

He who hesitates is lost—except a bachelor.

Bachelor: a man who has never come up with anything definite that a girl can put on her finger.

Bachelor: a chap who believes it's much better to have loved and lost than to have to get up for the 2 A.M. feeding.

154

Bachelor: the only species of big game for which the license is taken out after the safari.

What a pity it is that nobody knows how to manage a wife but a bachelor.

Advice to bachelors: if you're in doubt about kissing a girl, always give her the benefit of the doubt.

BALDNESS

Men worry more about losing their hair than their heads.

BANKING

A bank is an institution with so many vice-presidents that, when there's a director's meeting, it looks like a run on the bank.

Banker: a man who always takes an interest in his work.

"A banker," said Mark Twain, "is a fellow who loans you his umbrella when the sun is shining and wants it back the minute it begins to rain."

Did you hear about the woman who told the bank teller: "I want to make this withdrawal from my husband's half of our joint account."

Bankruptcy is often due to a lack and a lass.

Woman to bank teller: "Very well. If you insist I've overdrawn I'll just have to cash it somewhere else."

BANQUETS

Banquet: a plate of cold chicken and peas entirely surrounded by warm appeals for donations or help.

From a circular letter to Lions Club members in an Indiana town: "All members are requested to bring their wives and one other covered dish, along with table service."

BARGAINS

Bargain: Something you cannot use at a price you cannot resist.

If you think you can drive a bargain—buy a secondhand car.

155

Bargain hunter: a woman who, because she buys what she doesn't need, often ends up in needing what she can't buy.

A woman will buy anything she thinks a store is losing money on.

Spotting a bargain is easy. A bargain is anything your wife buys and can't explain any other way.

Bargain: something that is marked down from the price it was marked up to.

BASEBALL

The baseball scout reported on a rookie: "He bats, throws, and shaves right-handed."

BATHING SUITS

Bikini bathing suits are showing up on the beaches again this year, but just barely.

BATTLE OF SEXES

The battle of the sexes will never be won by either side. There is too much fraternizing with the enemy.

BEAUTY

Beauty parlor: where the women get a faceful of mud and an earful of dirt.

On a drugstore display of hair tints: "Hue-it-yourself."

Nothing makes a modern girl blush like the corner drugstore.

Jack Donnelly told about the woman who had her face lifted so many times she was talking through her eyes.

Cosmetics are abundant proof that gals have the skin they love to retouch.

Beauty parlor: where the talk alone is enough to curl your hair.

Miss America: a girl who's pretty as a picture and has a nice frame, too.

Herb Shriner, attending a coming-out party of a New York debutante, was reminded of some society girls back in his home town.

"They were so ugly," he said, "the first time they came out we made them all go back again."

When the veteran movie star got her face lifted it was a job of drastic surgery.

Wrinkles are what women get in their complexions by worrying about their complexions.

Beauty: what every girl prefers because every man can see better than he can think.

A decided blonde is a brunette who decided to dye her hair.

As far as fancy paint jobs go, modern girls are getting a lot of competition from the new cars.

Sign in Columbus beauty shop: "Home permanents corrected here."

Beauty contest: a trial to see which are the most beautiful less-dressed women in America.

One way to keep lipstick from smearing is to eat a lot of garlic.

A man told his friend that his wife had recently gotten a mud-pack to improve her beauty and his friend asked "Did it?" The man replied, "It did for a couple of days and then it wore off."

Catty woman to friend, "How lovely you look, dear—you must have gone to a lot of trouble."

A lady, well past the early bloom of youth, walked up to a clerk in a drugstore and whispered, "Have you got anything for gray hair?" and he replied, "Nothing, madam, but the greatest respect."

From the Columbus *Citizen*: "A radiant smile, plus only a clean gingham apron, can transform an average woman into a very charming personality."

BEGGAR

Beggar: a man who lives from handout to mouth.

BEHAVIOR

Judging from the way many people are misbehaving themselves these days, they must think that hell has been air-conditioned.

In this crazy, mixed up era, people don't repent even at leisure.

Tears: the world's greatest water power.

A chip on the shoulder is usually a splinter from the wood above it.

Wife to husband: "Let's buy Junior a bicycle," and hubby asked, "Do you think that will improve his behavior?" The wife replied, "No, but it will spread it more over the neighborhood."

By the time most men learn to behave themselves, they're too old to do anything else.

A man can stand his own poverty better than he can stand the other fellow's prosperity.

Rheumatism has kept many people on the right path in life.

Actions don't always speak louder than words, but they generally tell fewer lies.

To really know a man, observe his behavior with a woman, a flat tire, and a child.

There are too many hydromatic people—shiftless and easygoing.

The way of the transgressor may be hard—but it isn't lonely.

We try to see some good in everybody we meet, but occasionally there are folks who make us realize our eyesight isn't as good as it was.

BELIEF

The very kids who don't believe in Santa Claus are the ones who grow up and play the horses.

Some people will believe anything if they happen to overhear it.

Believe only half of what you hear, but be sure it's the right half.

BETTING

One of the best ways to stop a runaway horse is to bet on it.

BIGAMY

Bigamy: when a man marries a beautiful girl and a good cook.

A bigamist is a man who serves two masters.

Bigamy: a crime whose extreme penalty is two mothers-in-law.

BILLS

Husband, after examining bills, told his wife: "We are now on a pay-as-you went basis."

Young couple, going over bills, came to the last two and the man said, "Gosh, honey, we're practically broke. I don't know which to pay—the electric company or the doctor." She answered, "Oh, the electric company because, after all, the doctor can't shut off your blood."

A Georgia firm stamps this message on their statements: "Pay us so we can pay them and they can pay him and he can pay you."

You know what the husband felt like when he told his wife: "Seems like every time we get any money saved it's because we forgot to pay a bill."

BIRTHDAYS

A birthday is an anniversary on which a man takes a day off and a woman takes a year off.

The best way to remember your wife's birthday is to forget it once.

A girl asked her brother, "What shall we give father for his birthday present?" and the boy answered, "Let's let him drive the car."

"All my mother wants for her birthday," a teenager remarked to another, "is not to be reminded of it."

BLAME

A bachelor is a man who has no one to blame but himself.

BLESSED EVENT

Blessed event: when your mother-in-law leaves.

BLONDE

Vera Vague, in describing a lady, said: "Any similarity between her and a blonde is purely peroxidental."

BOARDINGHOUSE

A boardinghouse is a place where one man's meat is another man's croquette.

BOOKKEEPER

Bookkeeper: a person who feels good when things start looking black again.

BOOKS

To buy a book try your drugstore, grocery store, and book dealer, in that order.

New book title: "He Beat Her in the Wigwam" or "Her Sufferings Were Intents."

Rare volume: One that comes back after you've loaned it.

A dime novel is one that's gone up to four dollars and a half.

Someone is going to make a fortune not in writing a book on building your vocabulary but on giving it a rest.

Nowadays, a dime novel would be.

Clifton Fadiman, after reviewing an autobiography, wrote: "As far as I can see, this book has only one defect; poor choice of subject matter."

A bookstore manager received this request by mail: "Please send me the name of a good book on personal hygiene. I think I've got it."

Clerk to skittish lady: "It's not dirty. It's earthy, which is a very different thing."

A scrawny miss diffidently hung around the desk of the librarian until the latter asked: "Is there any particular book you're trying to make up your mind to ask for?" and the girl blushed and whispered, "Do you think I could borrow 'Scouting For Boys'?"

Did you hear about the publisher who told the author, "Your novel is excellent, but right now I am looking for trash."

Indignant woman to luscious-looking librarian: "Funny you don't have that book—my husband said you had everything."

BORES

A bore is a person who never seems to have a previous engagement.

Bore: a person who knows the same stories you do.

A. A. Milne says that bores can be divided into two classes: those who have their particular subject and those who do not need a subject.

The bore has one thing in his favor: he doesn't talk about other people.

A bore is a person who keeps you from being lonely and makes you wish you were.

BOSSES

"I don't know the style or color of shoes, but I want low heels," a tall blonde told the clerk and he asked, "To wear with what?" She replied, "A short, fat, elderly executive."

During the war when help was scarce a supervisor told a bungling workman: "This is the last straw, Jerkins! I'm giving you two year's notice."

Usually the first thing the new stenographer types is the boss.

A boss is the man who when you get to work early comes in late, and when you are late, comes in early.

Stenographer to friend, "He was a perfect lamb when I asked him for a raise. All he said was 'Bah!'"

Our idea of an optimist is a man who marries his secretary and thinks he'll be able to continue dictating to her.

Always laugh heartily at your boss's bum jokes—he may be giving you a loyalty test.

A girl boasted to fellow employee that she felt like telling the boss where to get off again, and her friend asked, "What do you mean again?" and the girl said, "I felt like it yesterday, too."

Boss to new stenographer: "Briefly, Miss Harrison, your duties will be to take dictation, file reports, answer the phone, and stay single!"

Overheard at an office party: "Oh yes, I like working for him very much. He's a perfect gentleman; all you have to do is slap his face once in a while."

161

BOSTONIAN

Bostonian: an American, broadly speaking.

BOYS

Boy: a noise with dirt on it.

Pat Buttram says that mothers who are a little sad as they send their small boys off to summer camp can look at it this way: they're not losing a son—they're gaining two turtles, a frog, and a garter snake.

Mothers who scold small boys for carrying crazy things in their pockets should look in their handbags.

Towel: what a boy looks at to find out if his face is clean after washing.

A family suffering loss and injury in a tornado sent their small son to his aunt's house for a visit, until they could arrange for other housing. After three days came this telegram: RETURNING TOM. SEND TORNADO.

Another thing a small boy outgrows in a hurry is your pocketbook.

One trouble in raising a boy is that father always expects son to do exactly as much work as he never did.

The young man who's looking forward to stepping into his father's shoes ought to be reminded that Dad doesn't wear loafers.

A boy becomes a man when he walks around a puddle of water instead of through it.

A neighbor of ours is having trouble with her son—he's too young to be left alone with the baby but too old to be left alone with the baby sitter.

Small boy, speaking of his teacher: "She's mean but she's fair—she's mean to everybody."

Little boy, to playmate, as pretty girl passes by: "Boy! If I ever stop hating girls, she's the one I'll stop hating first!"

BOY SCOUTS

Home is the place a Boy Scout returns to after he has done his good deed for the day.

BRAGGING

Bragging is just a way of blowing off a little self-esteem.

Don't strut. The fact that you have a certain title or position doesn't prove anything except that maybe in selecting you, somebody made a mistake that will be rectified later.

I'm sure you know about the termite who boasted to his friends, "This'll bring down the house."

Bragger: a man who thinks he can push himself forward by patting himself on the back.

The man who has a right to boast doesn't have to.

Duties are tasks we look forward to with distaste, perform with reluctance, and brag about ever after.

As a rule the fellow who blows his horn the loudest is in the biggest fog.

Boast not too loudly of your open mind, lest you be judged as having holes in your head.

BRAINS

A lot of people are smarter than they look—and that's reassuring.

There is no wholly satisfactory substitute for brains, but silence does pretty well.

BRIDES

Young bride to husband: 'The two best things I prepare are meat loaf and peach cobbler," and he asked, "Which one is this?"

By the time the modern wedding day rolls around, the bride's father hasn't much else to give except a daughter.

BRIDEGROOM

Bridegroom: a man who exchanges good quarters for a better half.

BRIDGE

A bridge player is one who learns to take it on the shin.

"What kind of bridge does your wife play?" a man asked a friend, and the friend answered, "Judging by the cost, I'd say it was toll bridge."

Bridge is a game you don't play for money—but your opponents do.

Bridge is a game in which a good deal depends upon a good deal.

Our idea of a card trick is how to get out of making a fourth at bridge.

BROAD-MINDEDNESS

Broad-mindedness is the ability to smile when you discover your roommate and your girl are both missing from the dance floor.

BUDGETS

Woman to friend: "George and I like the same thing, only he likes to save it and I like to spend it."

A budget is a means of telling your money where to go instead of wondering where it went.

With so much of one's salary taxed to balance the budget, most people have trouble budgeting the balance.

Budget: a family's attempt to live below its yearnings.

A budget is a system of worrying before you spend it instead of afterward.

You'll understand the housewife who remarked, "We always have too much month left at the end of our money."

"You're terribly extravagant," a husband complained to his wife. "If anything should happen to me," he said, "you would probably have to beg." The wife snapped, "I'd get by. Look at all the experience I've had."

BUREAUCRAT

A bureaucrat is a man who shoots the bull, passes the buck, and makes seven copies of everything.

BURLESQUE

Burlesque is a kind of vaudeville where, if the girl's clothes don't drop off, the attendance does.

BUS

August: the month you can't open the bus window which you couldn't close in December.

BUSINESS

"You don't sell used cars? What kind of a drugstore is this?"

Pretzel manufacturer: a man who makes crooked dough and still remains within the law.

Business is what, when you don't have any, you go out of.

The executive who puts his feet on his desk to think must be careful not to snore.

Foreign-manufactured goods are flooding this country and under-selling our stuff. Now that we have taught the rest of the world how to mass-produce efficiently, we have to teach them how to do it expensively.

Sign in Long Island dry-goods store window: "ALTERCATION SALE—PARTNERS SPLITTING UP."

The book that fascinates any executive is the volume of business.

One businessman to another: "We're a nonprofit organization. We don't intend to be but we are."

One of the best ways for a wife to get her husband to tell her about his business affairs is to try to get him to buy a new car for the family.

Today's successful business executive seems to be a man who has an infinite capacity for taking planes.

One of the hard things about business is minding your own.

Moral: businessmen who want to stay in business had better learn the difference between stocks and blonds.

A well-known businessman says his success was due to luck. That certainly makes it hard on speakers at commencement exercises.

Marriage is one business that always has a silent partner.

The big guns in business are generally those who have never been fired.

A girdle manufacturer lives off the fat of the land.

A St. Louis announcer started off: "And this morning the station is happy to announce that a new member has been added to its horde of directors."

When a Salt Lake City gas station changed hands, the new owner put up the sign: "Open under New Optimists."

An American businessman got his first view of the Sahara Desert and exclaimed, "Man! What a place for a parking lot."

Adam and Eve were the first bookkeepers. They invented the loose-leaf system.

Those economic terms really aren't so hard to understand. A re-adjustment is when your neighbor loses his job. A recession is when you lose your job. A depression is when your wife loses her job.

One executive to another, "Another thing about our new electronic computer—it will never come prancing in some morning and announce it's leaving to get married."

Home-coming executive to wife: "Whew! I took an aptitude test this afternoon. Thank goodness I own the company!"

The minister concluded his sermon by saying, "And remember, friends, there will be no buying and selling in heaven," and a fellow in the back row said to himself, "Well, that's not where my business has gone anyway."

BUSY

A man is never too busy to talk about how busy he is.

CAFÉS

A waiter in the diner of a Canadian Pacific train approached a regal-looking lady and bent over her solicitously, then asked: "Are you the cold salmon?"

Pheasant under glass: small bird with a large bill.

Café slogan: "Something Superior for Your Interior."

CALENDAR

June: the month unmarried girls like to be well-groomed.

CALIFORNIA

California is a place where it never freezes until you have bought an orange grove.

CAMP

Raymond Duncan says that a lot of parents pack up their troubles and send them off to a summer camp.

CANDIDATES

"I wasn't born in a log cabin," the candidate said. "But my family moved into one as soon as they could afford it."

CAREER GIRLS

Secretary to boss: "I'm saving my coffee breaks. When I get enough together I'm taking Friday off."

Unlike their grandmas, older career girls now pray for the day when they will be sixty-two and eligible for social security.

CAREERS

A career girl is one more interested in plots and plans than pots and pans.

A profession is something you study years to get into and then spend the rest of your life trying to earn enough to get out of.

When Bishop Fulton J. Sheen registered at a Minneapolis hotel, he filled out the card at the desk. After the word "Representing" he wrote: "Good Lord and Company."

CASE HISTORY

Case history: the history of the modern woman which consists of a vanity case, a cigarette case, and a divorce case.

CAUTION

A cautious man is one who hasn't let a woman pin anything on him since he was a baby.

It's better to tighten your belt than to lose your pants.

CELEBRITY

A celebrity is a person who works hard to become well-known and then puts on dark glasses to avoid being known.

CEMETERY

A cemetery is the only place where they have a good word for you after you're down.

CENSORS

Censor: a man who knows more than he thinks you ought to.

Censor: a man who would like to get the goods on the nudists.

A book censor is a person who reads so much he gets asterisks in front of his eyes.

Blessed are the censors for they shall inhibit the earth.

CHARM

Charm: something you think you have until you begin relying on it.

CHEER

When folks tell you to cheer up, things might be worse, try it— you'll find they usually *do* get worse.

168

CHILDREN

There really is no trick to getting children to follow a straight and narrow path. Just live in a corner house and seed the lawn.

Juvenile delinquency, one man says, is the result of parents trying to train children without starting at the bottom.

When you observe children of five years in a tantrum, you wonder who will manage them when they are thirty.

Today's children start to school with a big advantage. They already know two letters of the alphabet—TV.

There are no problem children—only children with problems.

All parents think their children are gifted, and all children think their parents are retarded.

The only things that children wear out faster than shoes are Mom, Dad, and Teacher.

An allowance is what you pay your children to live with you.

Child psychology: what children manage parents with.

Nowadays it seems that the children run about everything but the lawn mower and the vacuum cleaner.

If you don't want your children to hear what you're saying, pretend you're talking to them.

The best inheritance a parent can give his children is a few minutes of his time each day.

Millions of Americans have only the mentality of children. But if you have tried to work your child's arithmetic you may not think that's too bad.

Many a parent can remember when its child was in the "no-it-all" stage.

The persons hardest to convince that they are at the retirement age are children at bedtime.

You can't tell whether a parent has been a success or failure till you find out what happens to the grandchildren.

Little boy to pal, as they leave a movie: "I like television better. It's not so far to the bathroom."

Nothing makes a child worse-behaved than belonging to a neighbor.

If you're going to make a pal of your boy, don't do it until after he has had quadratic algebraic equations.

William Franklin Gaines says that few children fear water unless soap is added.

Child psychology would be O.K. if you could just get the children to understand it.

It's a wise child who resembles a wealthy relative.

D. O. Flynn believes that a happy balance in child-parent relationship has been achieved when neither is afraid of the other.

One reason so many children are seen on the streets at night is that they're afraid to go home.

Children are natural mimics. They act like their parents in spite of every effort to teach them good manners.

It is said that the FBI has over 80,000,000 fingerprints. So has every house containing small children.

Papa Owl said to his wife, "I'm worried about Junior," and Mama Owl said, "Yes, he doesn't seem to give a hoot."

Child: something that stands halfway between an adult and a television screen.

Jack Paar once observed, "I grew up to be the kind of kid my mother didn't want me to play with."

A child is a person who is often spoiled because you can't spank the two grandmothers.

There is the case of the lonesome little cowboy in a whole neighborhood of space cadets.

Little girl: "The more I play with him the worse I like him."

Most kids only eat spinach so they'll grow up and be big and strong enough to refuse it.

Unless you are the victim, nothing is funnier than kids mimicking their elders.

A little girl was telling her teacher about her baby teeth coming out, and she ended by saying, "Pretty soon I'll be running on the rims."

New baby sitter, a bit on the apprehensive side, told the parents of two troublesome boys: "Here's my telephone number where my parents can be reached in case anything happens to me."

The children were in the midst of a free-for-all when father came into the room and asked, "Richard, who started this?" And the kid answered, "Well, it all started when David hit me back."

Nowadays, parents take a problem child to a psychiatrist. Grandfather used to keep a do-it-yourself in the woodshed.

The saddest words of tongue or pen: "We just sold Junior's buggy when . . . ."

A mother snatched up her toddler after it had broken a lamp and exclaimed: "That settles it! You're going to be an only child."

Down in the cattle country a teacher was discussing with her third-graders the importance of being in school every day. Said one small girl proudly: "I never missed a day from school until I had broncho pneumonia."

Mother rabbit to her small child, "A magician pulled you out of a hat—now stop asking questions."

On a Chicago–Los Angeles flight was a lively youngster who nearly drove everyone crazy. He was running up and down the aisle when the stewardess was serving coffee, and ran smack into her, knocking the paper-cupped coffee to the floor. As he stood by watching her clean up the mess, she glanced up at the boy and said, "Look, why don't you go and play outside?"

Mama mosquito: "Now if you children will be good, I'll take you to the nudist colony tonight."

A Sunday-school teacher told her class, "Now, children, you must never do anything in private that you wouldn't do in public," and one of the kids yelled, "Hurray! No more baths."

Galja Barish Votaw tells of the thank-you note from a nine-year-old: "I love the book you sent me for Christmas. I have been reading it night and day and am now on page ten."

A kid said that "a skeleton is nothing but a stack of bones with the people scraped off."

On viewing the ocean for the first time, a little boy exclaimed, "Look, Mother, it just keeps flushing and flushing."

"Darling," mother asked, "why are you making faces at your bull-dog?" and the child replied, "Well, he started it."

Kid, to his mother, at the table: "I want one of those olives with a little red taillight."

When a child takes "No" for an answer, he's probably thinking of another way to ask the question.

Most children are descended from a long line their mothers listened to.

After being urged to eat more by her parents a little girl answered, "I don't want to grow up big and strong. I want to be pale and interesting."

Boy, patting cat: "He must be talking to somebody—I can hear the busy signal."

Notice on community bulletin board in Memphis: "Ten-year-old boy would like garden work and odd jobs after school and on Saturdays to help support a dependent who eats like a horse. P.S.: It is a horse."

"You're prettier than your mother," a woman told a little girl and the youngster answered, "I should be—I'm a later model."

Little boy, crying (to floor walker): "Have you seen a lady without a boy that looks like me?"

Four-year-old's definition of nursery school: "A place where they teach children who hit, not to hit, and children who don't hit, to hit back."

Some parents we know have difficulty selecting a name for their new baby—others have wealthy relatives.

Child's definition of impatience: waiting in a hurry.

Child reciting the Golden Rule: "Do unto others before they do unto you."

Children grow by leaps and bounds—especially in the apartment overhead.

One of our neighbors observes that before marriage he had three theories about children and now that he has three children he has no theories.

Children, like canoes, are more easily controlled if paddled from the rear.

The behavior of some children suggests that their parents embarked on the sea of matrimony without a paddle.

Those who speak of it as being easy to take candy away from a baby should try it sometime.

CHOICES

Of two evils, choose the one least likely to be talked about.

CHOIRS

From Georgia weekly: "Youth choirs of St. Paul's Episcopal church have been disbanded for the summer with the thanks of the church."

CHRISTIAN

Christian: a man who will lend his neighbor one hundred dollars but cannot trust the Lord with ten.

CHRISTMAS

Of course money is the Christmas gift everyone in the family would appreciate most—but the trouble is, you can't charge it.

A Nebraska man sent his best girl this Christmas greeting: "You are a dear, sweet girl. May God bless you and keep you. Wish I could afford to."

Family ties always get stronger toward Christmas—and louder, after it.

Christmas gifts are divided into two classes: those you don't like and those you don't get.

The most popular holiday green still comes from the United States mint.

Christmas is one time of year when a man's wife believes in giving him all the credit she can get.

173

The Christmas cigar a man really appreciates is the one that burns a hole in his Christmas tie.

Christmas: season of guided mistletoe.

The man who would give you the shirt off his back probably got it for Christmas.

Santa Claus takes a week to distribute the presents—and we hold the bag for the other fifty-one.

Christmas: what kids look forward to for one whole year and parents pay for the next.

Christmas Eve is when you stay in to see how you came out.

The majority of us are likely to do our name-dropping when revising the annual Christmas-card list.

One of our present troubles seems to be that too many adults and not enough children believe in Santa Claus.

Give a man enough rope and the Christmas package will come apart in the mail.

George Gobel's advice to last-minute Christmas shoppers: "Get a five-pound box of money, gift-wrapped."

Al Magee says that there's nothing so shopworn as a last-minute shopper.

Sign in department store: "Five Santa Clauses. No Waiting."

Christmas is the season when we must get the children something for their father to play with.

From a Louisville church bulletin: "The youth choir will sing 'I heard the bills on Christmas day.'"

CHURCH

A collection is a church function in which most people take but a passing interest.

Good sermon: one which hits the man who wasn't there.

Some folks only attend church three times in their lives: when they're hatched, when they're matched, and when they're dispatched.

Many people find the sermon cold because they insist on sitting in "Z" row.

Some people are late for church because they have to change a tire; others because they have to change a dollar.

Some families think church is like a convention where you send a delegate—and it's usually mother.

News item from church bulletin: "Time will be given for a dull discussion of the budget."

Jack Herbert observes that some people who give the Lord credit are reluctant to give him cash.

Some people think the Sunday service is just like a convention—many families just send one delegate.

Sign on church: "Support your church. You can't take your money with you but you can send it ahead."

Said the old man to the preacher at the close of the service: "Fine sermon, everything you said applied to somebody or other I know."

Among other things to pray for when going to church is a place to park.

Sign on St. Louis church: "What on earth are you doing for Heaven's sake?"

A Niagara Falls church, tired of having its lawn constantly showered with confetti, posted this notice to bridal parties: "If you must throw something, throw grass seed."

This want ad appeared in the St. Charles (Minnesota) *Press*: "Wanted: Men, women, and children to sit in slightly used pews Sunday morning."

Minister, announcing a special attraction: "Come early, if you want a back seat."

Headline: Rev. Bonnell Resigns; Attendance Doubles.

From a Springfield, Missouri, church bulletin: "A new loudspeaker system has been installed in the church. It was given by one of the members in honor of his wife."

A distinguished Bostonian, stopping in Salt Lake City on his way to the Pacific Coast, made the acquaintance of a little Mormon girl.

"I'm from Boston—I suppose you know where that is," he asked her. "Oh, yes," she replied. "Our Sunday school has a missionary up there."

From a church bulletin in Duluth: "We were glad to have the Rev. William Bobyns of St. Paul a sour guest speaker on Sunday evening."

Two bookies were leaving an Easter church service: "The word is 'Hallelujah' stupid, not 'Hialeah.'"

On a broadcast of a church service over a radio station in Duluth a minister prayed: "Lord, there are those afflicted by the radio today, comfort them we pray . . . ."

From the Santa Ana newspaper: "In the evening he will speak on 'How to Keep Sane in the First Methodist Church under the direction of Rev. James Smith . . . .'"

CIRCUMSTANCES

You never know. Louis XIV was the first man to wear heels to make himself look taller. Then the French chopped off his head to make him look shorter.

CIRCUS

Did you hear about the circus elephant who told another: "I'm getting sick and tired of working for peanuts."

"You can't quit now," the circus manager told the human cannon ball. "Where can I find another man of your caliber?"

There's quite a legend going around about the man on the flying trapeze who caught his wife in the act.

CITIZEN

A good citizen is one who wants better schools, better roads, better public officials, and lower taxes.

CIVILIZATION

Civilization is a slow process in which advertising men create new wants to be satisfied.

176

The coating of civilization is so thin that it often comes off with a little alcohol.

One wonders if archaeologists of the future who excavate artifacts of our civilization will recognize the strange weapon found by almost every campsite for what it is: a can opener.

CLASSMATES

You don't realize how many of your old school chums have become highbrows until they remove their hats.

CLERKS

Did you hear about the young lady who went to the store and told the sales girl, "I'd like a refund on this perfume—I don't care for the man it attracted."

CLOTHES

A designer claims women dress to express themselves. If that's true, some gals have little to say.

"One month my tailor told me I could have no more cuffs on my clothes," Phil Baker quipped, "and the next month he said I could have no more clothes on the cuff."

There's nothing so cold as a woman who's been refused a fur coat.

Why is it? Every woman complains she has nothing to wear but needs several clothes closets to put it in.

Suspenders: the oldest form of social security.

When you look at the bill for your wife's new Easter hat, the term "overhead" takes on a new meaning.

Girls' sweaters come in two sizes—too large and too small enough.

A girdle is something a girl wears to hold in the wrong places when going to the right places.

Hat: something to take off in a crowded elevator, buy back from checkroom girls, and chase down the street on a windy day.

Clerk to sweet young thing in form-fitting sweater, "Would you like to step outside and try it for whistles before you decide?"

Girdle: polite name for a plain, old-fashioned pot holder.

Men are trying to conquer space. The clothes closets indicate that women are, too.

A guard at a nudist camp hailed a man at the gate and said, "I'm sorry, but you can't come in here wearing a blue suit." "Who's wearing a blue suit?" the man chattered. "I'm cold."

The old saying about making a silk purse out of a sow's ear is a little out of date. Now, the question is how to get a mink coat out of an old goat.

A mink coat, draped over the back of a chair in a New York night club, bore a huge inscription on the label, "Paid for by myself."

A girdle is a device to keep an unfortunate situation from spreading.

When a man has a rip in his coat and only three buttons on his vest, he should do one of two things: either get married or get divorced.

There is a word for a girl fascinated by an army uniform: khaki-wacky.

A cub scout told his mother that his pack leader's wife was going to have a baby, and she asked him "How do you know?" "Well," the youngster said, "she's wearing one of those eternity jackets."

Shopwindow sign over girdles: "Line Tamers."

Ad in New Jersey paper: "Visit our clothing department. We can outwit the whole family."

After an ingenious merchant brought out a new line of suits made of spun glass, a bright young advertising man suggested as a theme song, "I'll be seeing you in all the old familiar places."

CLUBS

President Charles Eliot of Harvard once confessed that the most unusual letter he had ever received came from a certain women's club. It read: "Dear Sir: Our committee, having heard that you are the country's greatest thinker, would be greatly obliged if you would send us your seven greatest thoughts."

A group of women searching for a name for their new club decided on "The Vicious Circle."

COACHES

Jeff Cravath once explained why he prefers running a ranch to his old job, coaching the Southern California football team: "Cattle don't have any alumni."

Football coach: "And remember that football develops individuality, initiative and leadership. Now get in there and do exactly as I tell you."

COED

Coed: a girl who would rather be well formed than well informed.

COLDS

A doctor is the only man who hasn't a guaranteed cure for a cold.

COLLECTIONS

A minister told his congregation, "So now let us give freely, generously, in accordance with what you reported on your income tax."

COLLEGE

A college education doesn't guarantee you a job, but it gives you four years to worry about it.

To be college bred means a four-year loaf, requiring a great deal of dough, as well as plenty of crust.

University: a place which has classrooms seating four thousand and a stadium seating fifty thousand.

A college president never dies—he just loses his faculties.

A college dean is a man who doesn't know enough to be a professor and who is too smart to be a president.

Many a college boy's education is just pigskin deep.

Lecture: a process by which the notes of the professor become the notes of the student without passing through the minds of either.

Every father knows he has to make allowances if he has a son in college.

A father, upon receiving his son's grades, remarked to his wife: "Roger is shirking his way through college."

Posing the farmer and his college-age son for a picture, the photographer suggested that the boy stand with his hand on his father's shoulder. "If you want it to look natural," said the parent, "he could put his hand in my pocket."

With the money it takes to send Junior to college we could buy enough comic books to teach him at home.

College professor: one who talks in other people's sleep.

A professor may be absent-minded but never enough to forget to flunk someone.

A college student majoring in political science objected vehemently to a course in political economy he was required to take. He growled, "That's a useless course. Nobody in politics economizes nowadays."

One father to another: "Well, last week he made his first money since getting out of college. Sold the typewriter we gave him for graduation."

We heard about a fellow so dumb that when he won his letter at college somebody had to read it to him.

A parent of a boy in college said, "Our son is a four-letter man— we hear from him fall, winter, spring, and summer."

Blind date: when you expect to meet a vision and she turns out to be a sight.

Announcement on preparation-for-marriage class: "Are You Fit To Be Tied?"

A husband returned from home-coming at his alma mater and remarked, "I spent the weekend surviving old memories."

In Georgia Tech's student newspaper, a want ad listing clerical jobs carried the headline: "Put Your Wife To Work."

The honor system derives its name from the fact that professors have the honor and the students have the system.

An Indiana University coed on kissing: "The important thing in saying good night is to keep your feet on the ground."

Elderly professor to colleague as coed in slacks strides past: "That young lady'd better be careful or she'll be penalized five yards for the backfield in motion."

Coed to her roommate: "Ronald is a perfect gentleman at all times, but I guess that's better than having no boy friend at all."

Coed to girl friend: "I have an uncomfortable feeling we're not being followed."

Said the college boy: "I like the shy, demure type of girl; you know, the kind you have to whistle at twice."

Heard at a college home-coming when the class of '18 held a reunion: "Looks like Ferguson beat us to the paunch."

He was voted by his class as the man most likely to go to seed.

During sorority rush at the University of Oklahoma prospects are asked to fill out a questionnaire. Opposite "List any personal attributes which would be beneficial to the sorority," one hopeful simply wrote: "35-23-34."

"Four years of college," sighed the coed, "and whom has it got me?"

The boy wrote home: "I'm getting along fine in everything but school."

A sophomore told his friend, "I'm working my way through college by carrying a spear in the opera at night," and his friend asked him how he managed to stay awake. He replied, "The man behind me also carries a spear."

College officials at a Western institution sorting through cards filled out by students found the usual number of Baptists, Methodists, and so on listed under "Church Preference." But a neatly lettered card filled in by a senior majoring in architecture stopped them; his church preference: "Gothic."

An Eastern college listed two of its evening classes like this: "Efficient Listening—Preparation for Marriage."

A university is a football stadium surrounded by several small buildings.

Sign on dormitory door: "If I'm studying when you enter, wake me up."

The students of Vassar are publishing a booklet of advice for girls on house-party dates, titled, "What Every Young Lady Should No."

181

A Boston brokerage house advertised for "a young Harvard graduate or the equivalent." Among the answers was one from a Yale man: "When you speak of an equivalent," he wrote, "do you mean two Princeton men or a Yale man half-time?"

If all the people who sleep in college classes were laid end to end—they would be more comfortable.

COLUMNISTS

Newspaper gossip columnist: top man on the quot'em pole.

A columnist gives us the low-down on the higher ups.

COMEBACK

Then there's the woman who was stopped by a cop for speeding. She retorted, "Well, if I was speeding, so were you!"

COMEDIANS

A comedian is a man with a fun-track mind.

Beirne Lay says that today's comedian is a man who has succeeded in making a complete asset of himself.

COMFORT

For some of us, roughing it means turning down the electric blanket to "medium."

Woman at party to her friend, "I'm just miserable, I've got on my sitting-down shoes and my standing-up girdle."

COMICS

Howard McLellan says it this way: "Junior grabbed the funnies and went into a semicoma."

COMMERCIALS

An announcer, in the midst of extolling the virtues of a new vitamin, declared: "They are made especially for people who have taken vitamins A, B, C, D, E, F, and G, and still look like H."

Radio announcer: "And now for the news that happened during the commercial."

Did you hear about the radio announcer who in delivering a commercial for a local laundry, blandly recited: "Ladies who care to drop by and drop off their clothes will receive prompt and individual attention."

COMMITTEES

A committee is a group that keeps minutes and wastes hours.

Committee: a group of the unfit, appointed by the unwilling, to do the unnecessary.

A committee of five consists of the one who does the work, three who pat him on the back, and the one who brings in the minority report.

Nothing dies faster than a new idea in a committee meeting.

One reason the Ten Commandments are so brief and concise is that they didn't come through a committee.

A little girl with a cold was urged by her mother to stay home. And the girl replied, "I can't, Mother, this is the day when we start to make a clay model of a cow, and I'm chairman of the udder committee."

A camel is an animal that looks like it was put together by a committee.

COMMON SENSE

A little common sense would prevent most divorces—and marriages, too.

COMMUNISM

They also have a slogan in Russia: "Vote for the party. The life you save may be your own."

A communist is a fellow who has given up all hope of becoming a capitalist.

A communist is a person who wants to share his nothing with everybody else.

Communist: one who borrows your pot to cook your goose in.

COMMUNITY CHEST

Most community chests follow this slogan: Put all your begs in one ask it.

COMMUNITY LIFE

From Eagle River, Wisconsin, newspaper: "Eagle River's centennial is the biggest celebration ever planned by the community and may not be repeated again for some time."

COMMUTER

A commuter is a man who spends his life riding to and from his wife.

COMPANY

A man is known by the company he thinks nobody knows he's keeping.

COMPENSATIONS

Things work out pretty well in the world. Other people's troubles are not so bad as yours, but their children are a lot worse.

COMPLAINTS

It seems that most knocking is done by folks who aren't able to ring the bell.

Winter is the time of year when many people spend the week yelling at the janitor for more heat and spend the weekend skiing.

COMPLEX

Any wife with an inferiority complex can cure it by being sick in bed for a day while her husband manages the household and children.

184

COMPLIMENTS

A compliment is something which you say to another and which both of you know is not true.

Some persons never say anything bad about the dead—or anything good about the living.

If someone tells you that you look like a million dollars, don't consider it a compliment until you find out if he means before or after taxes.

When a husband tells his wife her new dress looks nice on her, he probably hasn't seen the price tag.

CONCEIT

"I used to be terribly conceited," a Hollywood chap confided, "but my psychiatrist straightened me out and now I'm one of the nicest guys in town."

A man who's wrapped up in himself makes a mighty small parcel.

"No," said the club wit, "I never said he was conceited. All I said was that if I could buy him at my price and sell him at his own, I'd make a darn good profit."

CONFERENCE

A conference is a meeting at which people talk about things they should be doing.

CONFESSIONS

One woman to another: "Why don't you go to him in a perfectly straightforward way and lie about the whole thing?"

Confessions may be good for the soul, but they're bad for the reputation.

CONFIDENCE

A lot of people believe they have the world by the tail until they try to swing it.

CONSCIENCE

The line is often too busy when conscience wishes to speak.

Asked why he never listened to his conscience, Charlie McCarthy replied, "I get a very poor reception."

Conscience gets a lot of credit that belongs to cold feet.

Conscience: something that feels terrible when everything else feels swell.

Quite often when a man thinks his mind is getting broader it is only his conscience stretching.

A man's conscience is that feeling which makes a man tell his wife something he thinks she will find out anyway.

Small boy's definition of conscience: something that makes you tell your mother before your sister does.

Conscience is a device that doesn't keep you from doing anything—it just keeps you from enjoying it.

Conscience: that still small voice that makes you feel still smaller.

CONSERVATIVE

Standpatter: a man who doesn't think anything should be done for the first time.

Herbert V. Prochnow says that a conservative is a man who acts impulsively after thinking for a long time.

One way to grow conservative is to have a good job, a wife, two or three children, and a home.

CONTESTS

Item in weekly newspaper: "Mrs. Harville won the ladies' rolling-pin contest by hurling one 75 yards at the county picnic. And Mr. Harville won the 100-yard dash."

When the Pacific Telephone Company ran a slogan contest on "Why I Should Support the Community Chest," one employee's entry read: "This is one chest that should not be left flat busted."

CONVENTIONS

One of our friends vows that the chairman of a meeting of throat specialists in Minneapolis declared on the platform, "You have all heard the motion. All in favor say 'ah.'"

Which brings up the question, after the recent nudist convention—where does one tuck his napkin?

CONVERSATION

It takes three persons to make a really good conversation; two of them here and the other far enough away so she can't overhear.

Many a man who opened a conversation with a girl years ago is now wondering how he can shut it off.

If women talked only about what they understand, the silence would be unbearable.

One thing about being a person of a few words: you don't have to take so many of them back.

A man and wife were eating breakfast, and she talked as he tried to read the paper. After quite a time she said, "You needn't bother saying 'uh huh' any more—I stopped talking five minutes ago."

Charming conversationalist: a person who reminds you of things to say and then listens while you say them.

Dorothy Parker wrote, "He's the type of person who keeps the conversation ho-humming."

Bernard Shaw once remarked: "I often quote myself. It adds spice to the conversation."

Dumb? If anyone said hello to her she would be stuck for an answer.

The secret of polite conversation is never to open your mouth unless you have nothing to say.

Good conversation is often ruined by the refusal of some nitwit to change the subject which he brought up.

A momentary lull in conversation is regarded by some women as a social blunder, and a signal to jump back into verbal high gear.

Even the experts in the art of holding a conversation know when to turn it loose.

Chance remark: anything a man manages to say when two women are talking.

Good listener: a person who can think of something to say when you can't.

To say the right thing at the right time, keep still most of the time.

Repartee: what you think of on the way home.

Will Rogers, on conversation: "I always like to hear a man talk about himself because then I never hear anything but good."

Sydney Smith described a man who "has occasional flashes of silence that make his conversation perfectly delightful."

Take a lesson from the whale: the only time he gets harpooned is when he comes up to spout.

CONVICT

A convict is the only person we know of who likes to be stopped in the middle of a sentence.

COOKING

"How long was your last cook with you?" a woman was asked, and she replied, "She never was with us. She was against us."

Where there's smoke—there's toast.

Most wives would learn to cook if they weren't so busy trying to get meals.

He missed his wife's cooking—every chance he got.

Two small girls brought home a boxful of dirt and warned their mother to be very careful of it. When she asked why, they replied, "Instant Mud Pies."

Chef: a man with a big enough vocabulary to give the soup a different name every day.

One of the neighbors explained, "Our toaster is the kind that doesn't ring a bell when the toast is done—it sends up smoke signals."

Instead of "What's cooking?" the modern husband rushes into the house and asks, "What's thawing?"

Grandma may have had her troubles, but she didn't have to worry about frostbite while reaching for frozen food.

Many women will understand the feelings of the harassed wife, working over the hot stove, asking her husband: "Why don't you call up sometimes and say you're not coming home for dinner, the way other men do?"

Men who brag about their ability as cooks make other husbands wonder if they practice it as a hobby, or for self-preservation.

My wife does the most wonderful thing with leftovers—she throws them out.

She treats her husband like a Greek god: she places a burnt offering before him at every meal.

The way our grandmothers prepared meals without the aid of modern conveniences was positively uncanny.

CO-OPERATION

Co-operation would solve most problems. For instance, freckles would be a nice coat of tan if they could get together.

No woman ever makes a fool out of a man without his full co-operation.

CO-ORDINATION

Co-ordinator: the guy who has the desk between two expeditors.

COSMETICS

Women live longer than men because paint is such a great pre-servative.

COST OF LIVING

Twenty years ago lots of people dreamed about earning the salary they can't get along on today.

No wonder it's cash-and-carry in groceries these days. Most people can easily carry as much as they have cash to buy.

The high cost of living now has the ounce of prevention costing as much as the pound of cure once did.

Worrying about cigarettes can be beneficial—it takes your mind off the cost of eating.

COSTS

A businessman, after talking to another for a while, said: "Speaking of rising costs, how's your wife these days?"

A man will pay $2.00 for a $1.00 item he wants; a woman will pay $1.00 for a $2.00 item she doesn't want.

It's rather sad to find yourself living in a more expensive apartment—when you haven't even moved.

COURAGE

There's only a slight difference between keeping your chin up and sticking your neck out, but it's worth knowing.

A brave man is one who musters enough courage to tell the ladies' bridge club that it is time to go home so his wife can get supper.

As the harassed driver approaches an extremely narrow pass on a tortuous Rocky Mountain road, he is confronted by the reassuring sign: "Oh, yes, you can. Millions have!"

COURTESY

The real proof of courtesy is having the same ailment the other person is describing and not mentioning it.

"When you are driving at night and see an approaching car," says George Gobel, "dim your headlights. If you don't have headlights, turn the radio up real loud."

COURTS

Receiver: a person appointed by the court to take what's left.

Jury: the only thing that doesn't work right when it's fixed.

Lawyer: a man who helps you get what's coming to him.

Witness stand: a place where half the lies told by witnesses are not true.

Said the contrite prisoner who had blacked his sister-in-law's eye, "I thought it was my wife."

A woman told eleven exasperated men jurors: "If you men weren't so stubborn we could all go home."

Bill Vaughan says that our court dockets are so crowded today that it would be better to refer to it as the overdue process of law.

Sign outside a South Carolina courtroom: "It doesn't pay to speed— but you do!"

Lawyer to siren: "My client wants you and himself to go your separate ways—and he's willing to pay you ten cents a mile."

Judge asked a man, "Are you trying to show contempt for this court?" and the man replied, "No, Judge, I'm trying to conceal it."

A man appeared in court seeking a separation from his wife. The judge asked "On what grounds?" and the man answered, "On the grounds guaranteed in the Constitution. You know, Judge, free speech."

Judge finished his lecture to defendant in divorce case and said, "I've decided to give your wife fifty dollars a month." The husband's face lit up and he said, "That's fine, Judge, I'll try to slip her a couple of bucks now and then myself."

A Denver lawyer broke a lengthy cross-examination of a witness to exclaim: "Your Honor, one of the jurors is asleep." "You put him to sleep," replied the judge. "Suppose you wake him up."

A strip-tease artist was pinched on a morals charge and the newspaper carried this headline: "Three Judges Weigh Her Fan Dance; Find It Wanton."

A court official, swearing in a woman witness, asked: "Do you swear to tell the truth, the whole truth, and stop there?"

Years ago a frontier coroner gave the following verdict: "We find that the deceased came to his death by an act of suicide. At a distance of a hundred yards he opened fire with a six-shooter upon a man armed with a rifle."

Deeply religious woman from backwoods was called into court as a witness. She had never been to court before. The judge asked her to swear in and then she said, "If I have to, I have to. Hell, and be damned."

COURTSHIP

Love: the softening of the hearteries.

Many a romance starts with sentiment and ends with settlement.

Suitor: a young man who asks for the daughter's hand, but often gets the father's foot.

Wolf: a man who knows all the ankles.

A frivolous woman makes life mighty interesting to a man while he's searching for a sensible one.

We heard of one young fellow who spent so much on a girl he had to marry her for his money.

Walter Winchell told of a girl "whose baby stares are for guys to trip on."

Girl to chum: "He says he always wants to remember me just as I am now, so he broke off our engagement."

When a girl strokes a man's forehead, it's a sure bet it's his scalp she's after.

To the average girl, courtship is the art of not showing her hand until you ask for it.

Very often a woman's head on a man's shoulder accomplishes more than his does.

Courtship makes a man spoon, but marriage is what makes him fork over.

Coquette: a girl who says she loves you from the bottom of her heart, because there's another fellow at the top.

Making love is like making a good pie. All you need is a liberal supply of applesauce, dough, and a good spoon.

The modern proposal is a matter of popping the question without questioning the pop.

Young college freshman wrote his dad: "I've decided to quit school and get married. I'm engaged to a peach." Father answered: "Suggest it would be wise to take my advice and leave the peach to its parent stem until you are able to preserve it."

Noel Wical says that a young man falls for the same kind of girl who hurried dear old dad.

Did you hear about the young man who fell in love with a dimple and made the mistake of marrying the whole girl?

Courtship is sometimes spoken of as the interval between lipstick and mopstick.

Dignified young man pulling away from ardent siren: "Please, Miss Cokesbury, you're steaming my glasses."

You can't kiss a girl unexpectedly—only sooner than she thought you would.

A kiss is the shortest distance between two.

We remember during the war that one of the neighbor girls got herself a second lieutenant—the first one got away.

A good line is the shortest distance between two dates.

A girl's hardest task is to prove to a man that his intentions are serious.

Weak: what a man is when a pretty girl is telling him how strong he is.

The girl who thinks no man is good enough for her may be right— also, she may be left.

"How did you and mom get acquainted?" a kid asked his dad. And the dad replied, "None of your business, but it sure cured me of whistling."

The main influence of the moon are on the tide and the untied.

A boy proposed to a girl and she replied: "No, dear, but I shall long remember your good taste in asking me."

A young lady after a broken engagement returned all the gent's letters marked, "Fourth-Class Male."

It seems strange that a man will propose to a girl under a light he wouldn't think of choosing a suit by.

It's better to go broke than never to have loved at all.

A girl to a suitor who has just proposed: "Let me hear that part again where you realize you're not half good enough for me."

Just heard of another romantic breakup—he lost his capital and she lost her interest.

The lipstick that glows in the dark is a useless invention. The search is half the pleasure.

Love starts when she sinks in your arms and ends with her arms in the sink.

Young man to girl friend: "I wouldn't change a thing about you—but your name."

Successful courtship once depended a great deal on what a fellow sent a girl; now it depends on how.

"If you kiss me," the girl warned, "I'll call a member of my family." He kissed her and she whispered, "Bro—ther!"

A young man told the father of the girl he had been dating, "I've been dating your daughter for exactly ten years," and the old man replied, "Well, what do you want, a pension?"

A boy called his girl and the operator said, "I'm sorry, sir, but that number has been taken out," and he asked, "Oh is that so? Well, can you give me information as to just who has taken her out?"

Explained the persistent suitor who could get nowhere with the girl of his choice, "She has an impediment in her speech—she can't say yes."

She's the kind of girl who likes to whisper sweet nothing-doings in your ear.

Men who kiss and tell are not half as bad as those who kiss and exaggerate.

Young girl to chum: "He hasn't proposed yet, but his voice has an engagement ring in it."

You can learn a lot about romance at the movies—if you don't let the picture distract you.

Sweet young thing to another: "I don't know whether he's a perfect gentleman or just not interested in me."

A college senior dated a young lad from a near-by school a few times. Then some weeks passed and when she hadn't heard from him, she sent a telegram: DEAD, DELAYED, OR DISINTERESTED? He wired back: HUNTING, FISHING, OR TRAPPING?

Girl, describing her boy friend to chum: "He's a perfect gentleman from the word 'stop.'"

Newton's tenth law: the dimmer the porch light, the greater the scandal power.

Clerk: "Here's a pretty card with a lovely sentiment: 'To the only girl I ever loved.'" And the sailor replied, "Fine, I'll take a dozen."

The future tense of courting is caught.

Mother asked daughter, "What are Steve's intentions?" and the daughter replied, "Well, he's keeping me pretty much in the dark lately."

The trouble with a man's acting like a gentleman on a date is that the girl usually thinks he's mad at her.

A fickle bachelor was telling a married friend about the accomplishments of the girl he had just met: "And you know, she has brains enough for two," and his friend replied, "Then you ought to marry her right away."

Wolf: a man with a lot of pet theories.

The young lady had received an engagement ring the night before, and to her chagrin no one had noticed it. Finally, in the afternoon when she was visiting with friends in the drugstore, she exclaimed: "My it's hot in here. I guess I'll take off my rings."

Girl, after proposal, asked, "If I refuse, will you commit suicide?" and her suitor replied, "That's been my usual custom."

Love is the only game that isn't postponed because of darkness.

Love is like a mushroom. You never know whether it's the real thing until it's too late.

One young thing to another: "While she's waiting for the right man to come along, she's having a wonderful time with the wrong ones."

COWBOY

The cowboy's horse stopped suddenly. Injun trouble!

CREDIT

The easiest way to get credit is not to need it.

What this country needs is a vending machine that honors credit cards.

A merchant in his will: "I want six of my creditors for pallbearers— they have carried me so long they may as well finish the job."

Sign in an Oklahoma City second hand store: "Nothing Sold on Credit—Damn Little for Cash."

CREMATORIUM

A Texas crematorium is reported to be bottling ashes and selling them to African cannibals as "Instant People."

CRIME

Alcatraz: a pen that works above water.

Crook: a business competitor who is doing well.

To make certain that crime does not pay, G. Norman Collie suggests that the government should take it over and run it.

Counterfeiter: a man who wants money bad.

Convict: a person who is doing time for others.

Alcatraz: the pen with the lifetime guarantee.

America is unique in that it is the one country where we lock up the juries and let the defendants go free.

Eyewitness: someone watching something somewhere near the scene of the accident.

A clue is what detectives boast about when they can't find the criminal.

Crime doesn't pay—but policemen don't earn much, either.

He started out as an unwanted child, but he overcame that handicap. By the time he was nineteen he was wanted in twenty-three states.

Capital crime: a murder where there is usually no clue to the whereabouts of the police.

From an Arkansas weekly: "Officer Bert Denison arrested the prowler after a short chaser."

CRITICISM

Critic: one who is quick on the flaw.

Many persons are so busy telling the world what is wrong with it that they haven't time to improve themselves.

Time's summing up of the movie in which Bette Davis plays Queen Elizabeth: "The Virgin Queen is strictly corn of the realm."

Bernard Baruch once reminded us that two things are bad for the heart—"running up stairs and running down people."

When New York critics panned a performance (packed to the rafters) of a noted singer, he wired each one: "Your cruel remarks made me so unhappy I cried all the way to the bank."

It is well to remember the Chinese proverb: Those who have free seats at the play hiss first.

A critic is a person who goes places and boos things.

Joseph P. Ritz says that a critic is a person who finds a little bad in the best of things.

CUPID

The reason Cupid makes so many wild shots is that he aims at the heart while looking at the hosiery.

Cupid may be a good man with the bow and arrow, but he makes some awful Mrs.

CURIOSITY

Chinese proverb: He who asks a question is a fool for five minutes; he who does not ask a question remains a fool forever.

CYNICISM

Cynicism: the screen behind which youth hides its inexperience and disappointment.

DANCE

George Bernard Shaw, doing his duty at a benefit dance, asked a dowager to dance and as they waltzed, she asked, "Oh, Mr. Shaw, whatever made you ask poor little me to dance?" and he replied, "This is a charity ball, isn't it?"

The people who are most likely to make ends meet are those on a crowded dance floor.

Girl to friend: "I must learn the new dances like the rhumba or go on being a waltz flower."

In Honolulu they say that the hula girls just twiddle their tums.

A lemon squeezer is a fellow who dances with a wallflower.

A poor dancer is one who makes us feel more danced against than with.

Some people grow old gracefully—others attempt the new dances.

A little boy who went to the ballet for the first time with his father watched the girls dance on their toes for a while and then asked: "Why don't they just get taller girls?"

Rhumba: a foxtrot with the backfield in motion.

Wife: "Waltz a little faster, dear, they're playing a rhumba."

A hula is just a dance with a lot of waist motion.

Once there was a city guy who was bewitched by a fan dancer— he was hipnotized.

Bob Hope says that the rhumba is a dance where the front of you goes along nice and smooth like a Cadillac and the back of you makes like a jeep.

DANCING

The waiter dropped a tray of dishes and six couples got up to dance.

He who dances must pay the fiddler—also the waiter, the florist, the hat-check girl, the doorman, and the parking-lot attendant.

Percy Hammond, noted critic, once wrote of a musical comedy, "I have knocked everything but the chorus girls' legs, and here God anticipated me."

It used to be claimed that one evening of dancing was equivalent to walking ten miles. Now it's more like climbing a dozen trees.

You'll appreciate the man who described a young lady by saying, "Dancing with her is like trying to get on a merry-go-round after it has started."

The difference between wrestling and dancing, Arthur Murray says, is that some holds are barred in wrestling.

DATES

Fellow was asked, "Did you have a good time with the Siamese twins," and he answered, "Yes and no."

Biggest worry of a doting father is usually a dating daughter.

DEBT

Rubber check: something that may give you a long bounce.

Collector: the only fellow who will stick to a man when he hasn't a cent.

You don't appreciate what compound interest can accomplish until you get on the paying end of a five-year note.

Modern man is one who drives a mortgaged car over a bond-financed highway, on credit-card gas.

The nation is still based on a system of checks and balances. She writes the checks, and he tries to figure out the balances.

An actor down on his luck asked comedian W. C. Fields for a loan and he replied, "I'd be glad to help you, my good man, but all my money's tied up in currency."

The sum total of our national debt is some total.

DEBUT

A debut is the most expensive way for parents to show that their daughter is ready to get married.

DECISIONS

When a person says, "I'll think it over and let you know—you know."

DEEDS

Few of us get dizzy by doing too many good turns.

DEFENDANT

Defendant: one who is seldom as guilty as the judge and the jury—take him to be.

DEFINITIONS

Sandwich spread: what some people get from eating between meals.

Snoring: sheet music.

Kiss: nothing divided by two.

Intuition: suspicion in skirts.

Drip: a person you can always hear but seldom turn off.

Anatomy: something everybody has but which looks better on a girl.

DEMAGOGUE

Demagogue: a man who can rock the boat himself and persuade everybody there is a terrible storm at sea.

DEMOCRACY

Someone has said that democracy is a system whereby the person who never votes can cuss out the man the people elect.

Democracy is wonderful. You can say what you please but you don't have to listen unless you want to.

DENTISTS

Teeth are the things you have out just before the doctor decides it was your tonsils after all.

DEPRESSION

Depression is a period when you can't spend money you don't have.

A recession is a period in which you tighten your belt. In a depression, you have no belt to tighten; and when you have no pants to hold up, it's a panic.

DESIRES

She's the type of girl who wants everything twice as nice as everyone else—she'd insist on Chanel No. 10.

DETERMINATION

Prayer of a Scottish preacher: 'Oh Lord, guide us aright, for we are verra, verra determined."

DETOUR

A detour is a rough road which is opened for summer driving.

DIETS

She's been on a diet for three weeks and all she's taken off is her hat.

The second day of a diet isn't too hard—because by that time you are off of it.

Little kid asked his mother if she knew what made the Tower of Pisa lean and she replied, "No. If I did I would take some."

More diets begin in dress shops than in doctor's offices.

The trouble with the bulk of women is where it usually shows.

Reducing: wishful shrinking.

"A diet," a dowager explained, "is that you get fed up with not being fed."

A doctor can't persuade a woman to go on a diet half as fast as last year's bathing suit can.

The worst kind of reducing pill is the one who keeps telling you how she did it.

Obesity: surplus gone to waist.

Diet is the art of letting the hips fall where they may.

Mae West says that a curved line is the loveliest distance between two points.

Dietetics: the triumph of mind over platter.

Doctor, to stout matron: "—and no more meals. You're getting enough between meals."

Overweight often is just desserts.

Reducing salon: where they take your breadth away.

One woman to another: "I knew her—fifty pounds ago."

A diet is what you keep putting off while you are putting on.

A dietician says that people are what they eat—which makes us conclude that a lot of them must subsist largely on tripe and baloney.

If you are counting calories but gaining weight anyway, what you don't want is a set of bath scales that tells the truth.

What a lot of women would like to do with last year's dress is get into it.

The young man looked at the high prices on the night-club menu and said to his date, "What will you have, my plump doll?"

Bob Cummings believes that overweight is like sugar in iced coffee —after a while it settles to the bottom.

Dieting, Paul Fogarty explains, is the penalty for exceeding the feed limit.

We know a woman who's furious—seems her husband told her to keep her best chin forward.

Maxine, one of the Andrews Sisters, rushed up to her sister Patty and exclaimed: "Hey kid, I've lost four pounds!" and Patty replied, "Turn around, honey, I think I've found them."

DIPLOMACY

Today every diplomat must watch his appease and accuse.

Diplomacy: the ability to say "Nice doggies" while reaching for a rock.

Diplomacy is the art of making others believe that you believe what you don't believe.

Diplomat: a man who has learned that you can't bend a nail by hitting it squarely on the head.

Diplomat: a man who can convince his wife a woman looks stout in a fur coat.

Diplomat: a person who can juggle a hot potato until it becomes a cold issue.

A diplomat is one who can tell you where to go in such a way that you look forward to going there.

Elsa Maxwell credits three simple words for making guests at her parties feel welcome and at home. "When they arrive," she says, "I murmur 'at last' and when they depart I protest 'already?' "

Diplomacy: the art of convincing a man he's a liar without actually telling him so.

DISAPPOINTMENT

Among the things that never turn out as big as you expected is the welcome the office force gives you when you return from your vacation.

Nothing irks a college student more than shaking out the envelope from home and finding nothing in it but news and love.

DISC JOCKEY

Disc jockey: one who lives on spins and needles.

DISCRETION

Discretion is forgiving your enemies, especially those you can't lick.

DISCIPLINE

The time to start correcting children is before they start correcting you.

Spanking had one advantage over modern child psychology. It made the child smart.

Sam Levenson, former teacher, has this comment on why parental discipline is so ineffective these days: "Today when a child disobeys his mother, he is sent to his room. When he goes to his room he has a radio, TV, and a 17½-year-old babysitter—his father didn't have it so good on his honeymoon."

Stranger, talking to little boy: "Don't cry, little boy—you'll get your reward in the end," and the kid answered, "I suppose so—that's where I always get it."

A pat on the back develops character if administered young enough, often enough, and low enough.

DISILLUSIONMENT

Disillusionment is what takes place when your son asks you to help him with the algebra.

Disillusionment: opening your friend's mail.

The most disillusioned girls are the ones who are married because they were tired of working.

DISTANCE

Distance lends enchantment—but not when you're out of gas.

DIVORCE

After a divorce, a woman feels like a new man.

Divorces are caused where the blind have led the blind.

One American marriage in five ends in a divorce. The other couples fight it out to the bitter end.

Divorce is proof that some people marry for love, some for money, but most for a short time.

She's been to Reno so often she's a little swap-worn.

Alimony: the high cost of loving.

Reno: a town where the cream of society goes to be separated.

Hollywood motto: 'Tis better to have loved and lost than never to have had any publicity at all.

In Hollywood, the chief cause for divorce seems to be matrimony.

"And you say that you want a divorce because your husband is careless in his appearance?" the lawyer said to the client, and she replied, "Yes, he hasn't showed up for nearly five years."

The proper time for divorce is during the courtship.

People wouldn't get divorced for such trivial reasons if they didn't get married for such trivial reasons.

The man who divorces a talkative wife and remarries may just be getting his second wind.

DOCTORS

As we understand the doctors, you can live much longer if you quit everything that makes you want to.

Unethical doctor: a dirty quack.

There's a doctor in St. Louis who is so conceited that when he takes a woman's pulse, he subtracts ten beats for his personality.

Did you hear about the patient who told his doctor: "No, I don't feel listless. If I felt that good I wouldn't be here."

A woman told an ear specialist: "I've never had trouble hearing, but lately I'm having a little trouble overhearing."

A patient was discussing his diet with the family doctor and at the end of the visit the patient asked, "When do you think I'll be well enough to eat the things that disagree with me, Doc?"

Obstetrician: a doctor who makes all his money on the stork market.

Hypodermic needle: sick shooter.

Cure: what a doctor often does to a disease while killing the patient.

Patient asked doctor, "How can I ever repay you for your kindness?" and the doctor replied, "By check, money order, or cash."

A woman wrote, "Dear Doctor Whoosit: What can you do for my husband? He has insomnia so bad he can't sleep while he's working."

According to the magazines in my doctor's office, business is booming—and 1940 may be even better.

Specialist: a doctor whose patients are expected to confine their ailments to office hours.

Doctor asked man, "Did the medicine I gave your uncle straighten him out?" and the man answered, "Sure did. They buried him yesterday."

A patient asked his doctor, "Are you sure this is pneumonia? Sometimes doctors prescribe for pneumonia, and the patients die of something else," and the doctor answered, "When I prescribe for pneumonia, you die of pneumonia."

Did you hear about the doctor who was so busy giving penicillin injections during the cold and virus season that he tacked this sign to the door of his inner office: "To save time, please back into the office."

Woman to neighbor, "We think Junior is going to grow up to be a doctor—he's already saving old magazines."

A woman asked her doctor: "Would that blood pressure still be all right if I happened to be a little older than thirty?"

A man was being questioned by his insurance agent, who asked him, "Have you ever had appendicitis?" and the man replied, "I'm not sure. I was operated on but I've never been quite certain whether it was appendicitis or professional curiosity."

After waiting hours in a crowded waiting room of his doctor's office a man got up and said, "Well, I guess I'll just go home and die a natural death."

A young physician calls his suburban estate Bedside Manor.

Bob Hope says that virus is a Latin word used by doctors to mean "Your guess is as good as mine."

DOGMATISM

A dogmatist is a person whose mind is like concrete, all mixed up and permanently set.

Dogmatism is puppyism full grown.

DO IT YOURSELF

Charles Barr says that all a do-it-yourself man needs to make a bay window is a knife and fork.

DOORMAN

A doorman is versatile. He opens the door of your car, helps you in with the other hand, and still has one left to get the tip.

DREAMS

Dreams are unlucky when they come during office hours.

Some people who think they are dreamers are only sleepers.

Many a man believes in dreams until he marries one.

Then there was the Congressman who had a most horrible nightmare. He dreamed all the money he was spending was his own.

There is some consolation in the fact that, even though your dreams don't come true, neither do your nightmares.

DRESSES

The kind of dresses men admire are the kind they object to seeing on their wives.

Few daughters nowadays get to use Mother's wedding gown—Mom is still using it.

Many a woman thinks she bought a dress for a ridiculous price, when in reality she bought it for an absurd figure.

In Dallas, dress shop sign says, "Convertible sun dresses—very sporty with the tops down."

DRINKING

The trouble with a small town's alcoholics is that they are not anonymous.

We know a man who puts vitamins in his gin. He says they build him up while he's tearing himself down.

We know a fellow who, after a physical checkup, was told by his doctor that he was in pretty bad shape: "Too little blood in your alcohol stream."

Bar examination: a test to determine just how much you can hold.

Never yet have we seen a fellow who could keep himself and his business both liquid at the same time.

Glasses don't always improve the vision—particularly the refillable kind.

Five-cents-a-glass whisky is still available, a recent autopsy reveals.

Many people have no respect for age unless its bottled.

Drinking may be something a man does to forget, but he usually forgets when to stop.

Whisky: a drink that makes you well when you are sick and makes you sick when you are well.

Tavern: where two pints make one cavort.

Walter Winchell once said that sophistication is the art of getting drunk with the right people.

A girl told her date at a night club: "I think I'll have another drink—it makes you so witty."

Will Rogers, Jr., says that one swallow doesn't make a summer, but it sure breaks a New Year's resolution.

Party talk: "I've been on the wagon about a year now since last Monday."

Social drinking is a lot like spelling Mississippi—it's mostly a matter of knowing when to stop.

Cocktail party: where you meet old friends you never saw before.

The doctors report that it's all right to drink like a fish—if you drink what the fish drinks.

High noon: three martinis before lunch.

Gracie Allen explained how she knows when she's had too much to drink: "A little blurred tells me."

A pink elephant is a beast of bourbon.

The three cocktail lounges nearest the Pentagon are known as the Chief Joints of Staff.

The man who enters a bar very optimistically often comes out very misty optically.

208

Sign in a New York night club: "If you drive your man to drink, drive him here."

A tipsy gent dropped a nickel into a telephone coin box, dialed a number, and cried, "Hello, Hello," and a voice at the other end called back, "Hello yourself." The inebriated one banged down the receiver and bellowed: "This telephone has an echo!"

George Gobel reminds us "I know my capacity for drinking, but I keep getting drunk before I reach it."

Where all that North Carolina moonshine comes from is a secret still.

Hangover: the moaning after the night before.

DRIVING

A pedestrian is a person who failed to keep up the payments on his car.

Famous last words: "I wonder how much this car will do?"

Definition of a road hog: any other driver.

A man nicknamed his wife, who was just learning to drive, "O-ma, the Dent Maker."

Driving might be safer if every motorist who took a chance got a ticket for it.

Bill Vaughan calls our attention to the fact that among nature's mysteries is the way she arranges it so that the fellow who doesn't know how to drive in snow and ice is always first in line of one hundred stalled cars.

A woman, alighting from a taxi, was told by the driver: "There'll be no charge, lady; you did most of the driving."

If you drank like a fish—don't drive.

A woman will look into a mirror any time except when she's about to pull out of a parking place.

Power brakes aren't very expensive. But the windshield they throw you through is.

A blamed fool is the one who bangs into your front bumper with the side of his car.

A driver is known by the fenders he keeps.

If your wife wants to learn to drive the car—don't stand in her way!

Although most new cars come equipped with automatic transmissions, one-armed drivers still use the conventional clutch.

Motorist's definition of a split second: the interval of time between the change of a stop light and the fellow behind you tooting his horn.

A reckless driver is one who passes you on the highway in spite of all you can do.

Crossing: a place where you shouldn't try to beat another car because if the race is a tie, you lose.

Auto parts: what people who live near railroad crossings never buy.

The cop gave the woman driver a ticket and she asked, "Does this ticket cancel the one I got this morning, officer?"

Traffiic light: a little green light that changes to red as your car approaches.

A pedestrian is a man who always has the right of way—when he's in an ambulance.

Another thing about a woman driver: she doesn't let her right hand know what her left hand has signaled.

A woman driver demands only a quarter of the road—but allows only a quarter of the road on each side.

Women who drive from the back seat are no worse than husbands who cook from the dining-room table.

Tell a little girl not to stick her arm out of the car, and when she grows up and drives she will remember the advice before making a left turn.

When the worm turns, Frances Rodman observes, it may be because he got instructions from the back seat.

Best way to stop the noise in your car is to let her drive.

A woman driver is a person who drives like a man—only she gets blamed for it.

A truck, taking its cue from TV programs, has these rear warnings:

an arrow on the left labeled "This is Your Life" and one on the right marked "Medic."

It takes hundreds of nuts to hold a car together, but it takes only one of them to scatter it all over the highway.

A tree is an object that will stand in one place for years, and then jump in front of a lady driver.

If all pedestrians were laid end to end, it would greatly simplify the task for some automobile drivers.

Accident: what happens when two motorists go after the same pedestrian.

DRUGS

"Are you positive one bottle will clear up my liver trouble?" the customer asked the pharmacist, and the druggist replied, "Right." I've never seen anyone come in for a second bottle."

DUTY

Many a man who does his duty as he sees it should consult an optometrist.

Duty: something we look forward to with distaste, do with reluctance, and boast about forever.

ECONOMY

Sir Anthony Eden says that everyone is always in favor of general economy and particular expenditure.

Most people don't start economizing until they run out of money.

Fred Neher says that economy is anything your mother wants to buy.

Eve was a model wife because she cost her husband nothing to keep her in clothes.

Economy: a reduction in the other fellow's salary.

"Two can live cheaper than one," Abe Martin observed, "but very few girls want to live that cheap."

An economist is somebody who has a plan to do something with someone else's money.

A Scot was told by his doctor that his wife should have had her tonsils taken out when she was a little girl. He had the operation performed—and sent the bill to his father-in-law.

Just about the time you think you can make both ends meet, somebody moves the ends.

Edward R. Murrow says that an economist is somebody who tells you what to do with your money after you've already done something else with it.

EDUCATION

Edna May Bush says that what you don't know won't hurt you—and just look at all the people who haven't an ache or pain!

You can get along without formal education like Henry Ford and Thomas A. Edison did, if you are a Ford or an Edison.

It is not only the I.Q. but also the I Will which is important in education.

It now costs more to amuse a child than it did to educate his father.

There is nothing wrong with our educational system—every schoolboy is certain he knows more than his father.

A college education seldom hurts a man if he's willing to learn a little something after he graduates.

Back in the old days it was a boy himself, rather than his teacher, who had to explain why he could not read.

College graduate: a person who had a chance to get an education.

The only thing more expensive than education is ignorance.

"There is nothing as stupid," Will Rogers said, "as an educated man if you get him off the thing that he was educated in."

An educated man is one who has finally discovered that there are some questions to which nobody has the answers.

Education is a wonderful thing. It helps you worry about things all over the world.

Education is what a man gets when he sits in his living room with a group of teen-agers.

EFFICIENCY

Efficiency expert: a man who walks in his sleep so that he can get his rest and exercise at the same time.

"Now what I want," said the efficiency expert, "is a chart that will show me at a glance what charts we've got."

EGO

No one is up in the air more than a person with an inflated ego.

Self-made man: one who can't blame it on his wife.

An ego is the only thing that can keep growing without nourishment.

An egotist is a man who thinks he knows just as much as you do but doesn't hide it.

Like Benjamin Franklin says, "A man who falls in love with himself will have no rivals."

Narcissist: the man who is always getting himself esteemed up.

Egotism is something that enables the man in the rut to think he's in the groove.

There are two kinds of egotists. Those who admit it, and the rest of us.

A self-made man is usually a horrible example of unskilled labor.

An egotist is a person of questionable taste more interested in himself than in me.

Egotism: an anesthetic nature gives to a man to deaden the pain of being a darn fool.

ELECTIONS

It would seem more people vote on leading brands of cigarettes than do for president.

ELECTRICITY

Then there was the electrical engineer who jumped from his chair because he had amps in his pants.

EMERGENCY

Youngster at military school sent an emergency air-mail letter to his parents: "Please send me a rug right away quick. I need something to sweep under."

EMOTIONS

Mixed emotions: watching your mother-in-law go over a cliff in your new Cadillac convertible.

EMPLOYMENT

An assistant: a fellow who can't get off.

A high-school senior told a classmate, "If you want a summer job you had better get it quick before the teachers grab them all."

Classified ad in Tucson paper: "Woman desires position in small store, part time, will talk hours."

Personnel manager to applicant: "What we're after is a man with drive, determination, fire; a man who never quits; a man who inspires others; a man who can pull the company's bowling team out of last place!"

ENCOURAGEMENT

When Thomas A. Edison's desk was opened years after his death, this card was found among his papers: "When down in the mouth, remember Jonah. He came out all right."

ENDURANCE

Your idea of an endurance test is entertaining a pest who says nothing.

ENEMIES

Oscar Levant once said, "I have no enemies, but all my friends hate me."

An enemy is a friend who found you out.

ENERGY

You're getting old when it makes you tired just to watch your kids play.

It takes as much energy to wish as it does to plan.

ENJOYMENT

Eat, drink, and be merry. And tomorrow you'll wish you were dead.

ENTHUSIASM

These days a go-getter is the fellow who can get up from where he's sleeping and go to bed.

Enthusiasm: faith with a tin can tied to its tail.

Enthusiasm: a person who has discovered the secret of perpetual emotion.

EPITAPH

Many epitaphs should read: "Died at thirty—buried at seventy."

The code of the Old West is told on a natural rock gravestone in Cripple Creek, Colorado: "He called Bill Smith a liar."

A Louisiana man bet a friend he could ride the flywheel in a new sawmill, and as his widow paid off the debt the next week, she remarked: "Jake, he was a swell husband but he sure didn't know much about flywheels."

Sign on bebopper's tombstone: "Don't dig me now—I'm real gone."

Ilka Chase: "I've finally gotten to the bottom of things."

Clive Brook: "Excuse me for not rising."

ERRORS

To err is human—but when the eraser wears out before the pencil, look out.

To err may be human, but to admit it isn't.

ESCAPE

At a dull academic party, a fellow guest remarked to Albert Einstein, "I'm afraid you are terribly bored, Professor Einstein," and he replied pleasantly, "*Ach, nein,* on occasions like this I like to retire to the back of my mind; there I am happy."

ESTIMATES

What's more, estimates should include an estimate of how much more it will cost than the estimate.

ETERNITY

For a small boy, eternity is the interval between the time he gets home from school and the time that supper is served.

ETHICS

Historians of the future may refer to the present as the "Age of Chiselry."

The Golden Rule is of little value unless you realize that you must make the first move.

Nobody ever got hurt on the corners of a square deal.

ETIQUETTE

Chaos: four women with one luncheon check.

EULOGIES

Minister presiding at funeral: "Friends, all that remains here is the shell; the nut is gone."

EVIL

A necessary evil is one we like so much we don't care to abolish it.

EVOLUTION

Evolution is what makes the chimpanzee in the zoo ask, "Am I my brother's keeper?"

216

Evolution is the theory that man descended from the animals, though some men descended much farther than others.

EXAMINATIONS

A teacher asked "What was the principal cultural contribution of the Phoenicians?" and a kid answered, "Blinds."

A student wrote this note on his high-school exam paper: "Views expressed in this paper are my own and not necessarily those of the textbook."

EXAMPLES

Few things are harder to put up with than the annoyances of a good example.

Nobody is completely worthless. If nothing else, a person can serve as a horrible example.

EXCITEMENT

Doctor advised his patient, "You must avoid all forms of excitement," and the man complained, "Gee, Doc, can't I even look at them across the street?"

EXCLUSIVE

Groucho Marx resigned from the Friars Club with the simple, chilly explanation: "I don't want to belong to any club that would accept me as one of its members."

EXCUSES

Mother's note to teacher: "Please excuse Randy from being absent —he has a new baby brother. It wasn't his fault."

A San Antonio, Texas, driver, fined for driving without a license, protested he couldn't get one because of poor vision. His job: car jockey in a parking lot.

In Pittsburgh, Pennsylvania, a former convict, discovered trying the doors of a rectory with a bunch of keys, stated: "I was just looking for a place to pray."

Some men think twice before leaving their wives for an evening. First they think up an excuse for going out, then a reason why she can't go, too.

Hear about the boy who, when absent from school to go rabbit hunting, always indicated reason on permit in principal's office: "Taking shots"?

EXECUTIVES

Wife to husband in sick bed: "It's a sympathy card from your secretary to me."

An executive is a man who can hand a letter back to a redheaded stenographer for a fourth retyping.

An unbending capitalist is a man who keeps a pair of opera glasses hanging by his bathroom scales so he can read the figures without bending.

Many an executive who is a big noise at the office is just a little squeak at home.

The thing worrying most bosses today is the number of unemployed still on the payroll.

The thing that keeps some executives so wound up is the suspicion that a colleague is running them down.

Beatitude for executives: "Blessed are they who go around in big circles, for they shall be called big wheels."

Sign above a TV executive's desk: "In this office, flattery will get you nowhere but to the top."

A San Francisco newspaper ran this ad from the classified section: "Wanted, big executive, from 22 to 80. To sit with feet on desk from 10:00 to 4:30 to watch other people work. Must be willing to play golf every other afternoon. Salary to start: $1,000 a week. We don't have this job open, you understand. We just thought we'd like to see in print what everybody is applying for."

Motto posted on executive's desk: "Use your head. It's the little things that count."

218

EXERCISE

When you're pushing sixty, that's exercise enough.

Chided because he took little exercise, George Burns said: "But I get plenty of exercise. Every week I go to the horror movies and let my flesh creep."

EXHIBITIONIST

Exhibitionist: a girl wearing a new engagement ring for the first time.

EXPENSES

Two can live as cheaply as one, and they generally have to.

The cost of living is the only thing that defies the law of gravitation because it keeps going up without ever coming down.

Nowadays apples are so expensive that you might as well have the doctor.

The Great Beyond: living beyond your income.

A wife told her husband: "I wish you had the spunk of the government. They don't let being in debt keep them from spending."

Stork: the bird with the big bill.

Fashion report: The thing that keeps men broke is not the wolf at the door. It's the mink in the window.

Two can live as cheaply as one, if one is a vegetarian and the other is a nudist on a diet.

It's nice to be able to make both ends meet, Marjorie Johnson reminds us, but it's nicer if they overlap a little.

Irate husband: "Light bills, water, gas, milkman! You've got to quit this wild spending."

EXPERIENCE

Loyd Burns says that experience is still the best teacher—and an added advantage is that you get individual instruction.

An employer, interviewing an applicant, remarked: "You ask high wages for a man with no experience," and the prospect answered, "Well, it's so much harder work when you don't know anything about it."

Experience is the cheapest thing you can buy if you're lucky enough to get it secondhand.

"You will pardon me for using so many illustrations from my personal experiences," the speaker explained, "but they're the only kind I've ever had."

Experience: what you have left after you've lost everything else.

Experience may be a good teacher, but not many pupils bring her bright red apples.

Experience may make a person better—or bitter.

Experience is a good teacher. Trouble is she seldom teaches the subject that interests us.

Experience is the name men give to their mistakes.

EXPERT

Expert: one who has a good reason for guessing wrong.

An efficiency expert is a man smart enough to tell you how to run your own business and too smart to start one of his own.

Expert: a person who can take something you already know and make it sound confusing.

An expert is a person who is just beginning to understand how little he knows about the subject.

Expert: "X" is the unknown quantity; "spert" is a drip under pressure.

Expert: a man who is seldom in doubt but often in error.

He's known as a small-talk expert. It there's nothing to be said, he can say it.

EXPRESSION

A sour-puss is made, not born. God gives us our faces; we give ourselves expressions.

You can't control the contour of your countenance, but you can control its expression.

EXTRAVAGANCE

Extravagance: the way other people spend their money.

FACE

Be it ever so homely, there's no face like your own.

FAD

Bill Stern says that a fad is something that goes in one era and out the other.

FAILURE

Failure is the line of least persistence.

Wilson Mizner says we all have something to fall back on, and I never knew a phony who didn't land on it eventually.

A down-and-outer watched a successful man whirl by in a Cadillac and said, "There but for me go I."

Has-been: the proof that nothing recedes like success.

Defeatist: a man who is sure nothing can be done because he has done nothing.

FAIRY STORIES

Fairy stories can be used in two ways; to quiet a restless child or to fool a suspicious wife.

FAITH

A Negro preacher began his sermon by saying: "Brethren and sisters, here you is comin' to pray for rain. I'd like to ask you just one question: where is yo' umbrellas?"

FAME

Fame is an elevation to which people are raised so that the public may have a better chance to throw mud at them.

Connie Towers tells of being a guest where "there were so many celebrities that I was the only one in the room I'd never heard of."

FAMILIES

Two types of families are likely to have a house full of antique furniture—the kind with money and the kind with kids.

As an inducement to hard work and economy nothing beats a big family.

By the time a boy reaches the age where he realizies how much he owes his parents, a girl comes along and takes over the indebtedness.

Family tree: a genealogical diagram showing that you belong to a family better dead than alive.

Man to office pal: "I owe everything to my wife—and boy, is she collecting!"

Robert Quillen says that the boss of the family is anyone who can spend ten dollars without thinking it necessary to say anything about it.

The dining room is the place where the family eats while painters are doing over the kitchen.

Economy is anything for which your wife wishes to spend money.

Looking ahead to this parental plight: "Dad, may I use the rocket ship tonight?"

Some families who can trace their ancestry back three hundred years can't tell you where their children were last night.

Walter Winchell describes a young man who didn't exactly come from a good family—he was sent.

FANATIC

A fanatic is a person who is so enthusiastic about something that you aren't interested in it at all.

FARMING

Farm relief: relieving the farmer of his farm.

Farmer to friend, after paying for a ham sandwich, "According to what they charged for that ham sandwich, I've got a hog that's worth $2,800."

E. B. White says that a farmer is a handy man with a sense of humus.

All it takes to make a successful farmer is faith, hope, and parity.

A gentleman farmer is one who has more hay in the bank than in the barn.

Dairy farmer, interviewing prospective hired man: "Have any bad habits—smoke, drink, eat margarine?"

FASHIONS

One reason girls of today are such live wires is that they wear so little insulation.

FATHERS

We can understand why so many fathers worry about their sons—they used to be one themselves.

Teen-age daughter, introducing her date to her father: "Egbert, meet my answering service."

A father told his daughter's suitor: "My daughter says you have that certain something but I wish you had something certain."

Little kid entered an essay in "My Pop's Tops" sponsored by Midwest newspaper, and it contained this tribute: "Pop never passed the seventh grade, yet he is just as smart as if he was in the eighth."

A father is a person who should be neither seen nor heard.

Whenever you hear it said that there is a beautiful tie between father and son, the son is probably wearing it.

When my father found me on the wrong track, he always provided switching facilities.

Father to daughter's suitor: "Frankly, young man, you aren't making enough to support her, but that's all right—neither am I."

Usually the only voice that father gets in family affairs is the invoice.

Just about the time a father gets his daughter off his hands, he has to start putting his son-in-law on his feet.

Anyone who has tried to read a newspaper and answer a small boy's questions will appreciate the story of the little fellow who told his busy dad, "Wanna know what you said 'uh-huh' to?"

Kate Smith recalls that "My mother was always having trouble with either my father or the furnace. Every time she would watch one," she says, "the other one would go out."

One man, introducing friend to another: "We're paternity brothers—we paced the hospital floor together the night our sons were born."

Fathers are what give daughters away to other men who aren't good enough for them—so they can have grandchildren that are smarter than anybody's.

Young father, discussing baby, "We just can't go anywhere—he's such a wet blanket."

Sign in Niagara Falls bakery: "Remember Father and Buy a Devil's Food Cake."

A father of the bride has one consolation—he may be losing a daughter, but he may have gained a bathroom.

Paul Harvey says that a father is a thing that growls when it feels good—and laughs loud when scared half to death.

FATIGUE

From an Indiana newspaper: "Girl Scout Leader's hat—leader worn out—hat like new."

A little boy was sent to bed by his frazzled mother, and he told his brother: "I can't understand it—every time she gets tired we have to take a nap."

When you're tired, it's refreshing to observe somebody else yawn.

Have you reached the place in life where it takes you longer to rest up after an event than to do it?

"My wife was so tired at the end of the evening," explained the host, "that she could hardly keep her mouth open."

"If Heaven's a place of rest," Burton Hillis says, "my hired man's going to be all practiced up for it."

Some fellows are so farsighted they rest before they get tired.

FAULTFINDERS

Faultfinder: a woman who goes through life demanding to see the manager.

FEAR

Hal Boyle says that fears are the only thing that multiply faster than rabbits.

Patient told doctor: "Doctor, I'm scared to death—this is my first operation," and he said, "Sure. I know how you feel. You are my first patient."

FIGURES

Zac Freedman says of a girl, "She was only a build in a girdled cage."

FISHING

Woman asked her husband, "How many fish was it that you caught Saturday?" He said, "Six, darling—all beauties," and she said, "I thought so. That fish shop has made a mistake again. They've charged us for eight."

A fish out of water must feel like a moth in a nudist colony.

Fishermen catch the most in the early morn or just after dark or when they get home.

"Sure I caught a fish but it was so small to fool with that I had a couple of other guys help me throw it back in the lake."

The way most fishermen catch fish is by the tale.

A man gazing incredulously at a huge mounted fish said: "The man who caught that fish is a liar."

Lady inspecting fishing rod, to salesman: "What size fish does this one catch?"

Fishing is mostly a matter of timing. All you have to do is to get here yesterday when the fish were biting.

A man returned from a two-week fishing trip and his friend inquired, "Well, how were the fish in those parts?" and the man replied, "Really can't say. For two weeks I dropped them a line twice a day—but I had no reply."

A woman, cleaning fish for her angler husband, said, "Why can't you be like the rest of the men? They never catch anything."

A fishing rod, according to some wives, is a pole with a worm at both ends.

A fish probably goes home and lies about the size of the bait he stole.

On the door of a small restaurant outside Birmingham: "Gone for the week. Fishing-pox."

FLATTERY

In a hat shop a saleslady gushed: "That's a darling hat. Really, it makes you look ten years younger," and the customer replied, "Then I don't want it. I can't afford to put on ten years every time I take off my hat."

When a man says he can't be flattered, he wants you to flatter him by agreeing with him.

Flattery is having someone else say all the nice things that we have always thought about ourselves.

A woman detests flattery—if it is directed at another woman.

Hal Chadwick says that many a man is enough of a dope to be easily cleaned by the use of soft soap.

Flattery is the thinnest thing in the world—and the hardest to see through.

Flattery is all right if you don't inhale.

FLIRTING

Flirting: wishful winking.

In Hawaii men often make passes at girls who wear grasses.

FLYING

Don't worry about that uneasy feeling right after the plane takes off. It's only groundless apprehension.

FOOD

Appetizers: those little bits you eat until you lose your appetite.

An onion a day will give your diet away.

French-fried potatoes stay in your mouth a few minutes, in your stomach a few hours, and on your hips the rest of your life.

Vegetable soup: the same as hash, only looser.

Watermelon is the only fruit you can eat, drink, and wash your face in.

Why do they put so many holes in Swiss cheese when it's the limberger that needs the ventilation?

A hamburger by any other name always costs more.

Billy Rose defines canapes: a sandwich cut into 24 pieces.

Most people agree that the nicest way to serve spinach is to somebody else.

There may be a destiny that shapes our ends, but our middles are of our own chewing.

Groaned one moth to another: "I'll have to stop eating overcoats— I'm getting ulsters of the stomach."

Some people thirst after fame, some after money—but everybody thirsts after popcorn.

Practically any girl who knows how to cook can find a man who knows how to eat.

No man is lonely while eating spaghetti, Christopher Morley observed, because it requires so much attention.

Tranquilized steers, according to food experts, make tastier steaks, which in turn make tranquilized husbands.

One man's meat is another man's cholesterol.

More people commit suicide with a fork than with any other weapon.

Hamburger: a steak that didn't pass its physical.

A refrigerator is where you put dabs of food in dishes you don't want to wash.

From an ad in the Detroit *News*: "Here is the world's tenderest beef! It's cut to give you more meatless bone . . . ."

Indigestion is the failure to adjust a square meal to a round stomach.

You can't have your cake and somebody else's cookie too.

Too many cooks spoil the figure.

A balanced meal is one from which the diner has a 50–50 chance of recovering.

We may not be eating as much as our grandparents, but we're paying twice as much for it.

The main difference between Swiss cheese and Camembert is that the ventilations are a little better.

Marmalade: the stuff you see on toast, neckties, and piano keys.

FOOLS

There's no fool like an old fool. You can't beat experience.

FOOTBALL

Football is a clean sport because it's about the only one with scrub teams.

Two Greeks were watching their first football game, and one said to the other: "This is all American to me."

Definition of a football player: a contortionist, because he is always going around his own end.

Comment of coach after watching his team work out prior to the big game: "I wouldn't let my mother-in-law run behind that line."

Parke Cummings tells of the football player who said, "Honest, coach, a fellow just gave me this cigarette to hold while he stepped into the library for a moment."

Football season: the short warm-up between spring practice and the winter bowl games.

A college grad, writing his coach about a high-school prospect, said, "He's lean and mean and in the summer he hunts rattlesnakes for fifty cents a pound."

Bob Hope says, "I played football in school and was known as Neckline Hope. I was always plunging down the middle, but never really showing anything."

Football makes a nation strong. You build up a lot of strong resistance sitting on a cold concrete seat.

To many football fans the pint after the touchdown is the most important part of the game.

FORGETFULNESS

Some forgetfulness is not due to absent-mindedness but to absent-heartedness.

FORGIVENESS

A blonde asked a clerk: "Have you something I could send to a nice young man who got slapped harder than someone intended to slap him?"

FORTUNE

Wife, reading her husband's fortune on a weight card: "You are dynamic, a leader of men, and admired by women for your good looks and strength of character. It's got your weight wrong, too!"

A lady fortuneteller is a woman who has put her feminine intuition on a paying basis.

FRANKNESS

John Boland, speaking of a friend, says, "He's terribly frank—burns the candor at both ends."

FREE

There are mighty few sensations that are as pleasant as getting something for nothing.

FRIENDS

A friend is a person who goes around saying nice things about you behind your back.

The quickest way to wipe out a friendship is to sponge on it.

A friend is a person who has the same enemies as you have.

A friend is a person who knows all about you and loves you just the same.

A friend is a person who can't understand how you got there, but still doesn't knock you.

Russell Newbold says that a friend who is not in need is a friend indeed.

Be kind to your friends. If it weren't for them you'd be a total stranger.

"If you have her for a friend," quipped June Allyson, "you don't need any enemies."

You can have your close friends—give me generous ones.

Claire MacMurray says that friends are not made. They're recognized.

Al Spong says that when it comes to helping a friend some people will stop at nothing.

It was just a platonic friendship—play for him, tonic for her!

Bing Crosby remarked, "There's nothing in the world I wouldn't do for that guy, and there's nothing he wouldn't do for me—we spend our lives doing nothing for each other."

FRIGHT

A farmer was bragging about a marvelous scarecrow, and a friend asked, "Did it scare the crows?" He replied, "I should say it did. Why, that contraption skeered them crows so bad some of 'em fetched back corn they had stole from me two years before!"

Wilkie Bard, the droll English comic, wowed a New York theater audience with this line: "My feet are like marble. I don't mean white marble. I mean cold like marble."

FRUGALITY

Frugality: saving something while your salary is small because it's impossible to save after you begin earning more.

FRUSTRATION

Hear about the octopus who fell into the cement mixer? Just a crazy, mixed-up squid.

FUN

Fun is like insurance—the older you get the more it costs.

There's no fun in having nothing to do; the fun comes in having plenty to do and not doing it.

FUND-RAISING

Girl to another at the office: "You remember the collection we took up to buy a toaster for Sue when she got engaged? Well, she and Jim have broken up and we girls thought it would be nice if everybody chipped in to get her a consolation present."

FURNISHINGS

Throw rug: a small rug that usually throws anyone who steps on it.

FURNITURE

Have you ever noticed that a chair is an immovable object in the daytime but at night it slips up and kicks you in the shins?

Once upon a time you could fix a broken chair with baling wire. Now a chair is baling wire.

FUTURE

Cheer up! These are the good old days you'll be sighing for about twenty years from now.

The nicest thing about the future is that it comes one day at a time.

You can't have rosy thoughts about the future when your mind is full of blues of the past.

GAG WRITER

Gag writer: one who has hitched his gaggin' to a star.

GAMBLING

We have no idea of how much money we saved by not betting on race horses, or what became of it.

A horse-race enthusiast, when asked the results of his afternoon at the track, replied: ""I broke even, and oh boy, did I need it!"

A race track is one place where dollars and sense seldom appear together.

No horse can go as fast as the money you bet on him.

Gambling: a way of getting nothing for something.

A gambler's nine-year-old son, asked to count in school, responded promptly, "1, 2, 3, 4, 5, 6, 7, 8, 9, 10, Jack Queen, King."

Bookie: a pickpocket who lets you use your hands.

Mine wasn't only the last horse in the race—I think it was the last race in the horse.

Las Vegas: the land of the spree and the home of the knave.

Walter Winchell is of the belief that the less you bet the more you lose when you win.

It is said that the American people squander ten billion dollars a year on games of chance. This does not include weddings, starting up in business, or buying television sets.

GAMES

A childish game is one in which your wife can beat you.

Two matrons, leaving the bowling alley, commented, "Well, anyway, we didn't lose any of the balls."

If looks could kill, a lot of people would die with bridge cards in their hands.

According to a survey, there are only five real authorities on bridge in this country. Odd how often one gets one of them as a partner!

Poker: waiting for a chip that never comes in.

Friendly game of cards—one in which you cheat but not for money.

GARDENING

Garden: something most men prefer to turn over in their minds.

James Shuford reminds us that old gardeners never die—they just spade away.

Make a better lawn and the world will beat a path across it to your door.

Have you seen the new power mowers which are equipped with a bag of arsenic? It's for husbands who'd rather die than mow the lawn.

A lot of suburban dwellers have discovered that trees grow on money.

Our forefathers ran a farm with less machinery than we need to keep a lawn.

Little boy to clerk in garden-supply store: "My mother wants a spray that will kill crab grass, Japanese beetles, weeds, and spinach."

One of our friends says, "Next year I'm gonna plant weeds—and see if the flowers won't choke 'em out."

An optimistic gardener is one who believes that whatever goes down must come up.

Nothing discourages an amateur gardener like watching the family eat his entire garden at one meal.

Grass: the green stuff that wilts in the yard and flourishes in the garden.

Man over back fence to neighbor working in the garden: "I had phenomenal luck with my garden this year—not a thing came up."

Gardening is simply a matter of your enthusiasm holding up until your back gets used to it.

GENEALOGY

A great many prominent family trees were started by grafting.

A genealogist will trace your family as far back as your money will go.

GENIUS

A genius is a man who can do almost anything but make a living.

Genius: a person who can spread a pat of restaurant butter over two slices of bread.

It's great to have a genius in the family, providing the other members of the family can earn the living.

Genius: a man who shoots at something no one else can see and hits it.

An infant prodigy is a child with highly imaginative parents.

GENTLEMAN

Gentleman: a man who is always as nice as he sometimes is.

It's a fine thing to be a gentleman, but it's an awful handicap in a good argument.

Southern gentleman: one who hasn't kissed his wife in twenty years and would shoot any man who tried.

GIFTS

A rare gift is any kind a woman receives after five years of marriage.

Ed Wynn says, "It isn't the string of pearls a man gives a girl that worries her—it's the clasp that goes with it."

Just inside the door of a gift shop in the Rockies is a big easy chair on which is pinned a note: "Reserved—for husbands whose wives are looking."

Suggested sign for post office urging early mailing at Christmas: "Send your gifts early—besides facilitating the handling of mail, it gives the receiver a chance to reciprocate."

You never realize how fortunate you are until you enter a gift shop and see how many things your friends haven't sent you.

In Phoenix, Arizona, a group of ministers collected money for a gift in recognition of the dedicated service of Mrs. Faith Norton, decided on perfume, and gave her a bottle of My Sin.

Visit a gift shop and you'll realize how many things your home doesn't lack.

GIRLS

Signs of growing up: a girl starts wearing her mother's mink instead of her father's sweatshirt.

A smart girl is one who knows how to play tennis, golf, piano, and dumb.

Girl to chum: "He seems rather dull and uninteresting until you get to know him. After that he's downright boring."

Homely girl: all dressed up and no face to go.

The modern girl is one who is inclined to be underdeveloped and overexposed.

A flirt is as strong as her weakest wink.

We know a girl who can't swim a stroke but she knows every dive in town.

Asked about her likes, a girl said: "I prefer men who go for the more refined things in life—like oil."

Asked about a certain girl, Bob Hope replied, "Yes, I remember her. She was non-habit-forming."

Bank official to new stenographer, "Do you retire a loan?" and she replied, "No, I sleep with Mother."

The modern girl is afraid of nothing except a stack of dishes.

A girl is a creature who makes up her face more easily than she does her mind.

Girl, describing her boy friend, to chum: "He likes classical music, art museums, and he reads a lot, but nobody's perfect."

Mechanic: "A girl is so dumb that she thinks the universal joint is a bar in the United Nations Building."

Funny, when a girl's old enough for her parents to let her go out alone, she doesn't.

Another sign of growing up: The little girls who used to make faces at the boys are now making eyes at them.

To most female teen-agers, a thing of beauty is a boy forever.

When a girl wants her boy friend to start saving his money, there's a very good chance he's going to need it.

A deb is a young lady with bride ideas.

The modern girl knows little about making bread—but more about needing dough.

One girl to another, at perfume counter: "I've stopped buying perfume—my boy friend reacts only to cooking aromas."

It's the modern girl who says, "One false move and I'll appreciate it."

Girl, to chum: "Ordinarily I never chase after men, Alice, but this one was getting away."

She's the picture of her father and the sound track of her mother.

Some modern girls turn a man's head with their charm—and his stomach with their cooking.

A nurse at the blood bank asked a girl if she knew her type and she replied, "Oh, yes, I'm the sultry type."

Many an old-fashioned clinging vine now has a granddaughter who's a rambler.

A smart girl is one who can hold a man at arm's length without losing her grip on him.

236

Sweet young thing to another: "Why, sure, he loves you, Ethel—do you think you're an exception?"

A lot of girls find it hard to remember their mother's advice about men because they just can't seem to recoil at the moment.

The old-fashioned girl never thought of doing things girls do nowadays—that's why she didn't do them.

Young girl to chum: "Dorothy is one of those sweet, shy, unassuming girls. You know, a real phony."

Girls who try to be talking encyclopedias should remember that reference books are never taken out.

The modern miss may not know how to cook but she knows what's cooking.

Economics lesson for today: Girls without principle draw considerable interest.

Some girls count on their fingers, but a smart girl counts on her legs.

Luke Neely says that when her date's car stalls, a girl should be ready to do likewise.

Describing his girl friend, a young fellow said, "She has a figure like an hour glass and she certainly makes every minute count."

The modern girl dresses to kill and cooks the same way.

Sweet young thing to the perfume salesgirl: "He's acting like that already. All I want is just a dignified proposal of marriage."

Little girls want an all-day sucker—big girls want one just for the evening.

Some girls have both beauty and brains. It's a rare one, though, who displays both on the beach.

Some girls can get as happy as a lark on a few swallows.

A small girl watched a passing boy and girl and then said to her friend, "Goodness, she's old enough to be his sitter."

A girl is a pleasant dinner companion, Allan Prescott says, when she makes you think she is taking dinner with you and not from you.

A girl's life cycle: safety pins, fraternity pins, clothespins, rolling pins, safety pins.

GIVING

If you haven't charity in your heart, Bob Hope says, then you have the worst kind of heart trouble.

It is more blessed to give than to receive—and it's deductible.

GLAMOUR

Glamour, declares Dr. Paul B. Popenoe, is when the value of the package exceeds that of the contents.

One young thing to another as they watch glamour girl sweep past with escort: "I wish I was smart enough to be as dumb as she is."

Beauty contest—lass roundup.

Her face is her fortune—and it runs into a nice figure.

GOLD DIGGER

Gold digger: a girl who falls in love at purse-sight.

Gold digger: a girl who mines her own business.

GOLF

Some men play golf religiously—every Sunday.

Caddy: a boy who stands behind a golfer and who didn't see where it went, either.

From Toronto *Telegram*: "For sale, golf clubs—must sell or get divorce."

A golfer, who had lost his sense of direction in the woods, yelled to caddy: "Never mind about my ball, caddy, come find me."

Fran Allison says that "Golf is just a lot of walking, broken up by disappointment and bad arithmetic."

A caddy is a small boy employed to lose balls for others and find them for himself.

A woman golfer told another: "You're improving, Delores. You're missing the ball much closer than you used to."

A golfer, who had made a spectacularly bad shot and tore up a large piece of turf, took the sod in his hand and asked, "What shall I do with this?" His caddy said, "If I were you, I'd take it home to practice on."

The hangman tightened the knot and asked the condemned golfer if he had any last words, and he replied, "Yes, I wonder if I could take a few practice swings."

Golf is a game in which a small white ball is chased by men who are too old to chase anything else.

A golf course is another place where a girl likes to go around in as little as possible.

Our neighbor says his golf is improving—the other day he hit a ball in one.

The golfer's ideal is not to stand too close to the ball after you've hit it.

Golf: a long walk punctuated with disappointments.

Golf is a game in which a ball 1½ inches in diameter is placed on a ball 8,000 miles in diameter. The object is to hit the small ball, but not the large one.

"My wife says she'll leave me if I don't give up golf," and the golfer's friend said, "That is tough." The golfer replied, "Yeah, I'll miss the old girl."

Golfer (to foursome ahead): "Pardon me, but would you mind if I played through? I've just heard that my wife has been taken seriously ill."

Jimmy Durante tried to play golf one day and after going around in about 200 asked his opponent what he should give his caddy. "Your clubs," his friend replied.

A golfer is a man who really knows how to express his thoughts to a tee.

Bob Hope says that teaching your wife to play golf is the reverse of teaching her to drive a car. "With golf, she never hits anything; with a car, she never seems to miss."

A little girl and her mother were watching a golfer in a sand trap, and the little girl finally said, "He's stopped beating it, Mother. I think it must be dead."

Bob Hope says that a few years back on Father's Day his children gave him a book, *How to Play Winning Golf*, and the next year they gave him, *How to Improve Your Golf*, and the following year, *Don't Let Bad Golf Discourage You*. Now he expects a volume on "How to Cheat at Golf."

From New Jersey newspaper: "One of the most interesting events for ladies will take place when there will be a petting and approach contest on the golf course."

GOOD TIMES

Good times is the period when you accumulate debts you're unable to pay in bad times.

GOSSIP

What you hear never sounds half as important as what you overhear.

Mary McCoy says that a gossip is a person who puts two and two together—whether they are or not.

Mrs. Smith to Mrs. Jones over the back fence: "I don't like to repeat gossip, but what else can you do with it?"

A gossip talks about others; a bore talks about himself. The man who talks about you is the brilliant man.

Women like gossip because it gives them something to talk about while talking.

Overheard on a bus, "You know, I wouldn't say anything about Doris unless I could say something good, and oh, brother, is this good . . . ."

Then there's the story of the two flashy young women being introduced. "Oh, yes," gushed one, "I've heard so much about you. Now let's hear your side of the story."

One touch of scandal makes the whole world chin.

Gossip: a woman who drops a name into the conversation and then sits back to listen.

When she drops a name, she practically hollers, "Look out below!"

A gossip is a woman who tells everything she can get her ears on.

A person who doesn't gossip is one who hasn't heard the rumor.

Woman, describing another woman to her husband: "She was the center of distraction."

Hear no evil, see no evil, and speak no evil—and you'll never be a success at a cocktail party.

It isn't the people who tell all they know that cause most of the trouble in the world—it's the ones who tell more.

A sister wrote to a columnist: "My sister and I aren't exactly lonely way out here in the country, as we have each other to talk to. What we need is some other woman to talk about."

GOVERNMENT

Nowadays, God helps those who help themselves, and the government helps those who don't.

It's easy to understand why they call it an "Unbalanced Budget." It's so big it's just crazy.

Our government has too many people fact finding, and too few fact facing.

Political economy: getting the most votes for the least money.

Unfortunately, there are ten thousand ways for a government to spend money and only one way to save it.

One of the hardest tasks of an independent man today is keeping the government from taking care of him.

Our national budget needs more pruning and less grafting.

GRAMMAR

When the Yale Athletic Committee telegraphed Harvard before a football game, "May the best team win," Harvard wired back, "May the better team win."

GRANDPARENTS

Was there ever a grandparent, bushed after a day of minding noisy youngsters, who hasn't felt the Lord knew what He was doing when He gave little children to young people?

GRATITUDE

Victor Borge, pianist and comedian, announced at the close of a television show: "I wish to thank my mother and father, who made this show possible, and my five children, who made it necessary."

One of the nicest things about old age is that you can whistle while you brush your teeth.

Remember the youngster who wrote: "Dear Aunt Mame, I want to thank you for all the gifts you have sent me in the past, and all you intend to send in the future."

Sylvia Strum Bremer tells of the kid who wrote: "Thank you for the fire injin. It's almost as good as the one I really wanted."

GREATNESS

The cemeteries are filled with people who thought the world couldn't get along without them.

GROUCH

If you feel dog-tired at night it's probably because you have growled all day.

GUESTS

Guest towel: a small body of absorbent linen entirely surrounded by waterproof embroidery.

"I do hope we haven't kept you from going to bed," said the belatedly departing guest. "Oh, that's all right," replied the host, "We'd have been getting up soon in any case."

A yawning host looked at his watch and then said to a visiting couple: "Who pays attention to time when good friends are together —why, it's only twelve eighteen and a half."

HABITS

Oscar Levant, describing his morning routine: "First I brush my teeth, then I sharpen my tongue."

242

HAIR

Bernie Kamber was told by a friend that his hair was getting thin, and he replied, "So what! Who wants fat hair?"

HAPPINESS

"For twenty years," mused the man to his friend, "my wife and I were ecstatically happy," and the friend asked, "What happened?" The man answered, "We met."

We've just been told about a fellow who is so interested in his wife's happiness that he's hired a private detective to check into the reasons for it.

"It's not the work I enjoy," said the cab driver, "it's the people I run into."

Optimist: happychondriac.

Some people cause happiness wherever they go; others, whenever they go.

A woman is happy if she has two things: furniture to move around, and a husband to move it around for her.

Cheer up! Remember it's better to light a candle than to curse the darkness.

The happiest days of your life are school days, providing your child is old enough to attend.

Holbrook Jackson says that happiness is a form of courage.

Happiness is one of the few things that doesn't go up in price during periods of inflation.

Contentment: a mental condition that consists of not knowing any better.

Philip Wylie spoke of a man who had "a grin like an ear of corn."

HARD LUCK

An officer stopped a motorist and told him he was going to give him a ticket for driving without a tail light. The motorist got out to investigate and started wailing. "It's not as bad as all that," the cop said. And the man replied, "It's not the tail light I'm worried about. What's become of my trailer?"

We know of a fellow who is so unlucky that he runs into accidents which started to happen to somebody else.

Then there was the man who bought a waterproof, shockproof, unbreakable watch—and lost it.

Guess you heard about the poor fellow who burned a hole in the coat of his two-pants suit.

Hard luck: the college student who was working for his board and room and suffered from insomnia and loss of appetite.

HASTE

Jumping to conclusions doesn't always make for happy landings.

HEADLINES

The New York *Daily News* once carried the following headline over a story on meat prices and inflation: "PRICES SOAR, BUYERS SORE, COW JUMPS OVER THE MOON."

Headline in California newspaper: "EGG-LAYING CONTEST WON BY LOCAL MAN."

Headline in Oakland, California, *Tribune*: "TWO CONVICTS EVADE NOOSE; JURY HUNG."

HEALTH

And then there was the dowager who told her doctor, "Since there is nothing wrong with me, I presume I owe you nothing."

We take a cold shower every morning—after the family have all taken hot ones.

Practical nurse: one who falls in love with a wealthy patient.

Woman asked neighbor, "Does your husband take any special exercise?" and neighbor replied, "Last week he was out seven nights running."

"You are very run down," said the doctor to the patient. "I suggest you lay off golf for a while and get in a good day at the office now and then."

"A permanent set of teeth," a kid wrote on his exam paper, "consists of eight canines, eight cuspids, two molars, and eight cuspidors."

One woman told another in doctor's waiting room: "Oh, I feel so much better now that the doctor's found out there's really something wrong with me."

Franklin P. Jones reminds us that wives suffer just as many ulcers as husbands do. The same ones.

Hay fever: much achoo about nothing.

A cold is both affirmative and negative: sometimes the eyes have it, and sometimes the nose.

Her ailment is not only chronic but chronicle.

Reducing slogan, "A word to the wide is sufficient."

Halitosis is better than no breath at all.

Car sickness: that feeling you get every month when the payment falls due.

After a complete examination, the doctor told the patient: "Quit smoking and drinking, go to bed early every night, and get up at the crack of dawn. That's the best thing for you." The man thought for a moment and said, "Frankly, Doc, I don't deserve the best. What's the second best?"

Doctor: a man who tells you if you don't cut out something, he will.

There's a new wonder pill so powerful that you can't take it unless you're in perfect health.

A hypochondriac is one who can't leave being well enough alone.

Slogan used in the chest X-ray campaign by the Winnipeg health department: "Every Chest or Bust!"

You will live longer if you don't drink, smoke, gamble, or stay out late. Anyway, it will seem longer!

Another tourniquet that will stop your circulation is a wedding ring.

245

Jack Barry boasted, "I got up at the crack of dawn, stuffed up the crack, and went back to bed."

HEARING

When asked why he didn't get a hearing aid, Grandpa Jenkins replied, "Don't need it, son. I hear more now than I understand."

HEAVEN

The average person probably hasn't stored up enough treasure in Heaven to make the down payment on a harp.

HELP

Elmer Leterman says that the best place to find a helping hand is at the end of your arm.

HEREDITY

Kid asked dad, "What is heredity?" and the man replied, "That's what a man believes in until his son begins to act like a fool."

A youngster being called down for a poor report card, asked, "What do you think the trouble is, Dad—heredity or environment?"

The law of heredity is that all undesirable traits come from the other parent.

HERO

Our idea of a movie hero is one who can sit through a double feature.

HEROINES

Heroine: a girl who is game but not everybody's.

HIDING

"A person who buries his head in the sand," Mabel A. Kennan says, "offers an engaging target."

246

HIGHBROW

Highbrow: a person who enjoys something until it becomes popular.

A highbrow is a man who has found something more interesting than women.

Highbrow: a person who can use the word "whom" without feeling self-conscious.

HIGHWAYS

Another traffic improvement might be divided highways marked "His" and "Hers."

HISTORY

Heard at the internal revenue office: "You claim a lot of dependents Mr. Solomon—uh—Your Majesty, I mean."

Mummy: a person pressed for time.

"History was a lot easier when I was in school," Strum Bremer says. "Not only was there less of it, but it seemed to stay put more."

The origin of the expression "hurrah for our side" goes back to the crowds in the streets when Lady Godiva made her famous sidesaddle ride through the streets of Coventry.

The worst thing about history is that every time it repeats itself the price goes up.

Knight: a one-man tank in the Middle Ages.

The pioneers who blazed the trails now have descendants who burn up the roads.

Columbus discovered America so that if some other country needed money, there would be a place to borrow it from.

HOBBIES

Fathers who have hobbies rarely lose their minds. However, you can't say the same thing of their families.

From a high-school basketball program: "His hobbies include hunting, skiing, tinkering with his hot rod and Elizabeth."

From a classified ad in a St. Paul newspaper: "Will sell fine collection of old whisky labels. Giving up hobby on doctor's orders."

A hobby is something you get goofy about to keep from going nuts about things in general.

Hobby: a favorite pastime which prevents people from becoming psychopathic but does not prevent those who have to live with them.

HOLIDAYS

A holiday is a day off that's generally followed by an off day.

A. G. Gardiner observes that it is when the holiday is over that we begin to enjoy it.

Too many people think Easter Sunday is Decoration Day.

New Year's: the time to send cards to friends who unexpectedly remember you at Christmas.

Holiday weekend: one in which people engage in a great weekend, testing whether this motorist or any motorist can long endure.

Thanksgiving: a holiday instituted by the Pilgrim fathers for the benefit of parents whose sons survived the football season.

HOLLYWOOD

Then there's the story about the Hollywood writer who left instructions that he be cremated and 10 per cent of his ashes thrown in his agent's face.

Hollywood: where the bride keeps the bouquets and throws away the husbands.

Heard in Hollywood: "He's a character actor: when he shows any character, he's acting."

A former chorus girl, who knew nothing about acting, was trying out for a dramatic role. Finally the director roared, "Can't you show me any emotion?" and she pouted, "How can I when all you've been photographing is my face?"

News photographers in Hollywood seem to favor the clothes-up picture.

248

One actress told another: "Darling, I sometimes wonder if you don't play too large a part in your life."

In Hollywood the eternal triangle consists of an actor, his wife, and himself.

In a rage of indignation, a Hollywood actress remarked about another star, "I knew her when she didn't know where her next husband was coming from."

A famous movie star was dining with a lady, and someone asked who the gal was. "That's his wife," he was told. "His wife!" he exclaimed. "Boy, what a publicity stunt."

Jimmy Durante divided Hollywood citizens into two categories: "Those who own swimming pools—and those who can't keep their heads above water."

Hollywood is the only place in the world where girls ask their husbands for consent to marry.

A comedian was touring bases during the war, and one night a soldier yelled at him, "Why aren't you in service?" The funny man said, "I'm 4-X," and the soldier asked, "What's that?" The comedian replied, "Coward."

They were discussing a rising young starlet: "You can talk all you want to about her," observed one man, "but she'll probably make a good wife for five or six guys."

A movie actress has just remarried her first husband—it must have been his turn again.

Sir Cedric Hardwicke said, "Hollywood may be thickly populated but to me it's still a bewilderness."

Many a Hollywood actress marries so often that wedding bells sound to her like an alarm clock.

A cinema star was getting married for the sixth time and the officiating clergyman, flustered by all the publicity and glamour, lost his place in the ritual book. The star yawned and whispered, "Page 64, stupid."

Wondering about a certain executive, one actor said to another, "I hear that he's changing his faith," and the other replied, "You mean he no longer believes he's God?"

HOME MOVIES

Home movies: the strange views people take of things.

HOMES

J. M. Strauss reminds us that any man who has lived through spring cleaning knows why hurricanes are given feminine names.

There's a couple down the way from us who live in a beautiful little apartment overlooking the rent.

A woman who lived in a trailer told a friend, "The worst thing about living in a trailer is that there's no place to put anything except where it belongs."

The only trouble with some of these new homes is their location— on the outskirts of your income.

Be it ever so humble, there's nothing like a new home for exceeding the original estimated cost by at least 50 per cent.

Some modern architect is going to design a home that consists of a garage, putting green, and bedroom.

The only voice a man has in the furnishing of a home is the invoice.

Men who yearn to die with their boots on should wear them into the living room on cleaning day.

A grouchy-looking wife told her grouchy-looking husband, "Look, I'll make a deal with you. You don't tell me about your day—and I won't tell you about mine."

Howard W. Newton says that an antique is an object that has made a round trip to the atttic.

A man's den is a private room where a husband retreats at the end of the day and growls when he finds his belongings aren't on the floor where he left them.

Home is a place where a man can say anything he pleases because no one pays the slightest attention to him.

Home: the place where the college student home for vacation isn't.

Screen door: something the kids get a bang out of.

Everything in the home nowadays is controlled by a switch except the children.

Medicine cabinet: a home drugstore without sandwiches.

Home is a place where we grumble the most and are treated the best.

There's nothing like a dish towel for wiping that contented look off a man's face.

The pleasure caused by a crackling fire in the fireplace is tempered to a degree by the crackling of your joints when you bring in the wood.

HOME TOWN

Your home town is the place where people wonder how you ever got as far as you have.

HONESTY

A father looked over his kid's report card and exclaimed, "One thing in your favor—with these grades you couldn't possibly be cheating."

Old lady rented room to two boys whom she did not know, and she worried some at first. She stopped fretting and told a neighbor, "They must be nice boys. They have towels from the Y.M.C.A."

HONEYMOON

Harold Coffin says that the honeymoon isn't over until the bride who thought she was mad about you finds out she's just mad at you.

The honeymoon is over when the cooing stops and the billing starts.

HORSES

"I'm a horse follower," Joe E. Lewis admits, and "the horses I follow, follow horses."

Dan Bennett says that the first time a man bets on the horses, he plans to win. The rest of the time he plays to get even.

Joe E. Lewis, describing a horse he bet on: "I won't say he ran slowly—but this is the first time a jockey took along copies of *The Reader's Digest* and *Cosmopolitan*."

Maurice Seitter believes that about the only thing you get right from the horse's mouth is the horse laugh.

Christopher Stone once said, "I hate horses—they are uncomfortable in the middle and dangerous at both ends."

HORSE SENSE

In this complicated world, horse sense is hardly enough, even for horses.

Horse sense is that sense which keeps a horse from betting on the human race.

Horse sense, naturally, dwells in a stable mind.

HOSPITALS

A hospital is a place where if they find you asleep they wake you up to give you a sleeping pill.

Nurse: "I think he's delirious, doctor. He keeps asking for his wife."

From a South Dakota newspaper: "McCall was said to be resting easily by a hospital nurse."

A woman, talking about her friend in the hospital, said, "She was so ill that they had to feed her inconveniently."

A doctor, to shapely nurse: "Just walk past the patient's bed occasionally—all he needs is a will to live."

Hospital: where many a patient takes a turn for the nurse.

Sign in maternity ward of hospital: NO CHILDREN ALLOWED.

HOTELS

Small boy's definition of a hotel: where you stay when you ain't got no cousins.

Hotel: a place where a guest often gives up good dollars for poor quarters.

Arthur Godfrey asks, "Why are hotel rooms so thin when you sleep and so thick when you listen?"

Wife (opening package): "Darling, how thoughtful. That hotel you stayed at last week sent me a blue nightgown."

HOUSEKEEPING

Groucho Marx tells us that the world is full of men who started out helping girls with their homework—and wound up doing their housework.

Our neighbor and his wife share household duties. She washes the dishes and he breaks them.

Women will understand the complaint of the hostess who said, "No matter how many ash trays I leave around, I still have to empty the carpet."

From an ad in the Birmingham *News*: "It requires no rubbing or scrubbing—just whisk a dam mop across it."

Red Skelton remarked of a certain movie queen: "She's an excellent housekeeper. Every time she's divorced, she keeps the house."

A good housekeeper is one who takes great pains—mostly in the small of the back.

HOUSES

Man passing a new development already beginning to look run down: "Those houses weren't what they were tacked up to be."

Real estate ad from Tennessee paper: "You can't heat this one— nine room and two-bath home."

A man told a real estate salesman, "What we had in mind was something in the ten-to-fifteen thousand dollar range that sells for no more than thirty thousand."

Your equity in the house may be small, but cheer up. If it weren't for the mortgage, you probably wouldn't even own that much.

If the world beats a pathway to your door, the architect must have made a miscalculation.

Attic: the place where you keep things you will never want until you have thrown them away.

253

Homer Phillips reminds us that what it takes to make a house lived in is Sunday.

The young couple down the block call their nursery the "bawlroom."

A penthouse is a type of apartment preferred by people who are fond of high living.

Before the split-level craze, the fellows kept it a secret if they lived over a garage.

An interior decorator suggests a plan evidently on the theory that you inherited your money.

What the modern builder accomplishes may not please you, but, at least, he's doing his split-level best.

The ranch-type house did away with the unsightly clutter in the attic and the basement. Now, it's in the garage.

Stucco—what a lot of house hunters are getting these days.

They call it a "dream house" because it usually costs twice as much as you dreamed it would.

Apartment: a place too small to throw anything except a party.

Window screen: a device for keeping flies in the house.

HULA HOOP

The hula hoop craze spread to the Far East—America's revenge for Asiatic flu.

HUMAN NATURE

Inferiority complexes would be fine if the right people had them.

A person we'd like to meet: a hostess who doesn't insist on introducing us to people we ought to know.

It's easier to understand human nature by bearing in mind that almost everybody thinks he's an exception to most rules.

One good thing about an introvert—he spends all of his time minding his own business.

Luck: what enables another fellow to succeed where you have failed.

254

Meddler: one who suffers from an interferiority complex.

Man may not be able to live by bread alone, Bill Gold says, but he notices that some folks seem to get by pretty well on crust.

Billy Rose once observed that "It's hard for a fellow to keep a chip on his shoulder if you allow him to take a bow."

Man, speaking of an associate with a cold personality, "He's a chip off the old glacier."

The division between the sexes, Hy Sheridan believes, is more than balanced by the multiplication.

Some people are good losers and others can't act.

For every woman who makes a fool out of a man there is another woman who makes a man out of a fool.

No two people are alike and both of them are glad of it.

A neurotic is a person who, when you ask him how he feels, tells you.

Poise is the power to raise the eyebrows instead of the roof.

Nuisance: a man you like better the more you see him less.

Dorothy Parker once quipped, "People are more fun than anybody."

A lot of people do the right thing too late or the wrong thing too soon.

What makes men and rivers crooked is following the line of least resistance.

Human nature is what makes a man find time to do the things he wants to do.

Morton Thompson believes that "the trouble with human nature is that there are too many people connected with it."

Nothing works out right. In a town where you can park as long as you want to, you don't want to.

Woman, describing another, "It takes all kinds of people to make a world, but she's the kind that ought to go somewhere and make one of her own."

Trade secrets—that's what women do.

Average man: the man you see everywhere except in your mirror.

Tom Masson reminds us that the best time to study human nature is when nobody else is present.

"Not even Dale Carnegie could help that fellow," said Burl Ives of an actor. "He bored me to death, even though he was talking about me."

People always want something new. If TV had been invented before radio, they'd rush out to buy that new invention that does away with unsightly pictures.

Ilka Chase told of a fellow "who said we were trying to make a fool of him, and I could only murmur that the Creator had beat us to it."

HUMAN RELATIONS

Kindness is one thing you can't give away. It always comes back.

Success in dealing with other people is like making rhubarb pie— use all the sugar you can and then double it.

HUMOR

A gagman is a person who when he dies is at his wit's end.

There are two sides to every story—one for mixed company and one for the men.

Mother always laughs at Dad's jokes—not because they are clever but because she is.

A joke is proof that the good do not die young.

Sense of humor: what a woman often shows in the choice of a husband.

Why is it? The harder you work at building up your funny story at a party, the more likely it will fall flat.

It's a wise crack that knows it's own father.

Milton Berle says that every humorist is an exhumerist.

Women have a keen sense of humor. The more you humor them, the better.

The lack of a sense of humor may make a person very funny.

Did you hear about the television comedian who went from gags to riches.

Comic relief: when the life of the party goes home.

HUMORIST

A professional humorist, Irvin S. Cobb once said, is a person who has a good memory—but hopes others haven't.

HUNCH

Hunch: what you call an idea that you're afraid is wrong.

HUNTING

A prominent display in the Van Patrick living room was a moose-head—but it was hung upside down. Mrs. Van Patrick's explanation was, "Papa shot it while it was lying flat on its back."

Almost any hunter's wife knows that a bird in the hand is worth about $15 a pound.

A hunter climbed into a tree so nobody would take him for a deer. It worked, too—he was shot for a bear.

A careless pheasant hunter crawled through the fence with his gun cocked. He is survived by his wife, three children—and a pheasant.

HUSBANDS

A husband is a man who wishes he had as much fun when he is out as his wife thinks he does.

Husband: a man who exchanges a bushel of fun for a peck of trouble.

Woman to neighbor: "This is the first season I've had the screens up in time to do any good. Bert didn't get around to taking them down."

Our idea of an early bird is one who gets up to serve his wife breakfast in bed.

Sometimes a man pulls the wool over the wife's eyes with the wrong yarn.

One man says he always has the last words with his wife when he leaves in the morning and it is "Oh, don't get up!"

Most men have two sides to them—the side their wives know, and the side they think their wives know.

Any man who thinks he's more intelligent than his wife is married to a smart woman.

Tip to lawn mowers: To distinguish between weeds and flowers, cut them all down. If they come up again, they're weeds.

Backyard conversation: "My husband would never chase another woman. He's too fine, too decent—too old."

It's better to have a husband who comes in handy around the house than one who comes in unexpectedly.

One way for the husband to get that last word in is to apologize.

Some husbands buy expensive perfume as truce juice.

Give a husband enough rope—and he'll want to skip.

Every man knows how a wife should be managed—but few seem able to act on the knowledge.

One husband explains that his wife is leading a double life—hers and his.

The man who says his wife can't take a joke forgets himself.

He met misfortune like a man—he blamed it on his wife.

Music-minded husband: one who goes out fit as a fiddle and comes in at night tight as a drum.

A wife told her thoroughly cowed husband: "Keep quiet when I'm interrupting."

The man who doesn't know his own strength should become better acquainted with his wife.

An old-fashioned husband is one who expects his wife to help him with the dishes.

The average man stacks up like this: Around chest, 40—around waist, 44—around golf course, 98—around home, 0.

258

A husband is a man who lays down the law to his wife and accepts all of the amendments.

Henpecked husband: one who wears the pants at home—under the apron.

A husband is what's left of a sweetheart after the nerve has been killed.

HUSTLE

The man who brags about sitting on top of the world might remember that it turns every twenty-four hours.

HYPOCHONDRIAC

Hypochondriac: a woman who hates to hear how well she looks.

HYPOCRITE

Our idea of a hypocrite is a man who prays on Sunday and on his neighbors the rest of the week.

A hypocrite is a fellow who isn't himself on Sundays.

IDEAS

Idea: a funny little thing that won't work unless you do.

Man is ready to die for an idea, provided that idea is not quite clear to him.

Ideas are very much like children—your own are wonderful.

Have you ever noticed that the smaller the ideas, the bigger words you need to express them?

Tom Pease, speaking of a certain man, said: "If there's an idea in his head it's in solitary confinement."

IGNORANCE

There's one thing to be said of ignorance—it sure causes a lot of interesting arguments.

The difference between most of us is that we are ignorant on different subjects.

A conference is a group of people with no information who pool their ignorance.

ILLNESS

Convalescent: a person who is not well but who is better than he was when he was worse than he is now.

"Are you homesick?" the nurse asked the little girl who was crying in the hospital, and the child answered, "No, I'm sick right here."

A chronic invalid is one who has every disease and ailment described by television announcers.

Wife, outside husband's bedroom door, to doctor: "I'm worried, doctor. He hasn't moaned or complained once."

IMAGINATION

Imagination is what makes the average man think he can run the business better than the boss.

Daydream: being lost in thought because you are a stranger there.

Ideas have to be hitched as well as hatched.

Imagination is what makes a politician think he's a statesman.

If you build a better mousetrap, chances are that you'll catch better mice.

Imagination: something that sits up with a wife when her husband's out late.

Imagination is what makes you think you're having a wonderful time when you're really only spending money.

It takes very little to capture a man's imagination—especially when the right girl is wearing it.

We've always imagined this would be an amusing sight: an absent-minded nudist striking a match.

Imagination was given man to compensate for what he is not, and a sense of humor was provided to console him for what he is.

260

IMITATION

Children are natural mimics. They act like their parents in spite of every effort to teach them good manners.

A boy and his little brother told a stranger that the smaller one would imitate a chicken for a dime and the man answered, "Will he cackle?" and the older boy said, "Heck, no. He'll eat a worm."

IMMORTALITY

Two angels were sitting on a cloud, chatting idly. Finally one said, "Do you believe in the heretofore?"

IMPATIENCE

Funny thing: a man will sit in one spot without catching a fish for three hours and then raise the dickens if his wife is five minutes late in fixing supper.

IMPORTANCE

Halo: what every average man thinks he has when he has a swelled head.

It is easy to be the most important citizen in town. The difficulty comes in finding a town small enough.

IMPRESSIONS

If we could see ourselves as others see us, we'd never speak to them again.

INCOME

When you see red, start living within your income.

Income these days is something you cannot live without or within.

Raise: the increase you get just before going a little more into debt.

A small child asked his father if he had any work around the place by which he could replenish his finances, and his father said he could think of nothing. "Then," answered the kid, "how about putting me on relief?"

"I'm living so far beyond my income," H. H. Munro says, "that we may almost be said to be living apart."

Folks who try to live within their income are just trying to mess up our prosperity.

Too often we live beyond our means to impress people who live beyond their means to impress you.

Kathleen O'Dell reminds us that about the middle of April even the dullest minds make some clever deductions.

Man, on filling out his income tax form: "Who said you couldn't be wounded by a blank?"

Many a taxpayer feels that he is being fined for reckless thriving.

Income-tax expert: someone whose fee is the amount he saves you in making out your tax.

It's along in April that we discover that we owe most of our success to Uncle Sam.

Victor Borge's explanation of how he left Las Vegas with all his salary: "All work and no play."

Practically every husband would be satisfied with the income his wife hopes the neighbors think he has.

Frances Rodman says that two can live as cheaply as one, but it takes both of them to earn enough to do it.

Arthur Godfrey points out that it isn't too hard to live on a small income if you don't spend too much trying to keep it a secret.

Today's cheerful thought: living within your income may be hard, but living without it would be a lot worse.

When Victor Borge, whose taxable earnings are among the top in show business, was paid $175,000 for a TV show, he quipped: "It's the kind of money Uncle Sam has always dreamed I'd make."

"From what I understand," a man wrote in a letter of complaint to the Atlanta Internal Revenue Service office, "that which you want me to send you I don't have at all."

A newlywed was filling out his income-tax return, and in the section marked "Exemption claimed for children" he wrote, "Watch this space."

Rumors are that next year's income-tax forms will contain only three questions: How much money have you? Where is it? How soon can we get it?

INDIGNATION

Moral indignation: jealousy with a halo.

INDISPENSABILITY

When Thomas Jefferson presented his credentials as U. S. Minister to France, the French premier remarked, "I see that you have come to replace Benjamin Franklin." "I have come to succeed him," corrected Jefferson. "No one can replace him."

INDIVIDUALITY

Individuality is the quality that makes any two children different —especially if one is yours and the other isn't.

INFERIORITY

James Montgomery Flagg, the artist, cured a friend's inferiority complex by telling him, "Anytime you feel as if you're neglected, just think of Whistler's father."

INFERIORS

When a woman was described as rude to her inferiors, Dorothy Parker is said to have asked: "Where does she find them?"

INFLATION

Inflation: a drop in the buck.

One thing you can still get for a dime these days is a sneer.

Inflation: another national headache caused by asset indigestion.

Inflation: the art of cutting a dollar bill in half without touching the paper.

Inflation: when you take your money out in a shopping bag and bring home your purchase in your pocket.

We read the papers not so much to see what's going on as what's going up.

INFLUENCE

Influence: what you think you have until you try to use it.

INGENUITY

Ingenuity: getting others to do the work you dislike.

An accomplished wife is the one who knows ten ways to use up stale bread.

INSOMNIA

To the insomniac, it's a great life if you don't waken.

Insomnia: inability to sleep until it's time to get up.

INSTALLMENTS

Teen-ager to chum: "I just love charge accounts—they sure go farther than money."

Theme song for the fellow who buys everything on installments "Backward, Turn Backward, O Time in Thy Flight."

Wealthy people miss one of the greatest thrills in life—paying the last installments.

Most couples these days have a plan for the future. It's known as the installment plan.

The world is so full of a number of things that it's hard to keep up payments on them.

As our neighbor remarked: "Boy am I in debt? I've got more attachments on me than a vacuum cleaner."

The world's greatest humorist continues to be the man who calls them "easy payments."

Time mends all—except the thing you buy on it.

Installment plan: a dollar down and a dollar whenever you fail to dodge the collector.

New cars have the forward look, the panoramic look, the dynamic look, and the motoramic look. But, at least, our old heap has that nice, comfortable, paid-for look.

From a jeweler's ad in the Hot Springs newspaper: "You don't need cash! Instead use our revolting credit plan."

INSULTS

Indignant at an insulting remark, Monty Wooley cried: "Sir! You are speaking of the man I love!"

INSURANCE

Insurance agent asked man, "Do you want a straight life policy?" and the man answered, "No, not exactly. I'd like to play around a little on Saturday night."

Will Rogers once said that life insurance is something you have to buy when you don't want it to have it when you do want it.

The best insurance against automobile accidents is a Sunday nap.

INTELLIGENCE

Human intelligence is millions of years old, but it doesn't seem to act its age.

INTERNATIONAL SITUATION

Insolationist: somebody who's against supporting the rest of the world in the style to which we are accustomed.

Uncle Sam has finally outdone Atlas. He is carrying the world with both hands in his pockets.

The trouble with America's foreign relations is that they are all broke.

A diplomat leads a terrible life. When he isn't straddling an issue, he is dodging one.

Dictatorship: a system of government where everything that isn't forbidden is obligatory.

Bernard Shaw once said that England and America are two countries separated by the same language.

Foreign country: where people tell us Americans to go home and leave them a loan.

Ambassador: a politician who is given a job abroad to get him out of the country.

Today's foreign policy seems to be speak softly and carry a big stick of candy.

Nothing stimulates an interest in foreign affairs like having a son of military age.

Carl Forsstrom says that the only discovery left for the Russians to make is that nobody believes them.

It is said some nations do not know what we stand for. Just about everything is probably the answer.

In a concert of nations there is the question of who plays the wind instruments and who plays second fiddle.

American money not only talks—it does so in almost every foreign tongue.

There are two things the Russians never seem to get: all they want and all they deserve.

Anybody who says he understands international affairs these days is two weeks behind the news.

A Bostonian returned from a visit to the United Nations, and her friend asked her what it was like. "Dreadful," she said, "the place was simply crawling with foreigners."

Cold war: nations flexing their missiles.

Howard F. Friffiths says that a Russian diplomat is an abominable no-man.

We hear there's a popular new television show in Europe. It's called "Break the U. S. Bank."

The United States also seems to have the highest standard of giving in the world.

When you look at the world's debt you are inclined to think that they that take the sword shall perish by the tax.

266

INTUITION

Intuition is what enables a woman to size up a situation in a flash of misunderstanding.

If women's intuition is so all-fired good, why do they ask so many questions?

The only place a woman's intuition doesn't work is when she is trying to decide which way to turn the car at the corner.

Intuition: that strange instinct that tells a woman she is right, whether she is or not.

Feminine intuition is the process by which women draw false conclusions from the absence of facts.

Margaret Evelyn Singleton says that famed intuition, the feminine hunch, never tells what a husband is having for lunch.

Intuition: what enables a woman to put two and two together and come up with any answer that suits her.

Women's intuition is just suspicion that clicks.

Intuition: feminine radar.

INVENTIONS

The automatic washer most young mothers want takes about ten years to perfect and often is named Junior.

Let's cross electric blankets with toasters and pop people out of bed.

A lot of labor-saving devices have been invented for women, but none have ever been as popular as a husband with plenty of money.

INVESTIGATOR

Investigator: busybody on a salary.

INVESTMENTS

Safe investment: doubling your money by folding it once and putting it in your billfold.

Wall Street: a place where people make and lose money that nobody ever had.

INVITATIONS

When a couple is supposed to go anywhere, the woman's first thought it, "What shall I wear?" and the man's, "How can I get out of it?"

JEALOUSY

Jealousy is the friendship one woman has for another.

JEWELRY

Sign in Hollywood jewelry shop: WE HIRE OUT WEDDING RINGS.

JOBS

To some people an occupational hazard means being offered a job when they report to pick up their unemployment check.

The personnel manager asked the young man seeking a job, "What have you done?" and the young fellow answered, "Me? About what?"

A young woman filling out an application blank in a California airplane plant, pondered over the last question, "What are your aims and ambitions?" then wrote, "I want to go as far as my education and sex will allow."

Applying for a position, the young thing came to the question "Marital status," and replied without hesitation, "hopeful."

John J. Plomp says that many a modern woman holds down a job outside the home to get a little leisure time.

Want ad in Nebraska newspaper: "Woman, 21, would like running elevator in office building. Has no experience and would like to begin in low building."

Personnel manager to girl applicant: "We offer several fringe benefits—two weeks' vacation, paid-up insurance, a pension plan, and two unmarried vice-presidents."

JOKES

Some women know their husbands' stories backwards—and tell them that way.

It is interesting to note that of all the comedians and humorists who get off wisecracks on Communism, none of them live in Russia.

Stalemate: a husband who keeps telling the same jokes.

Morey Amsterdam says that he is so corny with his jokes that when he dies they won't bury him—they'll just shuck him.

JUDGMENT

Good and bad luck are synonyms many times for good and bad judgment.

Good judgment comes from experience, and experience comes from poor judgment.

JURIES

Jury: twelve persons chosen to determine which side has the better lawyer.

Jury foreman: "We find the defendant gorgeous, breathtaking, sweet, lovely—and, oh yes, not guilty."

KINDNESS

One woman to another in a Hollywood night spot: "She's so kind to animals—why, she'd do anything for a mink."

KISSES

To her question—was she the first girl he had ever kissed—he replied: "As a matter of tact, yes."

Bob Hope declares that people who throw kisses are mighty near hopelessly lazy.

KNOWLEDGE

Oddly enough, it's the person who knows everything who has the most to learn.

Most of us carry our own stumbling block around with us. We camouflage it with a hat.

Someone has figured out that the peak years of mental activity must be between the ages of four and eighteen. At four, we know all the questions, and at eighteen, all the answers.

The less a man knows, the easier it is to convince him he knows it all.

Quip heard in Washington, D. C.: "If you're not confused, you're not well informed."

After all, the two most important things to learn are where to get the knowledge you need and how to get along without it.

Some students drink at the fountain of knowledge—others just gargle.

Man describing friend, "He knows so little and knows it so fluently."

In the business world an executive knows something about everything, a technician knows everything about something, and the switchboard operator knows everything.

A philosopher keeps learning more and more about less and less, until finally he knows everything about nothing.

No one is more infuriating than the chap who thinks he knows it all —and does.

John J. Plomp says that you know children are growing up when they start asking questions that have answers.

LADY GODIVA

Lady Godiva was the world's greatest gambler because she put her all on a horse—she didn't win but she showed.

LANGUAGE

Little kid: "The cow says 'moo moo'; the dog says 'bow wow'; the duck says 'quack quack'; and Mommie says 'no, no!' "

A Brooklyn teacher asked student to use the word "bewitches" in a sentence and a boy said, "I'll bewitches in a minute."

And you've heard of the man who was tossed out of the crematory after he walked in and asked, "What's cooking?"

LAUGHTER

Laugh and the world laughs with you. Cry and they say you're drunk.

LAWS

A Western sheriff confiscated a bunch of slot machines on the basis of a law banning the use of steel traps for catching dumb animals.

If you think there ought to be a law, there probably is.

A town in Kansas has this law: "When two trains approach each other on the same track, both shall come to a full stop and neither shall proceed until the other has passed."

LAWNS

The line between properties is never more closely defined than when your neighbor mows his lawn.

LAWYERS

He got his client a suspended sentence—they hung him.

A lawyer is a fellow who steps down when an irresistible force meets an immovable object.

The lawyer was hurt—the ambulance backed up suddenly.

A lawyer is a man who will stay up all night to break a girl's will.

He is indeed a wise lawyer who will have his client appear before a jury of women with three buttons off his coat.

LAZINESS

Even if you are on the right track, you will get run over if you just sit there.

Our yard man is the world's slowest-moving creature. One day, in desperation, I asked, "Joe, is there anything you can do fast?" and he answered, "Yes, sir, I gets tired fast."

A woman approached her husband who was sprawled in an easy chair and asked, "Aren't you afraid your self-winding watch will run down?"

Doing nothing is the most tiresome job in the world because you can't stop and rest.

Sign on Missouri farm: "Attention Hunters—Please Don't Shoot Anything on My Place That Isn't Moving. It May Be My Hired Man."

Some folks never travel far because they plan their course by lassitude and loungetude.

Then there was the lazy man who started taking trombone lessons because it's the only instrument on which you can get anywhere by letting things slide.

One comforting thing about being called a procrastinator is that you'll probably never get around to looking up its meaning.

Some fellows always reach for the stool when the piano is to be moved.

A do-nothing is a man who waits for things to turn up, only to find that his toes do it first.

Idler: a man who likes the parable about the multitude that loafs and fishes.

Easy street is always a dead-end street or a blind alley.

Some folks get up early so as to have more time to loaf.

LEADERSHIP

If you're not afraid to face the music, you may someday lead the band.

The trouble with being a leader today is that you can't be sure whether the people are following you or chasing you.

One man in a thousand is a leader of men. The other 999 are followers of women.

LEARNING

Moron: one who wrinkles his brow while reading the comics.

About all that man has learned in the past twenty-five years is how to work faster, work less, spend more, and die quicker.

LEISURE

There's enough leisure for everybody; trouble is the wrong people seem to have it.

Leisure: the two minutes' rest a man gets while his wife thinks up something for him to do.

LETTERS

Never write to a chorus girl. Those who can't read have lawyers who can.

A New Yorker on vacation received a letter from her mother. On the envelope, in her father's writing, was the notation: "Carried by slow male for three days."

LIBRARIES

Indignant woman: "Sir, will you kindly address me as 'librarian' and not as 'bookie.'"

LIES

A lie is a poor substitute for the truth, but it's the only one discovered to date.

Four-fifths of the lies in the world are told on tombstones, women, and competitors.

LIFE

Millions long for immortality who can't even amuse themselves on a rainy Sunday afternoon.

Matt Weinstock tells of a comment he heard in an office-building elevator: "The only time I believe in reincarnation is five o'clock in the afternoon when all the dead people come to life."

Life is like a taxi—the meter keeps going whether you are getting somewhere or just standing still.

Psychologists believe that no one should keep too much to himself. And so do Uncle Sam's tax collectors.

Things could be worse. Suppose your errors were tabulated and published every day, like those of a ballplayer?

Life for some people is to sow wild oats during the week and then go to church on Sunday and pray for a crop failure.

Life is made up of sleeping, eating, working—and interruptions.

Six things we can never afford: intolerance. indolence, injustice, indifference, intemperance, and ingratitude.

Life is a continuous process of getting used to things we hadn't expected.

LIKES

No one has ever found out which a woman likes best—to hear nice things about herself or awful things about another woman.

LINGUIST

Linguist: a man who has mastered every tongue but his wife's.

LITERATURE

Modern literature may be divided into three types: neurotic, erotic, and tommy-rotic.

The worst thing about banning so many comic books that might be harmful to children is that many adults will be deprived of their main reading matter.

LIVING

Many of us need the prayer of the old Scot, who mostly feared decay from the chin up: "Lord, keep me alive while I'm still living."

Too many men conduct their lives on the cafeteria plan—self-service only.

We should all live within our means—even if we have to borrow to do it.

It's getting so the kind of living the world owes you today isn't the kind worth collecting.

To live happily in the country one must have the soul of the poet, the mind of a philosopher, the simple tastes of a hermit—and a good station wagon.

LIVING COSTS

After the customer complained at the high cost of the mink, the salesman said, "Bear in mind, madam, the cost of living for minks has risen, too."

Overheard on a bus: "I hope they don't raise the standard of living any higher. I can't afford it now."

LOANS

You can always borrow all the money you want if you can prove you don't need it.

A friend once asked W. C. Fields for a loan of a dollar and the comedian replied, "I'll see what my lawyer says—and if he says yes, I'll get another lawyer."

Acquaintance: a fellow we know well enough to borrow from.

LOGIC

A man who thinks he can convince his wife he's right soon finds out he's wrong.

LONELINESS

Nobody is lonelier than the parents of teen-age children in a one-car family.

Loneliness, declares Harold W. Ruopp, is not so much a matter of isolation as of insulation.

LONGING

For every girl who yearns for that schoolgirl complexion, there's a man who longs for that schoolboy digestion.

LOSING

You're a good loser if you can grip the winner's hand without wishing it was his throat.

LOVE

A man, hearing a sermon on love, told his minister at the close of the service, "I'd just like to see you love my neighbors."

Love may not be blind. Perhaps there are just times when it can't bear to look.

Love is a form of government under the two-party system.

Love may not make the world go around, but it manages to make millions of phonograph records do so.

Platonic love is like a gun that seems not to be loaded but always is.

It was a case of love at first sight. She first saw him in his Cadillac convertible.

Love is the feeling that makes a man think almost as much of a girl as he thinks of himself.

Take a young man of twenty—all he thinks about is love. Take a middle-aged man—all he does about love is think.

LUCK

The less luck some people have, the more they believe in it.

Luck is when preparedness catches up with opportunity.

Lighting three cigarettes on a match isn't unlucky—it's unlikely.

You cannot be a lucky dog if you spend all your time growling.

Did you hear of the guy who'd been unlucky all his life, but things changed—when they dug his grave they struck oil.

LUXURY

A luxury is anything the neighbors have which we can't afford.

MAGAZINE

Confession magazine: a periodical in which people write their wrongs.

MAGICIAN

One magician said to another, "What happened to that pretty wife of yours you used to saw in half in your act?" and the fellow replied, "Oh, she's living in Boston and Seattle."

MAIDS

The new maid told her employer, "I don't use the vacuum, ma'am— it spoils the television programs for me."

MAIL

A good husband is one who feels in his pockets every time he passes a mailbox.

Dead-letter office: a husband's pocket.

Absentee: the last person to read a post card.

MAN

Connie Moore says that "Man is a perpetual-notion machine—and it's always the same notion."

A man is known by the company he keeps avoiding.

Man is an individual who spends most of his life looking for an ideal woman—and in the meantime gets married.

The typical man is the only animal who can be skinned more than once.

A man is a person who wishes he were as wise as he thinks his wife thinks he is.

A boy becomes a man when he stops asking his father for money and requests a loan.

MANNERS

The test of good manners is to be able to put up pleasantly with bad ones.

We expect our children to learn good table manners without seeing any.

Cannibal chief to son, "How often have I told you not to talk with someone in your mouth?"

Etiquette: learning to yawn with your mouth closed.

It's easy to identify the children whose parents ignore child psychology. Just look for youngsters with manners.

A polite man today is one who offers a lady a seat when he gets off the bus.

Social tact is making your company feel at home, even though you wish they were.

MARRIAGE

Marriage: a business in which the husband is the silent partner.

A woman, eighty-six, and a man, seventy-eight, were married the other day but friends didn't throw rice. They threw vitamins.

It isn't tying himself to one woman that a man dreads when he thinks of marrying—it's separating himself from all the others.

Some men are perfectly content to have an angel for a wife; then they get lonesome and marry again.

Many wives have been awakened from love's young dream with a snore.

Take your choice—be an old maid and look for a husband every day or marry him and look for him every night.

Marriage is a romance in which the hero dies in the first chapter.

It is impossible for a man to make a fool of himself—if he has a wife.

Speaking of a marriage, Jackie Gleason said, "When they were married, they were mispronounced man and wife."

278

One of our friends had an impediment in his speech—every time he opened his mouth, his wife interrupted.

A bachelor remarked, "I know marriage is a matter of give and take, but so far I haven't been able to find anybody who'll take what I have to give."

In some parts of India a man doesn't know his wife until he marries her. Same here.

They say he married her because her uncle left her a million dollars. He claims he would have married her no matter who had left it to her.

When a man changes his mind as much as a woman, chances are he's married to her.

A happy marriage results when both parties get better mates than they deserve.

Even the men who aren't born meek get married and get that way.

Marriage encourages thrift, says a banker. Demands is the word.

Marriage is the transition from a bachelor apartment to a dog house.

Poetic justice is when a man who'd rather play golf than eat marries a woman who'd rather play bridge than cook.

Girls, it is simply impossible to be married to the same man for fifty years. After the first twenty-five years, he's just not the same man.

You've probably heard of the Chinese sisters who never married. They were Tu Yung Tu, Tu Dum Tu, and No Yen Tu.

A man was asked, "Does your wife pick your suits?" and he replied, "No, just the pockets."

Marriage is a system in which a wife makes allowance for her husband's shortcomings, and the husband for his wife's outgoings.

"Keep your eyes open before marriage," Benjamin Franklin advised, "and half shut afterward."

Dorothy Dix once received this note from a reader: "I would like you to help me as you have helped others in trouble. The trouble is I'm married."

The honeymoon is over when the dog brings your slippers and your wife barks at you.

Sign on steps of courthouse: "This way for marriage licenses—Watch your step."

Sign on door of Marriage License Bureau: "Out to lunch. Think it over."

Don Marshall believes that most domestic quarrels could be checked by a timely use of arms.

The honeymoon is over when a husband doesn't notice his wife has something new until he gets a bill for it.

Wife to friend: "When we were first married, we hit it off swell. But as we were leaving the church . . . ."

Marriage license: a treaty pledging two powers to coo-existence.

Hal Chadwick says that it only takes a few years of marriage to change necking to pecking.

The art of being a good life-mate is to make molehills out of domestic mountains.

A married man is never interrupted when he talks in his sleep.

Yawning is a device of nature to enable husbands to open their mouths.

When a woman marries she gives up the attention of several men for the inattention of one.

Tolerance is the quality that keeps a new bride aware that she must not reform her husband right away.

There's nothing like marriage to break up a good romance.

By the time he whispers, "We were made for each other," she's already planning alterations.

A woman who makes a match for her daughter usually intends to referee it as well.

When there is a meeting of minds in a marriage, the wife's generally presides.

The wise husband meets a marital crisis with a firm hand—full of candy or flowers.

Marriage is another institution that offers only on-the-job training.

Two people can live as cheaply as one what?

280

Weldon Owens reminds us that a man who thinks that marriage is a 50-50 proposition doesn't understand two things—women and fractions.

Before they are married, a man holds an umbrella over a woman's head to keep her from getting wet; afterward, to keep her hat from getting wet.

Hal Boyle observes that the difference between marriage and a good circus is two rings.

Young lady: "I hear that Doris is engaged to an X-ray specialist. I wonder what he sees in her?"

There's one advantage of being married: you can't make a fool of yourself without knowing it.

The rich man employs a butler, a valet, a secretary, a laundress, a cook, and a housekeeper. The poor man just gets married.

King Solomon had one hundred wives so that he could come home from a hard day at the office and find at least one in a good humor.

When a man isn't a mouse, his wife keeps her trap shut.

Overheard on the cocktail circuit: "Marriage was the first union to defy management."

The wise wife asks for something she knows her husband can't afford so she can compromise on what she really wants.

Old-fashioned girls learned to cook to find a way into a man's heart, but modern girls thaw an easier way.

Said old Zeke the mountaineer to his child-bride, "Another report card like this, Fanny Mae, and I'm gonna git a divorce from you!"

The honeymoon is over when the wife complains about the noise her husband makes while fixing his own breakfast.

Sizes are often deceiving. Sometimes a woman's thumb has a man under it.

Solomon: one who loved not wisely but too many.

We used to hear about youngsters running away from home to get married. Nowadays, they get married and run back home.

Altar: where a woman stops making over a man and starts making him over.

Anniversary: the day on which you forget to buy a present.

"You are wearing your wedding ring on the wrong finger," one young thing mentioned to another. "Yes, I know," said the second woman, "I married the wrong man."

Sammy Kaye says that after all is said and done, it's usually the wife who has said it and the husband who has done it.

The trouble with a lot of marriages is that the husband is so busy bringing home the bacon that he forgets the applesauce.

Some people marry for love, and some marry for money, but many seem to marry for a short time.

Overheard: "They're starting out with just what they have to have— a bed, a stove, and a TV set."

The chain of wedlock is so heavy that it takes two to carry it— sometimes three.

A man picks a wife the same way an apple picks a farmer.

Marriages may be made in heaven, but man is responsible for the maintenance work.

Matrimony is an institution of learning in which a man losses his bachelor's degree without acquiring a master's.

Marriage entitles a woman to the protection of a strong man who steadies the ladder for her while she paints the kitchen ceiling.

It takes two to make a marriage—a girl and an anxious mother.

Bridegroom: a guy who began handing out a line and ended by walking it.

In marriage, like boxing, the preliminaries are often more entertaining than the main event.

Ken Kraft reminds us that marriage is like a door hinge. It permits great freedom of movement as long as you aren't going anywhere.

"I'm sure I heard a mouse squeak," a woman whispered in the wee small hours. Her husband groaned, "What do you want me to do—get up and oil it?"

MATURITY

You are only young once, but you can stay immature indefinitely.

MEALS

"If I ask my husband any questions at breakfast," one wife complained, "I have to take a lot for grunted."

MEDICINE

Richard Armour says that anyone who can swallow a pill at a drinking fountain deserves to get well.

MEDITATION

Every executive should sit back and meditate at some time during the day—and try not to snore.

Think twice before you speak—especially if you intend to say what you think.

MEETINGS

Our hero is the man who moves that the minutes of the last meeting be accepted without reading them.

MEMORY

Did you hear about the poor fellow who had a good memory for faces until he joined a nudist colony?

If you want to test your memory, try to recall the things that worried you last Monday.

A memory expert is a woman who has once been told another woman's right age.

Nothing makes a man forget a passing fancy like something fancier.

A woman is perturbed by what a man forgets—and by what a woman remembers.

Our idea of futility is the elephant who went away to forget.

Franklin P. Jones reminds us that "Nothing's more responsible for the good old days than a poor memory."

Sign in Nebraska post office: "Have you mailed your wife's letter?"

Olin Miller says that of all liars, the smoothest and most convincing is the memory.

An executive found this message on his desk: "Your wife called. Wanted to remind you of something which she couldn't remember but thought you would."

"There I was—forced down on a desert island with a beautiful red-head," the man told a friend and the friend asked, "What did you do for food?" The storyteller said, "Darned if I can remember."

MEN

Time tells on a man—especially a good time.

History has recorded only one indispensable man: Adam.

Baldness is a condition whose advantage is that, when you expect callers, all you have to do is straighten your tie.

Description of a Hollywood wolf: a very fine fellow once you get to "no" him.

Men may be more intelligent than women, but you never see a woman marrying a dumb man because of his shape.

Married men are said to be more inventive than single men. They have to be.

Some men are like a watch—hard to regulate.

This is the land of opportunity. That's why so many married men get into trouble.

Men can be divided into three classes: the handsome, the intellectual, and the great majority.

South Sea Islander's comment on bald-headed man, "Old fellow top-side no grass."

Counting sheep is no fun. Most men would rather count calves.

A man will always pay a fancy figure for checking his hat.

A man will squander money on buckets of paint, fishing tackle, or automobile gadgets, then knock the family out to reduce the heating bill ten cents.

One Internal Revenue clerk received an unusual inquiry this year.

"Can I put under charity," asked the taxpayer, "money spent for clothes to replace good suits that my wife gives to rummage sales?"

Richard Armour says that women have their permanent waves but all that men ask for is permanent hair.

One nice thing about being a man is that you don't have to kiss someone who hasn't shaved for two days.

MEN AND WOMEN

In the battle of the sexes, you never meet what you can truly call a conscientious objector.

MEN'S STYLES

One of our friends has a light summer suit made of that ever-durable miracle fiber—called wool.

MENTAL HEALTH

Mental health has become such an issue today that people go crazy in pursuit of it.

MERMAID

Mermaid: not enough fish to fry and not enough woman to love.

MESSAGE

A man in mountains of Arizona found an Indian sending up smoke signals. When he asked how big a fire he usually built, the Indian said, "It all depends on whether it's local or long distance call."

METEOROLOGIST

Meteorologist: a man who can look into a girl's eyes and tell whether.

MIDDLE AGE

When the young complain to you about the old and the old complain to you about the young—you're middle-aged.

Middle-age spread: the destiny that ends our shapes.

The forties are that period when both your mind and your waistline reach their full capacity.

Middle age is when you can do just as much as ever, but don't.

Middle-aged: someone ten years older than you are.

You've reached middle age when it's the doctor who tells you to slow down instead of a policeman.

Jules Henry Marr says that middle age is when you go all out and end up all in.

Middle age: thin on the top and not on the bottom.

Someone reminds us that middle age is when you look forward to a dull evening.

Noel Wical says that all you have to do to lick middle age is to keep looking like your old self without feeling it.

Middle age: when you divide your time between worrying how your children will turn out and when they'll turn in.

Middle age: when you're grounded for several days after flying high for one night.

It's called middle age because that's where it usually shows most.

A man has reached middle age, Franklin P. Jones says, when the girl he winks at thinks he has something in his eye.

Dan Bennett says that middle age is when a daily dozen is followed by several days of daily doesn't.

You've reached middle age when all you exercise is caution.

A man is getting old when he inspects the food and not the waitress.

One thing about getting along in years—you feel your corns more than your oats.

Maturity is the time of life when, if you had the time, you'd have the time of your life.

MIDDLE CLASS

Middle class is that strata of society which isn't rich enough to scorn gossip nor poor enough to escape it.

286

MINDS

Minds, like streams, may be so broad that they are shallow.

A mind, like a parachute, functions only when open.

Every husband should have a mind of his own so that he can figure out how he would have handled the situation if he had had anything to say about it.

One of our friends has a mind like a water bug—it just skates over the surface.

MINISTERS

Benjamin Franklin observed many years ago that "none preaches better than the ant, and she says nothing."

A man usually considers it a good Sunday sermon when he feels that the minister didn't refer directly to him.

We like the preacher who said, "I have learned that it does not make a sermon immortal to make it everlasting."

Clergyman: a man who preaches that the best way to rise to the heights is to stay on the level.

A preacher is about the only person we know who can keep dozens of women quiet for an hour.

A church member, describing her minister, said, "Six days of the week he's invisible and one day of the week he's incomprehensible."

Minister to congregation: "I have always said that the poor are welcome in this church, and I see by the collection plate that they have come."

He was said to be a great preacher—at the close of every sermon there was a great awakening.

A minister who conducts a gospel program on a Wichita station reads excerpts from listeners' letters of encouragement, taking care to tell the donation which accompanied each one. Once he resumed, "And now, dear funds . . . ."

The sermon went on and on and the preacher asked, "What more, my friends, can I say?" and a voice from the back of the church said, "Amen."

A Methodist minister, retiring, happily announced the first permanent home "Dunmovin."

"I feel so sorry for Rev. Smith," a man told his neighbor. "He bought a used car but he doesn't have the vocabulary to drive it."

From a New England newspaper: "Bishop Harlow surprised the congregation of the Episcopal Church last Sunday. The Bishop preached a fine sermon."

From a Montana church bulletin: "We regret to report that the minister does not plan to be away over any Sunday this summer."

MINORITY RULE

A perfect example of minority rule is a baby in the house.

MINUTE MEN

The minute men of today are those who can make it to the refrigerator and back with a sandwich while the commercial is on.

MISER

Miser: one who's perfectly content to let the rest of the world go buy.

MISFORTUNE

A pious friend was telling a Quaker of the misfortunes suffered by a poor relation. "I certainly did feel sorry for him," said the man sadly. "Yes, friend," replied the Quaker, "but did thee feel in the right place—in thy pocket?"

MISTAKES

Another thing that is often opened by mistake is a charge account.

To err is human—to keep it quiet is not.

If you can manage to make mistakes when nobody is looking, you stand a fair chance of becoming successful.

The man who invented the eraser had the human race pretty well sized up.

The biggest mistake you can make is always to be afraid you'll make one.

Learn from the mistakes of others. You can't live long enough to make them all yourself.

If you say the wrong word at the wrong time, you'll understand about the fellow who asked a woman, "How's your husband standing the heat?" and she answered, "I don't know—he's been dead for two years."

Man falling through the air from an airplane: "Gad, that wasn't the washroom after all."

MIX-UPS

Some people are like blotters. They soak it all in but get it backwards.

Somehow or other, wrong cards were attached to two imposing floral wreaths at the florist shop. The one that went to a men's store moving to an expensive new building read "Deepest Sympathy," and one intended for the funeral of the town's leading banker read "Good Luck in Your New Location."

On a North Dakota radio station, an announcer reported: "The local Boy Scout troop had a cook out and cramp session over the weekend."

MODERN AGE

Nowadays, when the bread fails to rise, there's something wrong with the toaster.

Old saw rewritten: What goes up must come down unless it orbits.

It takes a lot of jack to lift a modern car and to raise a modern kid.

Yes, modern women still build castles in the air, but nowadays they are supplied with things like automatic heating, TV, electric washers and dryers, and electronic ovens.

This is the age of chiselry.

A modern mother is one who is sure her children are smarter than their father.

It's nice to have these modern time-saving appliances in the kitchen. But you have to get up thirty minutes earlier to plug in everything.

Two things can worry you these days—one, that things may never get back to normal, and the other, that they already have.

One good thing about an electric razor is that nobody has yet found a way to sharpen pencils with it.

Man to co-worker, "I was reading in this atomic age a scientist says they'll soon be able to heat an apartment with one lump of coal," and his companion snorted, "My landlord has been doing that for years."

The modern child, hearing the Cinderella story, inquires whether when the pumpkin turns into a golden coach, it's straight income or capital gain.

MODERN GIRL

It's just as hard to find a needle in a girl's hands today as in a haystack.

MODERN LIFE

Ashes to ashes and dust to dust—if cigarettes don't get you, the fallout must.

MODERN TIMES

It might be interesting to note that about the time the old-fashioned back-yard hammock went out, ulcers came in.

MONEY

Women, we think, are the reasons that even love sometimes needs refinancing.

They say that a paper can be used to keep a person warm. Yes, we had a mortgage that kept us sweating for twenty years.

A financier is always ready to back his decisions with your last cent.

Budget: an attempt to live below your yearnings.

Money is like fertilizer—what good is it unless you spread it around?

Wife to husband at the airport, "Darling, be sure to write, even if it's only a check."

Money is what you swap for what you think will make you happy.

The real trouble with money is that you can't use it more than once.

Wife to husband: "All right, I admit I like to spend money. But just name one other extravagance."

Everybody tells you that you can't take it with you, but hardly anybody mentions the fact that you can't travel far without it.

Millionaire: a billionaire after he pays his taxes.

It seems that economists have just discovered a simple truth that Dad has known for years: Money is tight.

A joint checking account is never overdrawn by the wife—it is just underdeposited by the husband.

Money can be lost in more ways than won.

Women prefer men who have something tender about them—especially the legal kind.

What with withholding taxes, payroll deductions, and now credit cards, ordinary dough will soon join the dodo.

The only time most of us hear money talking is when it's doing a countdown before taking off.

When money talks she doesn't miss a word.

A dollar is something else that has more "bying" power now than ever before.

Hush money: the proof that silence is golden.

Of course money isn't everything. It isn't plentiful, for instance.

If money talks, why isn't it doing some explaining?

And there was the woman who entered the bank and told the cashier: "I'd like to open a joint account with someone who has money."

You've probably never thought about it, but we imagine no one has more trouble keeping up with the Joneses than old man Jones.

Hal Chadwick says that check stubs offer a convenient record of how you managed to overdraw your account.

Our idea of breaking even is to owe money to as many people as you don't owe.

Latest definition of cash: the poor man's credit card.

Sometimes a man's deeds can be a worry to him—especially if they are heavily mortgaged.

Classified ad in Taos, New Mexico, paper: "For Sale: Summer home on Red River. Away from road. So quiet you can hear the notes fall due at the bank."

Hard cash—the softest thing to fall back on.

Earl Wilson says that about the only thing that'll give you more for your money now than ten years ago is the penny scale at the drugstore.

Anybody who gets more for his money than he used to is probably weighing himself.

Money gets around so fast these days that the term "jumping jack" has taken on a new meaning.

Another reason you can't take it with you—it goes before you do.

The dime isn't entirely worthless—it still makes a pretty good screw driver.

The way some people are spending money, you'd think it was going out of style.

A fool and his money—are invited places.

Life is becoming so complicated because too many of us spend money we haven't earned to buy things that we don't need to impress a lot of people we don't like.

A fool and his money may part, but they were lucky to get together in the first place.

The man who doesn't know where his money goes obviously isn't married.

Save your dollar bill. It may be worth a dollar some day.

One of the main things about money is that you can choose your own misery.

Sure, money talks, but who can hold it long enough to start a conversation?

The best way to jingle coins in your pocket is to shake a leg.

If money did grow on trees, it would be just another surplus for the government to worry about.

Reactions you aren't likely to hear: "Sorry, I can't accept a raise. It would put me in a higher bracket."

One of our friends says, "Money isn't the best thing in the world. I just happen to like it best."

A man told his friend, "My wife dreamed last night that she was married to a millionaire," and the other replied, "You're lucky. Mine thinks that in the daytime."

Small boy to father: "Sure, I know the value of a dollar—that's why I asked for two."

Billion dollars—just a drop in the budget.

"Money talks" is an obsolete phrase. It goes without saying.

When money talks it is hardly ever interrupted.

Lots of people spend time making money and then spend money killing time.

"Maybe you can't take it with you," Pearl Bailey reminds us, "but where can you go without it?"

A nickel goes a long way today. You can carry it around for weeks before you can find something you can buy with it.

There seems to be plenty of money in the country, but everyone owes it to everyone else.

Money is one commodity that doesn't grow on sprees.

Our idea of a millionaire is a man who has so much money he doesn't even know his son is in college.

Say this for pickpockets—they try to keep money in circulation.

Dollars are made by those who are not forever depositing their quarters on easy chairs.

Road sign in Florida: KEEP FLORIDA GREEN — BRING MONEY.

You could get more for ten cents years ago—dimes sure have changed.

Many a man's wallet would be flatter if it weren't so full of credit cards.

Even if money did grow on trees, some people wouldn't shake a limb to get it.

Money is something you'd get on beautifully without, if other people weren't so crazy about it.

The average man knows that money isn't everything. The problem is to convince his wife that everything isn't money.

Wife to husband, "You keep on saying money isn't worth much these days and then you make a fuss when I spend some of it."

The man who sent his wife to the bank and kissed his money good-by wasn't so absent-minded.

Elastic currency is that which seems to shrink when we buy and stretch when we sell.

Waiting to see the manager of a finance company in California, a woman studied a mounted swordfish on the wall and said, "I've read about loan sharks, but this is the first time I've seen one."

Woman to neighbor: "I've just been to the bank to get some money. I really like banks—they never ask you what in the world you're going to do with the money."

A child commented on piggy banks as follows: "They teach children to become misers and parents to become robbers."

MONOTONY

Monotony is a form of marriage in which a man can have only one wife.

MOODS

Letter from soldier overseas: "If I sound blue, it isn't that I got up on the wrong side of the bed. It's that I got up on the wrong side of the world."

MORALE

Admiral Ben Moreel says that morale is when your hands and feet keep working together while your head says it can't be done.

MORONS

Did you hear of the moron who jumped off the bus backward when he heard a man say, "Let's grab his seat when he gets off."

Then there's the one about the moron who thought steel wool was the fleece from a hydraulic ram.

MOTEL

A little girl, just back from a vacation, described a motel as follows: "All the rooms except the bathroom are in the living room."

MOTHERS

Proud mother, holding infant for neighbor to see: "He's eating solids now—keys, newspapers, pencils."

Squaw (missing child as she walks into wigwam): "I could have sworn I was wearing him when I came in."

Did you hear about the Louisville mother who speaks of her nursery as the Inner Spanctum?

A mother's life is not a happy one. She is torn between the fear that some designing female will carry off her son and that no designing male will do the same for her daughter.

A lot of mothers in the last generation had their daughters vaccinated in places they wrongly thought would never show.

What a mother should save for a rainy day is patience.

Many a mother's life is disorganized around her children.

Mother: a woman who takes twenty years to make a man of her boy so that another woman can make a fool of him in twenty minutes.

Mother's definition of leisure: the spare time a woman has in which she can do some other kind of work.

MOTHERS-IN-LAW

Mother-in-law: what you inherit when you marry.

A mother-in-law is a woman who is never outspoken.

My mother-in-law is coming to see us—another mouth to heed.

A San Francisco executive excused himself from a meeting one afternoon with the explanation: "My mother-in-law is arriving on the four o'clock broom."

MOTTOS

Sign on wall of office: "Keep your eye on the ball, your shoulder to the wheel, your ear to the ground—now, try to work in that position."

MOUNTAIN CLIMBERS

Mountain climbers rope themselves together because there's safety in numbers—also, it keeps the sane ones from going home.

MOVIES

Wife to husband, as they came out of the movie: "It certainly wasn't worth stacking the dishes for!"

An Iowa theater offered this suggestion in an ad for a horror film: "Go with someone you hate."

Nowadays, a movie hero is the guy who sits through it.

A few reels of old vacation films usually put your guests in a traveling mood.

A gunman stuck a gun in the face of the movie cashier and growled, "The picture was horrible—give me everybody's money back."

Rocky Graziano, the boxer, told a crony he'd just seen Ingrid Bergman in *Anesthesia*, and his friend corrected, "You mean *Anastasia*, Rocky," and the boxer countered, "So how come I slept through it?"

The happy ending in some films is the simple fact that the picture has ended.

Sign on theater: Children's Matinee Today. Adults Not Admitted Unless with Child.

Sign on movie marquee: THE SEVENTH VEIL—GREAT EXPECTATIONS.

One small boy to another at wide-screen movie: "Let me know if anything happens on your side."

296

Most movies end just as the couples are about to get married, in order not to show anything brutal.

MUSIC

Song hit: taking an old composition and decomposing it.

Hillbilly singer: one who warbles through his nose by ear.

Quartet: four people who think the other three can't sing.

The sweetest music to any woman's ear is another woman playing second fiddle.

Jukebox: a device for inflicting your musical taste on people who wouldn't give a plugged nickel for it.

Of an operetta, Brooks Atkinson wrote: "The music is not as good as it sounds."

We are gradually reducing the number of illiterates in this country, which makes it harder and harder for writers of popular songs.

Harp: a piano in the nude.

Song writer: a man who can't carry a tune but who can lift a lot of them.

Star Spangled Banner: the song without words.

A sign in the Bronx says: "Piano lessons—special pains given to beginners."

Some people can carry a tune, but they seem to stagger under the load.

Violinist: a fellow who is always up to his chin in music.

Xylophonists must be superstitious—they go round knocking on wood.

A band is a group of musicians who travel in packs for purposes of self-defense.

Did you hear about the French-horn player whose toupee fell into his instrument, and he had to spend the rest of the evening blowing his top?

An ad in a St. Paul newspaper: "For sale, cheap; my son's collection of bebop and rock-and-roll records. If a boy's voice answers the phone, hang up and call later."

A California teacher discovered one of her youngsters singing with great seriousness: "My country, 'tis of thee, sweet land of liberty, of thee I sing; land where my fathers died, land of the pills inside . . . ."

A symphony violinist was was making such terrible faces while playing Brahms that the conductor stopped the orchestra and demanded, "What's the matter with you? Don't you like this piece?" And the man replied "Oh, it isn't that. It's just that I don't like music."

Brad Anderson tells of the music publisher who told his colleague: "I've never heard such corny lyrics, such simpering sentimentality, such repetitious uninspired melody. Man, we've got a hit on our hands!"

Every time we hear a disc jockey playing the top twenty popular tunes, we get the shakes thinking what the bottom twenty must be like.

Coloratura: a singer who carried a tune too far.

Perry Como asked Pearl Bailey, guest star of his TV show, whether she ever sang for the pleasure of singing. She replied, "Well, if you'll examine that musical scale, you'll find it begins and ends with 'dough.' "

Modern music is the kind that is played so fast you can't tell what classical composer is was stolen from.

One man, upon being asked if he played an instrument of any kind, replied, "Only second fiddle at home."

A true music lover is a man who, upon hearing a soprano in the shower, puts his ear to the keyhole.

A stringless violin was displayed in the window of a secondhand store in Chicago with this sign: "This is yours for $35—no strings attached."

Old songs will have to be modernized, so we suggest "Shine On, Harvest Sputnik" or "By the Light of the Silvery Satellite."

A popular song is one that has the happy virtue of making all of us think we can sing.

Classical music is music that threatens now and then to develop another new tune and always disappoints you.

Opera singer: a little aria coming out of a big area.

A four-year-old girl was heard singing *God Bless America* this way: "Stand beside her, and guide her, through the night with a light from a bulb."

Then there was the man who was going to write a drinking song but was never able to get past the first two bars.

News item in Arizona weekly: "Mrs. John Smith and Mrs. Fred Jones sang a duet, 'The Lord Knows Why.'"

Did you hear about the girl who told an over-amorous piano player to keep his dissonance?

News item from Iowa newspaper: "REGULAR WEEKLY BAD CONCERT WEDNESDAY NIGHT."

Theme song of the parachute corps: "It don't mean a thing if you don't pull that string."

Guide to classical music: Applause—a good thing for the amateur to avoid. If you do applaud, chances are it's only the end of the first movement and you'll be the only one in the concert hall who is making a sound.

News item: "The Middleton band director has prepared an appalling program."

Sign on a music shop in California: "Out to lunch. Usually Bach by one. Offenbach earlier."

NAMES

An Indian petitioned a judge in Arizona to give him a shorter name and the judge asked, "What is your name now?" The Indian replied, "Chief Screeching Train Whistle," and upon being asked what new name he would prefer he grunted, "Toots."

Two men were introduced and one said, "Pardon me for not getting up. You see, I'm ailing from arthritis," and the other replied, "Perfectly all right, I'm Goldfarb from Grand Rapids."

O'Brien boasted to a friend, "We named our new daughter Hazel" and the friend replied, "A fine thing; hundreds o' saints to name the child after and you name her after a nut."

Victor Borge, explaining his name, once said: "Actually, my full name was Robert Charles Arthur Victor Borge, but I dropped the first three. I got tired of being called RCA Victor."

NATIONAL AFFAIRS

Klyde Kaliher believes that the trouble with government seems to be too much overhead and too much underhand.

Red Skelton doesn't think we'll ever have a woman President. Then he asks, "What woman would openly admit that she is thirty-five years old?"

We sometimes forget that what the government gives, it must first take away.

Government should be like your stomach—if it's working right, you don't know you have it.

Capital and labor should pull together. We don't mean on the public's leg.

One natural resource, Sidney Brody observes, which is in danger of being completely drained is the taxpayer.

Americans have come to believe that it's easier to vote for something they want than to work for it.

One trouble with government is that it seems to think the individual owes it a living.

Washington should be referred to as The City Bureauful.

Metal plaque on California's twelve-million-ton Shasta Dam reads: "U. S. Government Property. Do not remove."

Calvin Coolidge possessed a sense of humor. One day he awoke from a short nap in the middle of the day, grinned, and asked a friend, "Is the country still here?"

"A census taker," a kid wrote on his quiz, "is a man who goes from house to house increasing the population."

NEED

It's reported that a new embassy attaché in Istanbul cabled home, "For heaven's sake, rush me a dozen Turkish towels."

NEIGHBORS

Enough is what would satisfy us if the neighbors didn't have more.

A little boy called on his next-door neighbor and said, "If that little boy next door ever bothers you practicing the piano, you might try complaining to my mother."

Anything you tell a woman usually goes in one ear and out to the neighbors.

A housewife told a salesman who knocked on her door: "I am not in the market for a vacuum cleaner, but try the Smiths next door. We borrow theirs and it is in terrible condition."

Stephen Schlitzer says, "To cultivate a garden takes too much time and labor; I'd rather live next door to one and cultivate my neighbor."

NERVOUSNESS

It was opening night and an actor asked another, "Are you nervous?" The other said, "Lean on me. I'm a regular Rock of Jello."

Tennessee Ernie described a friend as "being as nervous as a long-tailed cat in a room full of rocking chairs."

Upon entering the room a woman recognized the celebrity who was to address her group pacing madly back and forth. "Are you always nervous before you make a speech?" she asked and he replied, "Nervous! Why, no, I never get nervous." Then she asked, "Then what, may I ask, are you doing in the Ladies' Room?"

NEWS

Quickest ways of spreading news: telegraph, telephone, and tell-a-woman.

Usually the janitor is the last person to hear about a drop in the temperature.

The difference between gossip and news is whether you hear it or tell it.

Television will never supplant the newspaper. You can't fold up a channel and sit down with it beneath you on the grass.

Secret: something which everybody knows but which the small-town newspaper can't publish.

Readers of a Kansas weekly got a jolt recently when it appeared with one page blank save for an apologetic statement in small type: "Don't laugh. We had a helluva time filling the other three pages."

NIGHT CLUBS

Night club: an ash tray with music.

A floor show is something that goes in one eye and out the other.

It was one of those night clubs where they get away with murder and you face the charges.

Overheard in a jammed night club: "I'm so full of penicillin that if I sneeze in here I'm sure to cure somebody."

Accurate report from a night-club press agent: "The crowd was filled to capacity."

Herb Shriner, after a visit to a New York night club, remarked: "This place had a minimum. I don't know what it was, but the girls were wearing it."

A sergeant asked a private where he received such a black eye, and the boy answered, "I went to a dance and was struck by the beauty of the place."

NOISE

A report from a scientific conference is headlined: "DAILY NOISE LEVEL REACHING DANGER POINT." Exactly what we told the kids last night while trying to read the evening paper.

NORMALCY

Two friends were discussing a neighbor who had been thrown from a horse, and one asked the other, "Did old Jim finally get all right?" and the other answered, "No, he ain't all right, but he's back like he used to be."

NOTORIETY

There is only one thing worse than being talked about, and that is not being talked about.

NUCLEAR WEAPONS

Thermonuclear bombs come in three sizes—little ones, medium-sized ones, and where's everybody?

NUDIST

It's a mystery to us what a nudist does with the car keys after he locks the car.

NURSES

In an army hospital, one nurse warned another: "These are the dangerous cases. Almost well!"

OBSTACLES

If Columbus had turned back, no one could have blamed him, but no one would have remembered him.

OCCUPATIONS

Say this for flagpole sitters: they never lie down on the job.

Janitor: a floor flusher.

Taxidermist: a man who knows his stuff.

Taxi drivers must lead interesting lives—they run into so many people.

An elevator operator is the only person who makes a success of running other people down.

A former undertaker, who applied for a job with a Charlotte, North Carolina, business firm was asked: "What did you like most about your former job?" to which he replied "Working with people."

OFFICE

Desk: wastebasket with drawers.

OLD AGE

The best thing you can save for old age is yourself.

OLD DAYS

One thing we liked about the good old days was the fact that big spenders spent their own money.

Living in the past is lots of fun. Besides, it's cheaper.

When we were kids, ten cents was big money—how dimes have changed.

The good old days are becoming more difficult to remember. That's what makes 'em good.

These trying times are the good old days we will be longing for a few decades from now.

It is well known that the older a man grows, the faster he could run as a boy.

An old-timer is one who has seen the red-hot mama turn real cool.

Old-timer: a fellow who sits around making up definitions of an old-timer.

An old-timer is one who can remember when there was some criticism of the government for its extravagance in giving away free seeds.

An old-timer, Charles Ruffing says, remembers when you could go barefoot without going to bed.

An old-timer is a person who can remember when a sensational novel contained asterisks.

An old-timer is one who remembers when the baby sitter was called mother.

An old-timer is a man who can remember way back when a union suit was something you wore, instead of something you filed against your employer.

Antique: proof that your ancestors had very well behaved children.

In the good old days a woman looked well in anything she put on, and now her daughter looks well without anything she takes off.

Nothing makes the good old days better than a poor memory.

Old-timer: a man who can remember when the height of juvenile delinquency was to go out back of the barn and smoke corn silk.

The good old days date back to the time when marriages produced triangles on the clothesline rather than in the courtroom.

The term "Gay Nineties" does not refer to the temperature.

Grandma thought good appetite was a sign of health. Her grand-daughter thinks it is a waisting disease.

The Good Old Days—when rising early wasn't a sign of a "compulsion neurosis."

O. A. Battista says that an old-timer is one who remembers when a child had more brothers and sisters than he had fathers.

An old-timer is one who may remember when a girl didn't care whether spinning wheels had white side-wall tires or not.

An old-timer is one who can remember when allergy was just an itch and all you did for it was to scratch.

Things have been reversed, Harold Coffin says, since the good old days when we took a bath once a week and took our religion daily.

In the good old days a fellow could kiss a girl and taste nothing but the girl.

The beauty of the old-fashioned blacksmith was that when you brought your horse to be shod, he didn't think of forty other things that ought to be done to it.

Some old-fashioned mothers who can remember their husband's first kiss now have daughters who cannot remember their first husbands.

OLD MAIDS

Old maid: a gal that has been overlooked after she has been looked over.

An old maid is a woman in the prim of life.

An old maid is one who failed to strike while the iron was hot.

Old maid: a girl who knows all the answers, but no one ever asked her the question.

OPERATIONS

You'll need two anesthetics for your operation: one to put you to sleep, and another when you see the bill.

Minor operation: one performed on somebody else.

Hotels in Rochester, Minnesota, home of the Mayo Clinic, have signs reading: "Please do not discuss your operation in the lobby."

From a news column in a Minnesota weekly: "Mr. and Mrs. J. K. Parker left Wednesday for Rochester, where Mrs. Parker expects to have a garter removed by Mayo Brothers."

OPINION

Man to friend: "My wife is the most wonderful woman in the world, and that's not just my opinion—it's hers."

Never try to change a woman's mind—let her have the satisfaction of doing it by herself.

You can always spot a well-informed man. His views coincide with yours.

A woman makes up her mind and her face several times a day, and is seldom satisfied with the results of either.

The most embarrassing of all questions a man could be asked while under oath would be for an honest opinion of himself.

A smart woman always asks her husband's opinion—after she has made up her own mind.

Radical: anyone whose opinion differs radically from ours.

A Hollywood agent was describing a producer and he exclaimed, "No middle ground where he's concerned—you either hate him or despise him."

Drill sergeant to rookie: "Wipe that opinion off your face."

OPPORTUNITY

Opportunist: a chap who never puts off until tomorrow what he can get someone else to do today.

You can't control the other fellow's opportunities, but you can grasp your own.

Why are opportunities always bigger going than coming?

Our idea of an opportunist is a woman who meets a wolf at the front door and appears the next day with a fur coat.

A grapefruit is a lime that took advantage of its opportunities.

There's no point in going back looking for lost opportunity. Someone else has already found it.

Next to knowing when to seize an opportunity, the most important thing in life is to know when to forego an advantage.

Every American schoolboy has a chance to be President when he grows up—and that's just one of the risks he has to take.

If life hands you a lemon, squeeze it and start a lemonade stand.

OPTIMISM

An optimist is a manufacturer who includes a free comb with every bottle of hair restorer.

An optimist is one who lights a match before asking you for a cigarette.

An optimist is a person who looks forward to enjoying the scenery on the detour.

An optimist is a man who keeps the motor running while waiting for his wife.

Cheerful observation: "For years I thought I was in a rut, but now I've decided I'm just in orbit."

An optimist can have more fun guessing wrong than a pessimist can have guessing right.

There is no danger of developing eye-strain from looking on the bright side of things.

Optimist: a fellow who wipes off his glasses before starting to eat his grapefruit.

Optimist: a woman who leaves the dinner dishes because she will feel more like washing them in the morning.

An optimist is a guy who falls from a twenty-story building and at every story shouts, "I'm all right so far."

An optimist is a person who thinks humorists eventually will run out of definitions of an optimist.

Man is an incurable optimist. He believes he has a pretty good chance to win a lottery prize but there is scarcely the slightest chance of his getting killed in an auto accident.

Optimist: a bridegroom who thinks he has no bad habits.

An optimist, Richard Artridge explains, is a man who is just starting to shovel out a long driveway; a pessimist is one who has been working at it for five minutes.

A football coach, giving his team pre-game pep talk: "Well, here we are, unbeaten, unscored on, untied—and getting ready for our first game."

ORIGINALITY

Originality: undetected imitation.

A lot of people don't know what they think until they hear somebody else say it.

ORPHAN

Did you hear about the man who murdered both his parents and then pleaded mercy on the ground that he was an orphan?

OSTEOPATH

An osteopath is a man who works his fingers to your bones.

PANELIST

Bill Cullen says that a panelist is someone with an ability to think on his seat.

PARASITE

Parasite: a person who goes through a revolving door without pushing.

PARENTS

When two newlyweds feather their nest, it's not hard to find four parents that have been plucked.

The commonest fallacy among women is that simply having children makes one a mother—which is as absurd as believing that having a piano makes one a musician.

Who can remember the days when it took more patience than money to be a good parent?

Parents are people who always think their children would behave if they didn't play with the kids next door.

All parents should be on spanking terms with their children.

Parents spend the first part of the child's life getting him to walk and talk, and the rest of his childhood getting him to sit down and shut up.

We sometimes marvel when we think how little our parents knew of child psychology and how wonderful we are.

Picking up after children progresses from playthings to price tags and checks.

You can learn many things from children—how much patience you have, for instance.

Most parents look forward to the day when their teen-age daughter will marry and have a phone of her own.

Morrie Gallant says that parents should never stand in the way of a child—they're apt to get knocked down.

In a school essay on parents, the young hopeful wrote, "We get our parents when they are so old it is very hard to change their habits."

PARKING

Lady driver to friend: "The thing I dislike most about parking is the noisy crash."

Utopia must be the place where another driver doesn't slip in ahead of you and take the lone parking space.

A parking meter is an automatic device that bets a dollar to your nickel that you can't get back before the red flag pops up.

One of the greatest satisfactions in life comes from being able to park on what is left of the other fellow's nickel.

Claudia Reynolds says that a parking lot is a place where you pay fifty cents so you won't get fined a dollar while you go to get a ten-cent soda that costs a quarter.

A parking space is an unfilled opening on the other side of the street.

Husband to family as they climbed out of car: "Well, we finally found a parking place. Now let's see—does anyone remember where we were going?"

A woman, having difficulty parking a long car, was told by policeman: "Listen, lady, if you can't park all of it, park as much as you can."

PARTIES

A man can often tell what kind of time he has been having at a party by the look on his wife's face.

Too much celebrating has kept many from becoming celebrated.

A woman, planning to hold a club meeting in her home, asked the woman who came in to help once a week to come Wednesday morning instead of her usual day. "I'm going to have forty women here Wednesday afternoon—and you know what that means." "Yes," the woman replied, "eighty eyes."

A dull party has one advantage. You can get to bed at a decent hour.

Nothing is more irritating than not being invited to a party you wouldn't be caught dead at.

One little kid told another one as they left a party: " It was a swell party, Jimmie. I'm as sick as a dog."

Cocktail party: where everybody talks and nobody listens.

The employees of a certain fountain pen company recently threw a pen-point ball.

Discussing recipes, when Bing Crosby asked Dinah Shore what she did with party leftovers, she replied, "I call a cab."

One of our friends believes in the two-party system—one on Saturday and one on Sunday.

A woman, leaving the house with her husband, said: "Now if we find it's a dull party, just leave it that way."

If you're going to be the life of the party nowadays you'll have to talk louder than television.

310

Wife to husband, as they leave party: "I was so proud of you, Ray—the way you stood your ground and yawned right back at them."

Household hint: Two gold fish placed in a punch bowl will keep the sugar stirred up.

Nothing makes you more tolerant of a neighbor's party than being there.

An informal party is one at which you wear your own clothes.

There isn't much to talk about at some parties until after one or two couples leave.

A woman called a friend to ask what should be worn to a party, and her friend replied, "It's a hen party, dear, so come in an open throat and a back suitable for knifing."

Did you hear about the young lady who planned an Announcement Party, but when the engagement was broken she went ahead and had a Narrow Escape Party?

An office committee in charge of farewell parties was faced with stretching a slim budget to cover parties for two girls leaving simultaneously, one to be married and the other to meet the stork. The solution? A joint Troth and Consequences Party.

Bernard Shaw once received an invitation from a celebrity hunter: "Lady X will be at home Thursday between four and six." Shaw returned the card on which he wrote at the bottom: "Mr. Bernard Shaw likewise."

Headline from New Mexico newspaper: "LIONS WILL HAVE WOMEN FOR DINNER AT EAST SIDE FEAST."

From Tennessee weekly: "Mrs. Gertie Jerkins entertained the Ladies Social Club. She asked the ladies to come dressed like tramps, and that was easy for most of them."

PATIENCE

Patience may often be the inability to make a decision.

Too many people these days want to get to the promised land without going through the wilderness.

Patience is idling your motor when you feel like stripping your gears.

WHEN IT'S LAUGHTER YOU'RE AFTER

Because marriages are made in Heaven, married people have to have an unearthly amount of patience.

You can do anything if you have the patience. You can even carry water in a sieve if you wait until it freezes.

Patience: being able to wait for the first coat of paint to dry before adding the second.

Butcher, to woman who has asked question after question: "Anything else you'd like to know—perhaps the name of the cow?"

PATRIOTISM

Patriotism: that pain you feel in the neck when a foreigner wins the championship.

Sign under American flag in store: These colors don't run.

PAWNBROKERS

Pawnbrokers live off the flat of the land.

Pawnbroker's sign: "See me at your earliest inconvenience."

PAY

Maybe they call it take-home pay because there is no other place you can afford to go with it.

PEDESTRIAN

A pedestrian is a fellow whose wife beat him to the garage.

PEOPLE

Best people: the ones your wife knew before she married you.

Some people are born great, some achieve greatness—and some just grate upon you.

Frederick L. Collins once observed that there are two types of people in this world: those who come into a room and say, "Well, here I am!" and those who come in and say, "Ah, there you are!"

PERFECTION

Any time you doubt whether any person is perfect, read an ad of a politician running for office.

Practically every wife finds the perfect husband. He's married to the woman next door.

PERPETUAL MOTION

Perpetual motion: the family upstairs.

PERSISTENCY

It sometimes happens that a girl can get rid of a persistent suitor by marrying him.

STAYbility is just as important as ability.

PERSONALITY

Personality: what we call our own collection of peculiarities.

The trouble with inferiority complexes is that not enough people have them.

One girl told her chum, "My boy friend has a dual personality— sometimes he's a lot of fun, other times he's broke."

Will power: the courage to eat only one peanut.

One man to another: "The trouble with that guy is that someone once told him to be himself."

Lots of people get credit for their personality when they just have a good set of teeth.

Many a live wire would be a dead one except for connections.

Did you hear about the man who has the dual personality—Dr. Heckle and Mr. Snide?

PESSIMISM

How you can spot a pessimist: He turns out the light to see how dark it is.

Pessimist: a woman who thinks she can't get her car into the only available parking space.

Pessimist: a fellow who always looks both ways before crossing a one-way street.

A pessimist is a man who looks at the world through morose-colored glasses.

Dentist: one who always looks down into the mouth.

We know a woman who not only expects the worse but makes the most of it when it happens.

Pessimist: a man who once tried to practice what he preached.

He's quite a pessimist—always building dungeons in the air.

Don't be too hard on the pessimist, A. W. Perrine observes, because he may have gotten that way by backing an optimist.

A pessimist is a person who, when he has the choice of two evils, takes both.

Ade Kahn, in speaking of a disagreeable woman, remarked, "I don't know what's eating her—but it'll suffer from indigestion."

PHILANTHROPY

"I'll give until it hurts," a man said, "but I'm very sensitive to pain."

Philanthropy: giving away your money to strangers who appreciate it rather than leaving it to your relatives.

Hell hath no fury like the relatives of a philanthropist.

PHILOSOPHY

Philosophy is just common sense in a dress suit.

A philosopher is a man who doesn't care whether a thing is right or not as long as he can prove it.

PHOTOGRAPHS

One photographer has spent so much time in the dark room that he is faced with a life of mixed emulsions.

314

Overheard: "She says her photographs don't do her justice, but she doesn't really want justice—she wants mercy."

"If you look like your passport photo," Edward Arnold points out, "you need the trip."

Photographer's sign: "Come in and be enlarged, tinted, and framed for $15.50."

PIONEER

A pioneer is one who settled there before they raised taxes.

PLANNING

Young chap to friend: "He just doesn't plan for the future at all. He's getting married next month and hasn't even found her a job."

PLATITUDE

Platitude: an old saw that has lost its teeth.

PLAYBOY

Spike Jones says that when the tired businessman thinks of himself as a wolf, some starlet thinks of him as a mink.

PLAYS

George Kaufman, the playwright, was asked what he thought of a play on Broadway. "I thought it was frightful," he said, "but I saw it under particularly unfortunate circumstances. The curtain was up!"

POINT OF VIEW

Life is funny. If you're poor and do something peculiar, you're nuts. But if you're rich, then you're just eccentric.

POISE

Poise is an acquired characteristic which enables father to buy a new pair of shoes, at the same time ignoring a hole in his sock.

Poise is the art of raising the eyebrows instead of the roof.

Poise: the ability to be at ease naturally.

Poise is the ability to talk fluently while the other fellow pays the check.

You really have poise if you aren't disconcerted when a doorknob comes off in your hand.

POLICE

In Birmingham, Alabama, cruising police cars got a radio call: "Car X-Y-3, car X-Y-3, go to Third Avenue and 14th Street—a nude woman running down the street. . . . all other cars remain on your beat. That is all."

POLICIES

A middle-of-the-road policy may be all right in politics, but it's suicide on the highway.

The safest policy is to tell your wife everything, but be sure and tell her before someone else does.

POLITENESS

On a bus a man gave his seat to a woman. She fainted. On recovering, she thanked him. Then he fainted.

Politeness doesn't cost anything. It wouldn't be worth anything at all if it did.

POLITICS

Vesta Kelly observes that today's successful politician seems to be the one who can get into the public eye without irritating it.

Political double talk now costs twice as much. Inflation, you know.

There's a vast difference between a horse race and a political race. In a horse race the entire horse runs.

Roast: the main course at a political banquet.

Politics is the art of looking for trouble, finding it everywhere, diagnosing it wrong, and applying unsuitable remedies.

316

The White House is a little bit like Heaven—everybody who talks about it isn't going there.

Someone has said that what we need is a new code of ethics for public officials. They might take time to read the ten commandments.

Politics is a profession where the paths of glory lead but to the gravy.

Politics: the most promising of all careers.

Many an aspiring politician stakes his career on a few well-chosen wards.

Election year is when a lot of politicians get free speech mixed up with cheap talk.

It looks like people have been living in better homes long enough to produce some presidents who were born in them.

Statesman: a politician who is supposed to do something for everybody but who tries to do everybody for something.

When the political pot boils, it gives off the old familiar odor of applesauce.

Political platform: what a politician needs when he doesn't have a leg to stand on.

Adlai Stevenson says that a politician is a man who approaches a question with an open mouth.

Legislator: a person who brings disorder out of chaos.

Probably the reason many a politician stands on his record is to keep voters from examining it.

The time many a political candidate really stumps his state is after it has elected him.

Groucho Marx reminds us that America is the only country in the world where you can go on the air and kid politicians—and where politicians go on the air and kid the people.

Women voters are convinced they're called city fathers because of the clean-up promises they make but never keep.

An experienced politician is one who can toss his hat into the ring and still talk through it.

317

Politicians are fellows who've got what it takes to take what you've got.

The politician who keeps his ear to the ground may limit his vision.

The average politician can't stand on his own record—so he jumps on the other fellow's.

A candidate is a man who after passing you by for ten years suddenly greets you by name.

The adjective in "cheap politician" doesn't refer to what he costs the taxpayers.

A political orator is one whose expenditure of speech is too great for his income of ideas.

Chairman Meade Alcorn asked party leaders what was the one thing Republicans needed to do most. One leader sent a one-word reply: "Multiply."

It isn't necessary any more to fool all the people all the time—during the election will be sufficient.

Some politicians repair their fences by hedging.

Roy P. Stewart says that congressmen often suffer from foot-in-mouth disease.

It would be interesting if political parties would take a tip from world series telecasts and let the candidates tell where their lather comes from.

Item in Illinois newspaper: "During the short term he has been in the Senate he has displaced genuine ability."

You can't expect a politician to make up his own bed and lie in it. He's more likely to make up his own bunk and then lie out of it.

"I just got out of prison yesterday," a traveler told a man on the train, "and it's going to be tough facing old friends." And the man next to him said, "I can sympathize with you—I'm just getting home from the state legislature."

"I am not a member of any organized party," Will Rogers declared, "I am a Democrat."

Announcer, at conclusion of political speech: "The opinions expressed by the speaker were his own and not those of the station—or, for that matter, of anybody else in his right mind."

318

A sheriff, defeated in his fight for re-election, inserted this ad in the local newspaper: "I wish to thank all those who voted for me, and my wife wishes to thank all those who didn't."

Signing off a political speech, a Montreal announcer said, "You have been listening to the Honorable Wendell Eyres, Minister of Wealth and Hellfare."

POPULATION

Chinese checkers are census takers in Chinatown.

POVERTY

The easiest way to remain poor is to pretend to be rich.

It's no disgrace to be poor but it's mighty inconvenient.

Poverty may be no disgrace, but that is the only nice thing you can say about it.

"Did you see much poverty in Europe?" a man asked a friend just back from a trip abroad, and the man replied, "Not only did I see it— I brought some of it back with me."

PRAISE

A man is never so weak as when some woman is telling him how strong he is.

Giving praise is like making love to an old maid—you can't overdo it.

Emily Post once observed that "An overdose of praise is like ten lumps of sugar in coffee; very few can swallow it."

Billy Sunday said, "Try praising your wife, even if it does frighten her at first."

PRAYER

A minister asked a small boy, "Do you say prayers before eating?" and the lad replied, "We don't have to. Mom's a good cook."

Two twin girls knelt for their bedtime prayers. Little Susie prayed first, and then concluded by saying, "Amen. Good night, God. Now stay tuned for Isobel."

319

Our preacher says that "prayer is not a monologue. What you say is not nearly as important as what is said to you."

Little boy, kneeling at bedside, asked his mother standing near by, "Mom, do you suppose it would be all right if I put in a commercial about a new bike?"

Some people think the modern youngster's prayer seems to be: "Lead us not into temptation but tell us where it is and we'll find it."

Little girl, whose father had refused a request, said in her prayer that night: "And please don't give my papa any more children. He don't know how to treat the ones he's got."

Our boss invokes divine guidance: "Oh Lord, let me be thy servant. Show me my duty. Give me work to do, but oh Lord, let it be in a consulting capacity."

A pastor was asked why he had never asked one of the elders to give the before-sermon prayer and he replied, "What? And have him say, 'Now I lay me down to sleep . . .'?"

A six-year-old attended a prayer meeting, and that night when he knelt to say his prayers before going to bed he prayed: "Dear Lord, we had a good time at church tonight. I wish you could have been there."

Garry Moore tells this story: "A little boy finished his prayers by saying, 'And Dear God, take care of Mommy, take care of Baby Sister, and Aunt Jenny and Uncle Jim and Grandma and Grandpa—and please God, take care of Yourself, or else we're all sunk!' "

PREDICTIONS

Prophet: a man who is not honored in his own country because people grow tired of hearing him say, "I told you so."

No matter what happens, there's always somebody coming along who knew it would.

PREJUDICE

The difference between a conviction and a prejudice is that you can explain a conviction without getting angry.

A prejudiced person is anyone who is too stubborn to admit that I am right.

It is amazing that a narrow-minded person can stack so many prejudices in a thin vertical column.

Prejudice is a wonderful time-saver—it enables one to form an opinion without bothering to get the facts.

PRESENTS

People seldom think alike—until it comes to buying wedding gifts.

PRESSURE

The only trouble in trying to keep up with the Joneses is that about the time you have caught up with them you discover that they have refinanced.

PRICES

Nowadays, he who hesitates is cost-conscious.

In this age in reality, some men will never believe that lead can be transformed into gold—until they get a bill from the plumber.

People today are chiefly concerned about the higher things of life—like prices.

The doctor who says you should have pleasant thoughts at meals obviously doesn't know the price of meat.

If a man pays today's high prices for fireplace wood without complaining, then surely he has money to burn.

"Things are so high these days," Jack Paar says, and continues, "I hear that even the price of down has gone up."

PRIDE

Why does a woman slave to clean her house so she won't be embarrassed when the cleaning woman shows up?

Your pride really gets a lick when you see your secretary yawning over one of your snappy sales letters.

PRISON

Inmates of the Iowa State Penitentiary refer to it as "The Walled-Off Astoria."

PRIVILEGES

Marriage is when a man gives up privileges he never knew he had.

PROBLEMS

In problem solving, get more hose or get closer to the fire.

It's not the ups and downs of life that bother the average man. It's the jerks.

Too bad life's big problems don't hit us when we're eighteen. That's when we know everything.

Showing that anxiety is often worse than the problem, Josh Billings once recalled, "When I was a boy, I'd rather be licked twice than postponed once."

PROCRASTINATION

Procrastination: putting off until tomorrow something that we should have done day before yesterday.

PRODIGY

He was an infant prodigy. The trouble was that he kept on being an infant long after he ceased being a prodigy.

PROFANITY

About the time a man is cured of swearing, the monthly bills start coming in.

PROFESSIONS

Did you hear about the fellow who decided to become a chiropodist because he was always at the foot of his class.

PROFESSORS

"When the room settles down I'll begin my lecture," the professor said. One of his students spoke up, "Why don't you go home and sleep it off?"

Professor asked, "Who's smoking in the back of the room?" and a student answered, "No one. It's just the fog we're in."

Professors: those who go to college and never get out.

College professors get what's left after the football coach is paid.

Frances Fitzpatrick Wright, speaking of a teacher, said: "Our professor was a dismal soul—he embalmed the subject and let us view the remains."

The nurse in the maternity ward approached the new father, a professor, and said, "It's a boy, sir," and the professor replied, "What does he want?"

PROGRESS

Progress: exchanging old worries for new.

You have to do your own growing no matter how tall your grandfather was.

At the rate science is advancing, some genius will soon invent a sound that will travel faster than planes.

Another measure of civilization's progress is the way that the cost of relaxing keeps going up.

Civilization: the advance from shoeless toes to toeless shoes.

The genius of American industry is in building things to last twenty years and making them obsolete in two.

Mike Connolly defines this as progress: before you could dial a wrong number only locally; now you can dial 'em all over the country.

Gold was discovered at Sutter's mill in old California. It has taken over a hundred years, plus a lot of blood, sweat, and tears to get it all dug up and properly put underground again at Fort Knox in Kentucky.

Bill Vaughan says the airplanes they are making these days are so fast they can fly halfway across the country before they're obsolete.

Sign explaining torn-up streets in Corpus Christi, Texas: "When you gotta grow, you gotta grow!"

PROOF

A draftee claimed exemption on the grounds of poor eyesight—and brought along his wife to prove it.

PROSPERITY

Prosperity: the sweet buy and buy.

PRUDENCE

People of Haiti say, "Never insult an alligator till after you have crossed the river."

PSYCHIATRY

A New York billing clerk had to be put away for mental care. He kept hearing strange invoices!

Neurotic: a person who has discovered the secret of perpetual emotion.

Franklin P. Jones observes that anybody who's not neurotic these days is probably underprivileged.

Advertisement by a young psychiatrist: "Satisfaction guaranteed or your mania back."

A Los Angeles psychiatrist ran into one of his patrons at a restaurant. "Doctor," the woman said, introducing her spouse, "this is my husband—one of the men I've been telling you about."

Mother of small boy to child psychiatrist: "Well, I don't know whether or not he feels insecure, but everybody else in the neighborhood certainly does."

With all of the books on psychiatry being published, John Fuller is reminded of the psychiatrist who became so famous all the world beat a psychopath to his door.

Psychiatrist: a mind-sweeper.

Psychiatry is the study of what people are up to that they should be ashamed of.

A psychiatrist says that talking will cure a lot of our troubles. We don't believe it. Talking was what started most of them in the first place.

The psychiatrist asked a man, "Is there any insanity in your family?" and the man said, "There must be—they keep writing me for money."

Psychiatrist to patient: "When did you first discover you enjoyed paying your income tax?"

A worried businessman told a psychiatrist that he ate grapes all day long and the psychiatrist scoffed, "So what?" and the businessman gasped, "Off the wallpaper?"

A psychiatrist is a man who doesn't have to worry as long as other people do.

One psychiatrist to another, "You are fine—how am I?"

PSYCHOLOGY

A Princeton psychologist declares that men know more about women and vice versa. Much of what men know, however, consists of what the women told them, and it probably isn't so.

Psychology: the science which tells us things everybody knows about human personality in language which few of us understand.

"Tell me what you eat and I'll tell you what you are," a waiter told a group of diners. At that the little fellow at the table spoke up: "Cancel my order for shrimp salad, please."

Psychologists say that a hysterical girl is most efficiently quieted by a firm kiss. But how do you get them hysterical?

PUBLIC

Any institution or organization without a public-relations program is like winking at a girl in the dark. You know what you are doing, but no one else does.

PUBLICITY

It's hard to keep a good man down—and it is even tougher to hold down a mediocre man with a good press agent.

Publicity is what some stars say they don't want in order to get more of.

A good way to get your name in the newspaper is to walk across the street reading one.

Barbecue: an incinerator with a press agent.

PUBLIC OPINION

An indignant dowager once demanded of Dr. George Gallup why she had never been questioned on any subject. "Madam," he replied, "don't you realize that your mathematical chances of being interviewed are about equal to your chance of being struck by lightning?" "I have been struck by lightning," she answered.

PUBLIC RELATIONS

Public relations are the ones who show up as soon as you become famous.

Press agent: that which if you don't have one, no one will read about the things you didn't say.

Don Herold says that public relations is the letter you don't write when you're mad and the nice letter you write the so-and-so the next day after you've regained your sense of humor.

PUBLIC SPEAKING

Hint to speakers: if you don't strike oil in ten minutes, quit boring.

A noted traveler, in describing his experience in Africa to a Ladies' Study Club, said, "There I stood, drinking in the scene, with the giant abyss yawning before me," and one of the ladies interrupted, "Was the abyss yawning before you got there?"

PUNCTUALITY

Franklin P. Jones reminds us that punctuality is the art of wasting only your own time.

The trouble with being on time is that there's no one there to appreciate it.

No matter how careless neighbors are about other things, they send your children home at the hour you mention—if not a little before.

Punctuality is the art of guessing correctly how late the other party is going to be.

Some women are so particular about their appearance that they usually make it an hour late.

A boss was upset because his new stenographer was late every morning. The next morning she came in late as usual and he fumed, "You should have been here at nine!" and she asked, "Why? What happened?"

Punctuality: the art of arriving for an appointment just in time to be indignant at the tardiness of the other party.

PUNISHMENT

Richard Armour says that his idea of capital punishment is spending the summer in Washington, D. C.

An anthropologist says Eskimo children are rarely punished. And no wonder. When a spanked child wears fur-lined pants, the moral is lost on him.

QUARRELS

The easiest way to bury a hatchet is with the corpse.

QUESTIONS

He's the kind of fellow who asks you a question, answers it for you, and then says you're wrong.

One of our married friends said he would do less lying if his wife didn't ask so many questions.

Groucho Marx, assigned to teach a first-aid class, was driven to distraction by stupid questions. One woman asked, "Mr. Marx, suppose you went home and found your wife's head in the oven with all the gas jets on. What would you do?" "That's easy," growled Groucho, "I'd baste her every fifteen minutes."

Asked if he'd like to see a model home, the man replied, "Glad to. What time does she quit work?"

William E. Barrett points out that it "was one of those feminine questions which give a man his choice between two wrong answers."

327

RADIO

A radio announcer is one who works for the love of mike.

Radio announcer: "Tune in again next week—same station, same time, same jokes!"

Radio announcer: a man who talks until you have a headache and then tries to sell something to relieve it.

Radio commercial: jabbertising.

Radio announcer: "And now a word from our sponsor who has made this program impossible."

A radio program hitting the air at 6:00 a.m. each day received this note from a woman: "Before I tuned in your program, I could never get my husband out of bed in the morning. Now he can't get out of the house fast enough."

A dramatist employed to write stories from the Bible in radio form was astonished to hear the announcer say at the end of the broadcast: "Will Cain kill Abel? Tune in at this same time tomorrow morning and find out."

Radio announcer: "We have just received a bulletin of a catastrophe, the like of which has never been known to mankind—but first, a word from our sponsor."

A North Dakota radio station received a letter from a Minnesota listener which said: "I know you will be interested to know that after listening to your program for over a year I now have a baby."

READING

We know a man who reads just enough to keep himself misinformed.

Children are speedy readers. Most of them, in fact, can finish a comic book before the druggist tells them to put it back on the rack.

REAL ESTATE

A real-estate salesman ended his speech to a couple in this way: "This is truly a restricted development. No one is allowed to build a house they can afford."

328

A Wisconsin realty company displays this sign: "We Have Lots to Be Thankful for."

It may take a heap o' livin' to make a house a home, but before that it takes a lot of borrowing.

RECESSION

Recession: a period when sales are down 5 per cent and staff meeting are up 25 per cent.

RECOMMENDATIONS

A boss wrote of a former employee: "His leadership is outstanding except for his lack of ability to get along with subordinates."

RECREATION

Recreation: getting exhausted on your own time.

REDUCING

No reducing system is perfect. There ought to be some way to slim the hips and flatten the tummy without simultaneously inflating the ego.

Sign in New York reducing salon: DON'T GIVE UP THE SHAPE.

In the window of a Chicago reducing salon: COME IN AND SHOO THE FAT.

There's a fellow who has announced he expects to make a million dollars. He's invented a candy covered with chocolates and nuts. It's for women who are on a reducing diet—and has a plain lettuce center.

REFERENCE

Charlie McCarthy, applying for a job, was asked if he had a character reference and he said, "Yes, Old Man Duggan." The personnel director asked, "Do you think he's a good reference?" and Charlie answered, "Well, he's a character."

REFORM

Reformer: someone who wants his conscience to be your guide.

Earl Wilson observes that there's so much good in the worst of us, and so much bad in the best of us, that it's hard to tell which of us ought to reform the rest of us.

A reformer is the kind of guy who would have you believe that he gave Eve back her apple.

RELATIVES

Adam must have been a happy man because he didn't have a mother-in-law.

Everyone could use a rich and generous relative—and those who have them usually do.

A traffic-court judge has more kinfolks than most anybody.

There's no such thing as a distant relative.

Rich relatives: a kin we love to touch.

Relative: a person who wonders how you manage to be so well off.

When you save enough to eliminate rainy days for yourself, your relatives start sending in bad-weather reports.

Vesta Kelly reminds us that one thing a rich relative is sure to leave behind is a lot of people wondering how much.

"Mother," a kid asked, "are you the nearest relative I have?" and she answered, "Yes, dear, and your father is the closest."

A husband told his wife, "I'll say one thing for your relatives— I like your mother-in-law better than mine."

Milton Berle, referring to his brother, "I want him to learn a trade so at least he'll know what job he's out of."

RELIGION

An atheist is a man who goes to the Notre Dame–SMU football game and doesn't cheer.

A Smith College freshman scrawled as her denominational preference, "I'd like to be called Alice."

Most people have some sort of religion—they at least know which church they're staying away from.

Heaven: a place you'll reach if you turn to the right and then go straight forward.

When your religion gets into the past tense it becomes pretense.

A mother asked her little daughter, "Who said 'God's in His heaven —all's right with the world'?" and the little girl's answer was, "Mrs. God."

Heathen: folks who don't quarrel over religion.

Maybe the Lord gets some people into trouble because that is the only time they ever think of him.

Girl to mother: "I can't marry him, Mother, because he's an atheist and doesn't believe in hell," and the mother answered, "Marry him, dear, and between us we'll convince him."

From the parish magazine: "The bring-and-buy sale was like Heaven. Many we expected to see were absent."

Two goldfish in a bowl were talking. They were discussing religion and finally one said in disgust, "But if there's no God, who changes the water every day?"

Little girl said, "My Grandmother reads the Bible all the time. I think she's cramming for her finals."

REMINDERS

A wife came home carrying a big package and told her husband, "I'll bet you thought you'd forgotten my birthday."

REPENTANCE

Repentance was perhaps best described by a small girl: "It's to be sorry enough to quit."

REPORT CARD

Hollywood teachers do not use the routine type of report card with "Poor, Fair, Good, and Excellent." They grade work as "Sensational, Magnificent, Stupendous, and Colossal."

REPUTATION

Reputation is character minus what you get caught at.

RESISTANCE

Grandpa Snazzy celebrated his one-hundredth birthday and a reporter said to him, "Pop, I'll bet you've seen plenty of changes around these parts," and the old man answered, "Yep, and I've been against every durn one of them."

RESOLUTIONS

Resolutions: proof that the good die young.

If all New Year's resolutions were placed end to end, they wouldn't reach to the end of January.

RESORTS

Beach: a place where people lie upon the sand—about how rich they are in town.

An ideal summer resort would be where the fish bite and the mosquitoes don't.

A summer resort is often a pleasant strutting ground where nobody knows how unimportant you are at home.

Some of the best comic strips are on the beach.

When people go to summer hotels for a change and a rest, the bellboys get the change and the hotel the rest.

Father to small boy dragging top half of bikini bathing suit along the beach: "Now show daddy exactly where you found it."

Sign on mountain lodge: "Open to Take Tourists." Under the printed words someone has written, "And how!"

Resort: where cold water comes out of the hot water faucet, hot water comes out of the cold water faucet, and nobody ever comes out of the bathroom.

A girl sitting with youth on porch of resort hotel: "I feel a little chilly, Robert. Will you go inside and get me Frank Coulter."

Young thing, talking to her chum, at tropical resort: "It's just as I imagined it—beautiful blue sky, gently rolling waves, balmy breezes, and no men."

Vacationer, watching native building a small structure: "Pop, what's that?" and the old man replied, "If I can rent it, it's a rustic cottage, and if I can't it's a cowshed."

A dude ranch is a tourist resort where people who have never been on horses before expect to ride horses that have never been ridden before.

RESPONSIBILITY

Some people grow under responsibility—others merely swell.

RESTAURANTS

Menu: sheet of paper on which the best meal is usually scratched out.

"Do you serve lobsters here?" the man asked as he entered the café and the waiter replied, "Yes, sir, just have a seat."

Sign in Texas restaurant: "If our steak is too tough for you, GET OUT! This is no place for a weakling."

To get fast service at a restaurant, try to sit two at a table for four. The waiter will rush your order to get rid of you.

Waiter: one who thinks money grows on trays.

Sign in Washington, D. C., restaurant: "The Only Thing You Get on the Cuff Here Is Gravy."

After eating a meal in a first-class dining restaurant these days, you need an after-dinner mint, such as the one in Philadelphia.

Sign in Chinese restaurant: Not responsible for personal proprieties in dining rooms unless checked.

William Feather observes that what you don't like or can't afford is precisely what the menu offers.

My favorite restaurant serves half-and-half coffee—half in the cup and half in the saucer.

When you really need an after-dinner mint: when the waiter brings the check.

Artichoke: the only vegetable you have more of after you finish eating it than you had before you started.

Item on menu in New Orleans restaurant: "Yankee Pot Roast— Southern Style."

Next time you dine out in a ritzy place, notice the waiter's "tipical" smile.

A Cleveland restaurant featured a seventy-five-cent hangover breakfast: "One jumbo orange juice, two aspirins, and our sympathy."

A waiter asked a customer, "How did you find your steak, sir?" and the man replied, "It was just luck. I happened to move that piece of potato and there it was."

An impatient customer in a café told the waiter as he passed the table, "That food looks pretty good; I'd like to eat here sometime."

On St. Paul restaurant menu: "Chicken with muchroom on toast."

Man in restaurant eating pie asked waitress, "What kind of pie is this?" and she said, "What does it taste like?" He replied, "Glue." Then she thought a moment and said, "Then it's apple. The pumpkin tastes like soap."

Sign in Buffalo tearoom: "What foods these morsels be."

Man in restaurant to waitress: "What's our offense? We've been on bread and water for almost an hour."

Note in restaurant menu: "Customers who consider our waitresses uncivil ought to see the manager."

The farmer ordered roast beef. When the waitress brought him a small serving, he looked at it and said, "Yes, that's the kind I want. Bring me some of it, please."

RETIREMENT

One nice thing about being old and retired is you have more time to read about what your problems are.

Nowadays the thing to put aside for one's retirement age is all thoughts of retirement.

You can't win. As long as you stay with the old rat race, you're tense, and as soon as you leave it you're past tense.

American men, they say, never know what to do with themselves when they retire. As one puts it: "I get up early, read the obituary column, and if my name isn't there, I go back to bed."

RETROSPECT

Don't let yesterday use up too much of your today.

REVIEWS

Monty Wooley once wrote, "For the first time in my life I envied my feet—they were asleep."

A reviewer in *Time* wrote: "It's a run-of-the-morgue whodunit."

Child's review: This book tells more about penguins than I am interested in knowing.

REWARD

Milton Berle: "My sponsor threw me a big dinner—but it didn't hit me."

In Nunnally Johnson's *Woman in the Window* a Boy Scout said, "If I get the reward I will send my younger brother to some good college and I will go to Harvard."

RICHES

Wealth: a curse when the neighbors have it.

The rich man has acute laryngitis—while the poor man has a cold.

A tough break is to be born rich and never have the opportunity of bragging about carrying a paper route, living in a log cabin, or walking ten miles to school.

Texas mother to her tots: "Careful going to school today, kids— we had another well come in last night and it's slippery out!"

RIGHTEOUSNESS

A lot of people who talk so much about righteousness find that they have little time to practice it.

ROBBERIES

Said the old maid to the burglar: "Sure, I have money. Don't just stand there—frisk me!"

ROCKETS

A guided-missile office in the Pentagon is reported to have this sign on the door: "Out to Launch."

ROMANCE

The best way for a girl to keep her youth is not to introduce him to anybody.

An ideal romance is one in which the couple gets married and lives happily, even afterward.

A couple decided to end their romance so the girl said, "Look—let's compromise. I won't return your ring and I won't keep it. Let's sell it and split the cash."

And then there was the couple whose beautiful friendship ripened into another office collection.

RUMOR

Rumor: something that goes in one ear and out over the back fence.

A rumor goes in one ear and out many mouths.

A rumor is about as hard to unspread as butter.

Unimpeachable source: the guy who starts the rumor.

SADNESS

Every sad-eyed woman hasn't loved and lost. Some of them got him.

SAFETY

Sign in Texas town: "20 Miles an Hour or $25."

A fire plug never hits a car except in self-defense.

It isn't the used cars that are a menace on the highways—it's the misused ones.

"I did not say you were built like a truck," the man insisted to his wife. "I merely said people are afraid to pass you on the right."

Fellows who drive with one hand are usually headed for a church aisle. Some will walk down it; some will be carried.

Advice to one-armed drivers approaching railroad crossings: You can't pay attention to your brakes when your mind is on the clutch.

A lot of auto wrecks result from the driver's hugging the wrong curve.

Sign on back of truck: PLEASE DON'T HUG ME, I'M GOING STEADY."

In a traffic accident, the one who is right is not always the one who is left.

Our idea of a safe driver is one who honks as he goes through a red light.

One gal remarks that if women are crummy drivers, perhaps it's because their husbands taught them.

Safety zone: a protected area that permits a car to strike you only from one side.

A streamline train not only has the right of way at a crossing but can prove it.

Too many people who have passed their driving tests think they can pass anything.

Another traffic improvement might be divided highways marked "His" and "Hers."

Sign on highway near St. Louis: "Drive Right So More People Will Be Left."

A speed demon is a driver who is in such a hurry to get into the next state that he often gets into the next world.

There wouldn't be nearly as many pedestrian patients, Earl Wilson declares, if there were more patient pedestrians.

Slogan: Approach school like you did when you were a child— slowly!

The receptionist in Saint Peter's office probably hears a good many arguments about who had the right of way.

Power brakes may stop a car on a dime—but it usually costs about $100 to get the rear end fixed.

Today's safety slogan: "Watch out for school children—especially if they're driving cars."

Traffic warning: GO SLOWLY. THIS IS A ONE-HEARSE TOWN.

The National Safety Council reports that its records fail to show a single accident in a tunnel of love. Still, it's a great place to enjoy the thrill of a near miss.

Sign in motel: "DON'T SMOKE IN BED. THE ASHES THAT FALL ON THE FLOOR MAY BE YOUR OWN."

A copy of a safety warning: Treat all guns as if they are loaded and all ketchup as if it is going to pour.

A cop asked an injured pedestrian if he noticed the license number of the driver who struck him and he replied, "No, but I'd remember his laugh anywhere."

Warning at a New Mexico intersection: "Cross Road—Better Humor It."

Since the advent of the car, mankind is divided into two classes—the quick and the dead.

After installing a sprinkler system a hotel warned its guests: "Please Do Not Smoke in Bed—You May Drown Yourself."

Sign in a Delaware chemistry plant: "If You Insist on Smoking, Please Tell Us Where to Send the Ashes."

SALARY

Two best reasons for wanting a raise in salary: twins.

His monthly salary runs into three figures—his wife and two daughters.

A man who received by mistake a pay envelope without a check asked the accounting department: "What happened? Did my deductions finally catch up with my salary?"

SALES

Saleswoman showing girdle to a large woman: "I don't think it will support you in the manner to which you're accustomed."

338

In a Missouri shoe shop: "If your shoes aren't ready, don't blame us. Two of our employees have gone after a heel to save your soles."

A perfume salesgirl told a young lady, "If he's the sort who can resist this, honey, you wouldn't want him anyway."

A perfume salesgirl to young lady, "You've got to keep changing. They build up an immunity to them."

Sign in window of Seattle store: "Evening Gowns Cut down Ridiculously Low."

Sign in a woman's shoe store in St. Louis: "Ten per cent discount if you make your purchase within ten minutes after entering the store."

Husband, "I tried to find you at the sale when I was mangling with the crowd."

A salesman to an old lady, "I represent the Mountain Wool Company, madam, and I wonder if you'd be interested in some coarse yarns?" and she said, "Gosh, yes, tell me a couple."

A woman, trying on a hat, told the sales girl: "It's nice. But it's a little less than he can afford."

A perfume girl told a customer, "The first whiff is good, but it's the fallout that gets them."

Many a salesman uses liquids to make himself solid with his customers.

We like the bait seller who placed this sign near his house: "Worms with Fish Appeal."

A salesman is a man with a shine on his shoes, a smile on his face—and a lousy territory.

Sign on department store counter: "Extra large towels—just the thing to wear when answering the phone."

The shoe clerk told the woman customer: "Let's start with the larger sizes and work down until we get that stab of pain we're looking for."

Super salesman: someone who can make you feel that you've longed all your life for something you've never heard of.

Super salesman is one who can sell a double-breasted suit to a man with a Phi Beta Kappa key.

Car salesman, talking to prospective customer: "And it's priced just over the car which is priced a few dollars above the car which costs no more than some models of the lowest price car."

"Just look at this," the announcer said. "New shipments of Navy field jackets, and many other items too humorous to mention."

Monologue: a conversation between a realtor and a prospect.

"Just look at this," a sales manager demanded of the salesman. "Your expense account shows that you spent nine dollars for food in a single day in Sandusky, Ohio. How can that be?" and the man answered, "It's easy—you just skip the breakfast."

SATELLITES

Space satellites can scan the earth below and send back useful information. How about fixing up one that could radio the location of the nearest parking space?

SATISFACTION

As satisfying as an income-tax refund.

SAVING

It used to be that if you saved money, you were called a miser. Nowadays, if you save money, you're a wizard.

Husband to wife: "If we continue to save at the present rate—at retirement we'll owe two million dollars."

SCANDAL

Scandal: a breeze stirred up by a couple of windbags.

SCHOOL

Bobby soxer on phone: "I'd love to go but I feel that I should stay home and help father with my homework."

Small boy, scowling over report card, said to his dad, "Well naturally I seem stupid to my teacher. She's a college graduate."

A teacher asked her class, "What is a scale?" and a boy replied, "It's a freckle on a fish."

A teacher asked, "What is a millenium?" and a student said, "It's about the same as a centennial only it's got more legs."

"Hey Dad, I'm home from school again," the youngster said, and his father exclaimed, "What the devil is wrong this time?" and the boy stated, "Graduated."

A father was reading his son's report card and he commented, "He excels in initiative group integration and responsiveness—now if he'd only learn to read and write."

Upon being asked to define steam, a little kid blurted out, "It is water gone crazy with the heat."

"Were you a good boy at school today?" Dad asked his boy, and the kid answered, "How much trouble can I get into standing in the corner all day?"

From an Iowa paper: "Each of the attractive girl cheerleaders had a large golden H on her seater."

One child, in speaking of a tattler, "He's nothing but a school pigeon."

A little kid, trying to explain his poor grades on his report card, said, "And Dad, don't forget that we're studying all new stuff this year."

Father noticed comment on daughter's report card, "Betty is a good student but she talks too much," and he wrote just below it. "You should come by and meet her mother sometime."

The kid wrote in his essay, "In Christianity a man can have only one wife. This is called monotony."

A little kid was asked to define a flood and he answered, "It's a river that's too big for its bridges."

We spend $5,000 on a school bus so the children won't have to walk to school, then we spend $50,000 for a gymnasium so they can exercise.

A student remarked that the leaves began to turn the night before exams.

An underprivileged child today is one who doesn't carry a new leather briefcase to grade school.

Did you hear about the principal who told the small boy: "It's very generous of you, Donald, but I don't believe your resignation would help the crowded school situation."

Schoolboy in geography class: "The principal export of the United States is money."

There ought to be a course in school that teaches all to read the handwriting on the wall.

Fond mother: "Yes, Genevieve is taking French and algebra. Say 'Good morning' to Mrs. Smith in algebra, darling."

A little girl was surprised one night to find that her father had placed this sign in front of the TV: "The picture has been temporarily disconnected due to homework."

September is the month when most little boys develop class hatred.

The class yell in the school of experience: "Ouch!"

A student was asked to name the two genders and he replied, "We have two—masculine and feminine. The feminine are divided into frigid and torrid, and the masculine into temperate and intemperate."

A small boy's examination paper contained this definition: "The equator is a menagerie lion running around the earth's middle."

News item: "This will be the first time that the school chorus has appeared at a PTA meeting, and a real threat is anticipated."

Billy the Kid, the famous Arizona desperado, killed nineteen men before he was twenty-one, the teacher told her class. A kid held up his hand hurriedly and asked, "What kind of a car did he drive?"

Headline: "Feeble-Minded School Dean Resigns."

A street sign read, "School—don't kill a child." Beneath was a childish scrawl: "Wait for the teacher."

A teacher asked, "Where are elephants found?" and a kid answered, "Elephants are so big that they hardly ever get lost."

SCIENCE

The scientist who doesn't have his head in the clouds these days is working on the wrong project.

There's a miracle drug so new that the doctors haven't found a disease for it yet—but they will.

So far science has not figured out how a man can tell what a woman is thinking by listening to what she's saying.

Did you hear about the nuclear physicist who had too many ions in the fire?

Look at cows and remember that the greatest scientists in the world have never discovered how to make grass into milk.

One humiliating thing about science is that it is gradually filling our homes with appliances smarter than we are.

The revolutionary vanishing cream deodorant: you vanish and people wonder where the odor is coming from.

A diamond is one of the hardest substances known to man, particularly to get back.

A chemistry professor asked his class what they considered the outstanding contribution chemistry had made in the world, and a student in the front row said, "Blondes."

Adam was the first electronics engineer. He took some spare parts and made the first loudspeaker.

SCOTS

A Scot is a person who can come out of a five and ten with just one package.

And there was the Scot who bought only one spur; he figured if one side of the horse would go, the other side would go also.

SEASONS

Spring is that season of the year when farmers and golfers start their plowing.

Summer is the time when it's too hot to do the things it was too cold to do in the winter.

SECRETS

Secret: anything a woman doesn't know.

343

Secrets are things we give to other people to keep for us.

Secret: something which is hushed about from place to place.

A woman looks on a secret two ways: either it's not worth keeping or it's too good to keep.

Women can keep a secret just as well as men, but it takes more of them to do it.

One woman to another: "Why no, I didn't tell anyone—I didn't know it was a secret."

When asked about his plan of campaign, General "Stonewall" Jackson asked an inquisitive chaplain, "Can you keep a secret?" and the eager cleric answered, "Yes." Jackson replied, "Well, so can I."

We know a fellow who can really keep a secret—he got his salary raised six months ago, and his wife hasn't found it out yet.

A busybody, unable to contain her curiosity any longer, asked an expectant mother point blank whether she was going to have a baby. "Oh, goodness, no," the young woman said pleasantly. "I'm just carrying this for a friend."

SENSITIVITY

A man's body is extremely sensitive. Pat him on the back and his head swells.

SERMONS

A minister met a church member on the street and told him, "It's been nice to see you in church with your wife these past few Sundays," and the fellow replied, "It's a matter of choice. I'd sooner hear your sermons than hers."

SERVICE

Vesta Kelly says that service while you wait is usually what the other fellow is getting.

Some people go about doing good—other people just go about.

Chaplain asked man in electric chair: "Can I do anything for you?" and the man answered, "Yes, hold my hand."

344

Sign in rural service station: "To keep from having complaints about our free service, there will be no free service."

SHOPPING

Shoppers: women who bring back everything but prosperity.

When some women shop it looks like they are taking an inventory on the stock.

Woman said, "I strolled past the shops window-wishing."

If you're getting a big charge out of life, your wife and daughter have been shopping.

Wife to husband as the tailor measured his waist: "It's quite amazing when you realize it takes an oak tree two hundred years to attain that girth."

Husband to wife returning loaded down with packages: "I gather your object is to lick the depression singlehanded."

A wife told her husband just as she left the house, "I'm going to do some shopping. I'll be back in about forty dollars."

Man whose wife just came in from a shopping expedition: "It's amazing what women would rather have than money."

Parking meter: a device that enables you to do two hours of shopping in one.

A woman kept demanding that the clerk show her more shoes, and she finally said, "If you don't show me everything, how can I see what I don't want?"

Young bride asked for oysters in a sea-food store and dealer said, "Large or small, madam?" and she hesitated, "Well, I don't know for sure but they're for a man who wears a size 15 collar."

One aimless shopper to another, "If you don't plan to buy anything in this store, let's look at something more expensive."

Woman, talking to husband in supermarket: "Look at it this way, dear—the more it costs the more green stamps we get."

Woman, after being shown a dozen samples of wallpaper, exclaimed, "Now we're getting somewhere. That's the exact opposite of what I want."

A woman, pointing to a large steak, asked how much it was and the butcher replied, "Three ninety-five." She asked, "How can you tell without weighing it?" He answered, "Lady, that there steak has been weighed six times this morning."

SHOW BUSINESS

Then there was the fellow who saw *Tobacco Road* so many times he got nicotine in his eyes.

The actor's tour was a great success—he outran every audience.

Confronted by that time-honored query, "If you were marooned on a desert island, what would you like to have for reading matter?" a Broadway chorus girl gave the answer to end all answers: "A tatooed sailor."

SHOWS

Robert Garland, after seeing a Broadway show, wrote in his column, "This show has to be seen to be depreciated."

In most homes, the husband runs the show, but the wife writes the script.

SIGNS

Sign outside a women's club in Florida: Enter and Knock.

Sign framed on a bar in Newark, New Jersey: "When confiding in me, kindly confine your remarks to baseball, track, politics, and weather. All other subjects barred. I have my troubles, too."

Sign on newly painted wall in high school: "This is a partition— not a petition. No signatures are required."

Sign in a small mountainside filling station: "We sell no gas on Sunday—and darned little the rest of the week."

Sign over the marriage-license bureau: "Two Can't Live as Cheap as One, But It's Lots More Fun."

Meyer Berger found this sign plastered on a nonworking vending machine: "This machine taketh. It giveth not."

Sign in Florida cocktail lounge: "Please don't stand up while the room is in motion."

Sign on Memphis church: "Come in and have your faith lifted."

Sign on St. Louis kennel: "The only love that money can buy. Puppies for sale."

Sign in Portland dance hall: "The management reserves the right to exclude any lady they think proper."

Sign outside a service station in Atlanta, Georgia: "This is the wrong road to Chattanooga."

Sign over roadside fruit stand in Arkansas: "God Help Those Who Help Themselves."

A sign in the Navy Bureau of Research: "If it works, it's obsolete."

SILENCE

Blessed are they who have nothing to say, and who cannot be persuaded to say it.

Reticence: knowing what you're talking about but keeping your mouth shut.

SIN

Only the wages of sin have no deductions.

The fact that scientists have announced that no new sin has been discovered in the past five thousand years must give college freshmen quite a feeling of futility.

An Illinois preacher recently compiled a list of 457 sins. He has been swamped with requests for the list by people who are afraid they have missed something.

Instead of choosing the lesser of two evils, many choose the one they haven't tried before.

SIZE

Arthur "Bugs" Baer once confessed, "I'm a worldly man—bigger at the equator than at the poles."

Blessed are they who have big feet for they shall be well balanced.

SKEPTICISM

Skeptic: a person who believes only half of what he sees and nothing of what he hears.

SLACKS

Fred Allen once observed that he had never seen a pair of slacks that had much slack in them.

SLEEP

Rip Van Winkle was the only man who ever slept as long as he wanted to the next morning.

Sleepwalker: the only person who gets his rest and exercise at the same time.

Early rising: triumph of mind over mattress.

Early to bed and early to rise probably means that the TV is being repaired.

"To do each day two things one dislikes is a precept I have followed scrupulously," Somerset Maugham remarked. "Every day I have got up and I have gone to bed."

Doctor asked patient, "How much sleep do you ordinarily require?" and the man said, "About five minutes more."

A wife told her husband, "You swore terribly at me in your sleep last night," and he answered, "Who was asleep?"

SLOGANS

Revised slogan: "Join the Navy and See What's Left of the World."

Undertaker's campaign in running for office: "I'm the last man to let you down."

SLOWNESS

"I am slowly going mad over a beautiful woman," a patient told his psychiatrist, "but isn't there some way of speeding up the process?"

An irate husband called his wife upstairs and asked, "How soon will you be ready? Be specific—give me a date."

348

SMALL TOWNS

A small town is a place where a fellow has to walk around a dog enjoying a nap on the sidewalk.

A hick town is one where there is no place to go that you shouldn't.

Small town: where everybody knows which men beat their wives but also which ones need it.

"I once played in a town so small," said Milton Berle, "that they didn't even have a town drunk. All the men had to take turns."

Village idiot: man who used to be laughed at, but now is elected.

Here's one nice thing about a small town: most of your worrying is being done for you by others, who probably do a better job than you could do yourself.

In a small town you can chat for a while on the telephone even if you get the wrong number.

A small town is a place where they wonder where the doctor is going when he leaves his office in a hurry.

A hick town is one in which the nine o'clock curfew wakes most of the town.

Street sign in a southern village: NO U-ALL TURNS.

Tourist asked old man in small town, "Any big men born around here?" and the native replied, "Nope. Best we can do is babies. Different in the city, I suppose."

SMOKING

Ash tray: something to put ashes in when the room hasn't got a fine table top or rug.

A customer in a tobacco shop, after being told filter tips were sold out, asked: "What other kind of cigarettes do you have for someone who has quit smoking?"

SOAP OPERA

Soap opera: corn on the sob.

349

SOCIAL LIFE

Too much celebrating has kept many men from becoming celebrated.

SOCIAL SECURITY

Social security: something that promises you steaks for an age when you have no teeth.

SOCIETY

Tea wagon: a pushcart that has broken into society.

You've arrived socially if the place card is more important than the menu.

We know one socialite who boasts that she has friends she hasn't even used yet.

SONGS

It seems these days singers not only show off their best arias but also their best areas.

When Arthur Godfrey was a record jockey he told a lady listener that he had dedicated a new song to her, entitled, "I'll Send You a Kitten, Dear, You Could Use a New Puss."

SORROWS

Some people don't drown their sorrows. They teach them how to swim.

SPACE

The real space man is the one who can find a parking place.

The guy who figured out how to get 25,000 units of Vitamin A in one tiny capsule must have been a bus driver.

Perhaps we should show more concern about what a human can endure on earth and less about his survival in outer space.

Jet planes have passed the speed of sound and are fast approaching that of gossip.

350

A Martian lands in Paris, spots Brigitte Bardot and, electric-bulb eyeballs flashing furiously, demands: "Take me to your leader—later . . . ."

SPEAKERS

Man describing speaker, "He could speak for an hour without a note and without a point."

Franklin Jones says that a finished speaker seldom is.

It's all right for a speaker to talk like a book, provided he is also smart enough to shut up like one.

After-dinner speaker: a person who has only a few words to say but who seldom stops when he has said them.

Some speakers who don't know what to do with their hands, G. Norman Collie observes, should try clamping them over their mouths.

Some day—some place—on some occasion, the chairman will arise and say, "I now present a speaker who needs an introduction."

Frances Rodman says that one of the better-known after-dinner speakers is he who is always making an important phone call when the waiter presents the check.

Scheduled to make an after-dinner speech, a Seattle man became so nervous that he slipped out and went home. What this country needs is more introverts.

Some speakers electrify an audience—others gas it.

A lot of fellows classified as after-dinner speakers are merely after dinner.

An explorer is a person who makes a short trip and gets enough material for a lecture.

The Governor of the Virgin Islands was a guest in Washington. The toastmaster, in the introductory remarks, said the usual things and ended with, "It's a great pleasure to present the Virgin of Governor's Island."

Most women go from saying "I do" to "You'd better."

Unusual candor was shown by the toastmaster who rose after the dinner and said, "Gentlemen, it is high time we got the bull rolling."

351

Anyone may easily become a good speaker if he knows how to dilute a two-minute idea with a one-hour vocabulary.

It often takes a speaker twice as long to tell what he thinks as to tell what he knows.

Speaker to audience: "I am up here to talk to you. You folks are sitting out there to listen. If any of you get through before I do, would you please raise your hand?"

Man, describing wife: "She speaks 142 words a minute with gusts up to 185."

Frances Rodman says to think twice before you speak—and you'll find everyone talking about something else.

It's pretty hard to tell whether a man is a finished speaker until he sits down.

We heard of a ventriloquist so dumb he didn't know when to keep his dummy's mouth shut.

Your brain is a remarkable thing. It starts to function the moment you are born and doesn't stop until you get up to make a speech.

When Arthur Larson was serving as labor undersecretary, he spoke to a meeting of South Dakota farmers. Thinking that he had delivered his speech rather well, he asked one of the farmers what he thought of it. "Well," the farmer said, "it wasn't too bad but a half-hour rain would have done a damn sight more good."

A long-winded speaker complained, "Mr. Chairman, there are so many rude interruptions I can hardly hear myself speaking," and a listener piped up, "Don't let it bother you, you're not missing anything."

John G. Winant, once asked to make a speech in England, stood in agonized silence for four minutes, and finally said softly: "The worst mistake I ever made was getting up in the first place."

SPECIALIST

Specialist: a man who has discovered which of his talents will bring in the most money.

SPEECHES

Stutterer: the only man who thinks twice before he speaks once.

A clergyman's daughter was asked if her father ever preached the same sermon twice, and she answered, "Yes, I think he does; but he hollers in different places."

Speeches are like steer horns—a point here, a point there, and a lot of bull in between.

Oratory: the art of making deep noises from the chest that sound like important messages from the brain.

One man to another: "She's one of those women who regard free speech not as a right but as a continuous obligation."

Blowhard: a person who is always me-deep in conversation.

Herbert V. Prochnow says that the recipe for a good speech includes some shortening.

Irishism: "The sooner I never see your face again, the better it will be for both of us when we meet."

Husband interrupting wife talking to guests: "To make a long story short, dear, let me tell it."

What this country needs is more free speech that's worth listening to.

All work and no plagiarism makes a dull speech.

It takes a baby approximately two years to learn to talk and between sixty and seventy years to keep his mouth shut.

News item: "The chairman replied in a few appropriated remarks."

Every man knows that home is the place where a man can say what he pleases because no one pays any attention to him anyway.

A short speech may not be the best speech, but the best speech is a short one.

Upon being introduced as the toast of radio, toast of the movies, and toast of television, Dinah Shore responded with: "I love the way you buttered that toast!"

A good speech is like the latest Paris fashion—long enough to cover the subject and short enough to be interesting.

There's one consolation about being a poor speaker—you don't have to worry about having an off night.

Congressional speeches are printed and distributed by the government without the slightest profit, and many of them are read that way.

Most speeches on government are sound—all sound.

In the Orient, speeches at public dinners are delivered before the banquet starts. Now we have a better understanding of what is meant by the wise men of the East.

A man was to speak at a luncheon club and he asked the chairman, "How long shall I talk?" His host replied, "As long as you wish, but all of us leave here at 1:15."

Toastmaster's introduction: "Gentlemen, you have been giving your attention to turkey stuffed with sage. Now you will hear from a sage stuffed with turkey."

SPEED

Woman, describing an experience: "The hour flew by like time on a parking meter."

You really wonder how the other half lives—when you ride in a car with some of them.

The kind of lamb that Mary could follow in her modern car would be a Rocky Mountain goat that could run sixty miles an hour.

Things are moving so fast these days that people who say it can't be done are interrupted by someone doing it.

Two ants were running along at a great rate across a cracker box when one asked, "Why are we going so fast?" "Don't you see?" said the other. "It says here, 'Tear along dotted line.'"

Every year it takes less time to fly across the ocean and longer to drive to the office.

One of our neighbors says that the only thing he can remember about the speed of light is that it gets here too soon in the morning.

Motorists who make a practice of exceeding the speed limits are wrong—dead wrong.

In the old days, if anybody missed a stagecoach he was content to wait a day or two for the next one. Now he has a grandson who blows his top if he misses one section of a revolving door.

354

Airplanes are getting faster and faster. It is even conceivable that one day they might reach the speed of the office grapevine.

Now planes are so fast you don't have time to get acquainted with the hostess.

A man who was wildly enthusiastic about his driving ability was taking a trip with his wife, and after traveling a great distance, she consulted a map and told him they were lost. "What's the difference?" he said, "we're making great time."

Did you hear about the Oklahoma desperado who got so handy with his .38 that he could stand in front of a mirror and beat himself to the draw?

Bob Hope on transportation: "We left Spokane with two rabbits and when we got to New York, we still had only two rabbits."

Most speeding is done by people who aren't going anywhere in particular.

SPELLING

One secretary said to another: "If I can't spell the words in the first place how does he expect me to find them in the dictionary?"

SPORTS

Jack Carson says, "Interest your kids in bowling—get them off the streets into the alleys."

Did you hear about the girl who learned to ski in just ten sittings?

A baseball park, as everyone knows, is a hot-dog stand that has floor shows.

Advice of coach to athletes: "Boys, you can't fly with the owls at night and keep up with the eagles in the daytime."

Overheard through the locker room of a men's club—one fat man to another: "I'm in such bad shape that I can't even do the exercises to get in shape again."

Baseball fan: a spectator sitting five hundred feet from the plate who can see better than the umpire standing five feet from it.

Did you hear about the baseball pitcher with a sore arm who was in the throws of agony?

355

Newspaper story: "At this point the gallery deserted Mrs. Moore to watch Miss Smith, whose shorts were dropping on the green with amazing regularity."

Social security: when a boy has the only baseball in the neighborhood.

Robert Q. Lewis, learning to ski: "By the time I learned to stand up, I couldn't sit down."

Suddenly the church organ broke the stillness of the service with the strains of the National Anthem. Junior, an ardent sports fan, called loudly, "Who's playing today, Pop?"

Any baseball team could use a man who plays every position superbly, never strikes out, and never makes an error; but there's no way to make him lay down his hot dog and come out of the grandstand.

Woman, watching baseball in pouring rain, to husband, "This is probably another of my silly questions, but why don't we go home."

Why all this fuss about baseball needing a third major league? There already are three leagues—the American, the National, and the Yankees.

Swimming pool: a crowd of people with water in it.

Umpire: what a baseball player becomes after he loses his eyesight.

Indoor sports are all right if they go home at a reasonable hour.

Husband, eyes glued to baseball on TV, to wife: "But there will be plenty of time to talk on nights they are rained out."

Bob Considine tells of the fan, watching a prize fight in New York and disgusted with the lack of action, who called out: "Hit him now, you bum. You got the wind with you!"

John McGraw once told an erring first baseman: "You have more talent to the square head than anybody I know."

"I love rodeos," Ed Wynn declares, "because it's such a relief to see the bull throwing people for a change."

Sign on municipal tennis court: "IF LADIES' SHORTS BECOME ANY SHORTER, THEY WON'T BE ALLOWED ANY LONGER."

Most indoor sports are either illegal, immoral, or fattening.

356

SPRING

Dan Bennett says that spring is that time of year when motorists drain the antifreeze from their radiators two weeks too soon.

STALLING

Some people have made an art of being slow to pick up the check. You've really got to hand it to them.

STATESMEN

Congress: a lawmaker's body which has some of the best members that money can buy.

STATISTICS

A statistician is a man who comes to the rescue of figures that can't lie for themselves.

Statistics show that there are three ages when men misbehave—young, old, and middle.

Statistics are like a Bikini bathing suit. What they reveal is suggestive, but what they conceal is vital.

News item: "Statisticians find that nine out of ten women are knock-kneed." And for years I've been thinking that statisticians never had any fun.

STENOGRAPHERS

Office girl, leaving on vacation, told her substitute: "While I'm gone, you'll go right on with what I was working on—but that doesn't include Mr. Disney."

Want ad in Seattle newspaper: "Wanted: secondhand typewriter by young lady student with wide carriage."

An employer was pointing out to his secretary several errors she had made during the day when she interrupted with: "Mr. Smith, it's five minutes past five; you're annoying me on my own time."

Glamour girl to male fellow worker: "Yes, I can tell you how I got my raise, but I don't think it will help you much."

Steno to caller on the phone: "He's out to lunch now, but he won't be gone long—nobody took him."

From the New York *Times*: "Author-psychologist wants secretary, college graduate who has majored in any subject but psychology."

A secretary may not be able to add but she certainly can distract.

Many a steno feels she isn't getting along very well when the boss compliments her on nothing but her work.

Certainly the Dictaphone has one advantage. It never takes a man's mind off his work by crossing its knees.

From Miami newspaper: "Vacationing stenographer beaching daytimes would like to be occupied nights to make vacation money. Am fast and make no errors.

Shorthand can be a great blessing to a steno, especially if she doesn't know how to spell.

Sign on a secretary's desk: The boss may not always be right, but the boss is always the boss.

One steno complaining to co-worker: "That handsome young executive asked me if I had a date for this evening and when I said 'No' he piled all this work on my desk."

Steno: a girl you teach to spell and punctuate while she looks around for a husband.

Tardy secretary to boss: "I'm really not late. I took my coffee break before coming in."

STICK-TO-ITIVENESS

Diamond: a chunk of coal that stuck to its job.

STORIES

To make a long story short, don't tell it.

One of the frustrations of an elevator operator is that he never hears the end of stories.

The drawback to telling a good story is that it reminds the other fellow of a dull one.

One sure way to make a long story short is to start telling it to a traffic cop.

Anecdote: a brief account of an incident that never occurred in the life of some famous person.

STRUGGLE

From the time an infant tries to get his toes into his mouth, life's a continual struggle to make both ends meet.

STUDENTS

A student says his school is promoting a new do-it-yourself project —it's called homework.

Did you know that school children are getting stronger? To be sure that a new type of desk would stand up under juvenile squirming, it was tested by being hit 30,000 times with a 40-pound sandbag.

STYLES

If brevity is the soul of wit, then women's swimsuits are getting funnier.

Women were made before mirrors and have been before them ever since.

Some of today's styles show a woman's good tastes—and that isn't all.

Negligee: what a woman hopes she'll have on when there's a fire in the house.

Sign on a Los Angeles display of women's bathing suits: "Suits that let you slink or swim."

A fur coat is not to keep a woman warm, but to keep her quiet.

Every woman has a price on her head—if she wears a hat.

Women who wear ridiculous hats are just trying to avoid being conspicuous.

The modern girl wears less on the street than her grandmother did in bed.

The clothes that make the woman are the clothes that break the man.

Women's hats are all different, Earl Wilson says, because no one likes to make the same mistake twice.

W. J. McAuliffe makes the observation that women who are not interested in clothes are probably not interesting in clothes.

A husband asked his wife where she didn't get her new bikini bathing suit.

Fashion note: There'll be little change in men's pockets this year.

Many a man has stopped calling his wife "the little woman" after taking a good look at her in slacks.

In a night club a fellow pointed out a girl wearing a daringly low-cut gown. "That girl," he said to his companion, "is wearing a $1,000 gown." "True," was the reply, "but her heart isn't in it."

Some women are attractive in slacks, but that does not go for the bulk of them.

Arthur Godfrey once told of a girl "wearing one of those convertible dresses—with the top down."

Women wear funny things, but a stiff, tight collar isn't one of them.

A salesgirl told a woman in the fitting room: "On the other hand, Madam doesn't do anything for the dress, either."

Bob Hope says that evening gowns are getting more daring every day—the front is now daring the back.

And then there was the woman who looked as though her toreador pants had been put on with a spray gun.

Milo Anderson, fashion designer, makes the observation that most women in strapless gowns look like a chest of drawers with the top drawer left open.

A woman is a person who will spend $25 on a beautiful slip and then be annoyed if it shows.

The best camouflage for a woman's bow legs is a plunging neckline.

Herb Stein caught a glimpse of a Hollywood star in a very low-cut gown at a preview. "She comes from one of the Scandinavian countries," he was informed. "Yes, I see," agreed Stein appreciatively, "Jutland, no doubt."

Bikini bathing suit: something that begins nowhere and ends all at once.

The trouble with a lot of fashions for women is that you finally get used to them.

The strapless evening gown is held up principally by public opinion.

Oren Arnold muses that "I never mind when a woman looks poured into a dress, provided too much hasn't settled to the bottom."

Easter millinery: hatrocities.

Women wear two kinds of clothes—the fashionable and the comfortable.

Louis Sobol spoke of the woman "who was wearing a low-cut gown, with ample reasons."

A woman never knows what kind of dress she doesn't want until she buys it.

Bikini bathing suits: two dots and a dash.

Girls who wear blue jeans probably figure that the end justifies the jeans.

A new hat is not only a tonic for a woman, but it makes her feel strong enough to buy a suit and two pairs of shoes to go with it.

Blanche Bowman, describing a woman, said "She looked as though she had dressed in front of an airplane propeller."

Nowadays no woman will wear a hat or dress identical to another woman's—but all rules are off about mink coats.

A well-dressed woman is like a good actress—she never overplays her lines.

Angel: a woman who is always harping on something and never seems to have anything to wear.

Fashion: something that goes in one year and out the other.

Bob Burns, in describing a woman's hat, said: "It looked like a dish of chop suey with a choice of two vegetables."

Herbert V. Prochnow asks, "What would we say if men changed the length of their trousers every year?"

Will Rogers once remarked, "Every time a woman leaves off something she looks better, but every time a man leaves off something he looks worse."

The clothes that keep a man looking his best, Walter Woerner says, are worn by girls on beaches.

From an ad in the Cleveland *Plain Dealer*: "Look younger and simmer in Millay girdles."

The modern woman believes in love, honor, and display.

Many modern evening dresses are more gone than gown.

Jay E. House says that a new hat has the same effect on a woman as three cocktails have on a man.

The one way every man likes to have a woman dress for him is fast.

Most men lack imagination—that's why dress designers leave so little to it.

Sign on dressmaker's shingle in New Orleans: "Skirts that Strut."

An evening dress is another case where there's plenty of room at the top.

Eve was lucky. She didn't have to look behind her to see what other women were wearing.

Host introducing man to woman wearing a strapless gown: "This is Professor Heinzman, authority on structural engineering. He wants to ask you something."

Women's styles may change, but their designs remain the same.

Men get one break. At least they know where their waistline will be next year.

SUBMISSION

The man who gives in when he is right is weak, spineless, and probably married.

SUBSTITUTES

Children, after their regular teacher's illness, reported, "Oh, we liked the substitute teacher all right, but she wasn't as good as you. She had to use two hands to play the piano."

SUBURBANITE

Suburbanite: a man who hires someone to mow his lawn so he can play golf for exercise.

"The typical successful American businessman," Don Marquis once declared, "was born in the country, where he worked like hell so he could live in the city, where he worked like hell so he could live in the country."

SUCCESS

By the time you are important enough to take hours off for lunch, the doctor limits you to a glass of milk and a cracker.

The dictionary is the only place where success comes before work.

All that stands between some people and the top of the ladder is the ladder.

Success is the ability to make more money to meet obligations you wouldn't have if you didn't have so much money.

The trouble is that when success turns a fellow's head it doesn't wring his neck at the same time.

What lies behind us and what lies before us are tiny matters compared to what lies within us.

Success is getting up just once more than you fall.

We know a man who owes his success to his first wife, and his second wife to his success.

The gent who wakes up and finds himself a success hasn't been asleep.

You know a man is successful when the newspapers start quoting him on subjects he knows nothing about.

A successful businessman uses two desks—one for each foot.

Remember that you are not really successful until you hear from a fellow who proudly claims that he sat next to you in school.

Work faithfully eight hours a day, Robert Frost once said, and you may eventually get to be a boss and work twelve hours a day.

Did your hear about the fellow who climbed the ladder of success "wrong by wrong?"

Nothing recedes like success.

Success is a matter of either getting around you better than yourself or getting around better men than yourself.

It seems easier to succeed when one doesn't have the advantages others have.

A man owes it to himself to become successful. Once he is successful he owes it to the Bureau of Internal Revenue.

Nowadays a man can't consider himself a success until he has to borrow money to pay his income tax.

You're on the road to success, William G. Milnes, Jr., observes, when you realize that failure is merely a detour.

Everybody's a self-made man, but only the successful ones are willing to admit it.

You don't have to stay awake nights to succeed. Just stay awake days.

How to succeed: Hitch your wagon to a star, put your shoulder to the wheel, keep an ear to the ground, and watch the handwriting on the wall.

Behind every successful man can usually be found three people: his wife and Mr. and Mrs. Jones.

The most difficult part of getting to the top of the ladder is getting through the crowd at the bottom.

God gave us two ends—one to sit on and one to think with. Success depends on which we use most. Heads we win, tails we lose.

Remember: Triumph is just umph added to try.

The secrets of success are secrets to most people.

Success: Don't rust on your laurels.

People sitting on top of the world usually arrived there standing up.

Too many people miss the silver lining because they're expecting gold.

One of the biggest troubles with success is that its recipe is often the same as that for a nervous breakdown.

You can't leave footprints in the sands of time by sitting down.

Behind most successful men is a publicity department.

Success doesn't always go to the head—often it goes to the mouth.

When success turns a person's head, he is facing failure.

Success that goes to a man's head usually pays a very short visit.

Starting from scratch isn't so hard. It's starting without it that's tough.

The home run you hit yesterday won't win today's ball game.

You can't get a square deal in life by going around in circles.

If hard work is the key to success, most people would rather pick the lock.

You are a success today, Bill Vaughan says, if you own the smallest car and the largest power mower in the neighborhood.

Successful man: one who earns more than his wife can spend.

Successful woman: one who can find such a man.

The road to success is dotted with many tempting parking places.

If you don't believe that success is merely a matter of luck, ask any failure.

If at first you don't succeed—you are running about average.

SUMMER

It's a sure sign of summer if the chair gets up when you do.

The reason some girls are such live wires during the summer is that they wear so little insulation.

Reflection after a summer's inspection: "Bikini once referred only to an atoll. Now it's a swimsuit—nothing at all."

Summer: the season when children slam doors they have left open all winter.

SUMMER CAMP

Camp: where parents spend $1,000 to teach their daughter to make a 50-cent pot-holder.

SUNDAY

Some persons think if they wear their best clothes on Sunday they're observing the Sabbath.

SUPERIORITY

Having a party so you can snub certain folks by not inviting them is O.K. if you're entirely sure they would have come if you had invited them.

Some people are like owls. They get the reputation for being wise just by hooting at everything.

SURPLUS

Among the nation's unmanageable surpluses are wheat, cotton, and Girl Scout cookies.

SURVEYS

Recent surveys show that four out of five women haters are women.

SUSPICION

Wife to husband: "There's a corner torn off your pay check—what did you spend it for?"

Watching the ads on matchbook covers in your husband's pockets is a lot cheaper than hiring a detective.

Frances Rodman says that suspicion is trying to find out what you'll wish later you didn't know.

SWIMMING

Going to the beach is like going to the attic—you are surprised what you will find in trunks.

Robert Q. Lewis says that the trouble with a bathing suit is that it either shows you off or shows you up.

SYMPATHY

We know a woman who has a sympathetic disposition—but she wastes it on herself.

Sympathy is what one girl offers another in exchange for details.

Gracie Allen, on hearing of a friend's death: "Oh, that's too bad. I hope he didn't die of anything serious."

TACT

Did you hear about the woman who told her guests, "Oh, Fred and I are always on the go. We haven't had a dull moment since the last time we saw you."

"How did you manage to marry an heiress?" a man was asked, and he replied, "It was simple. I sent her twenty-five roses on her thirty-third birthday."

Arch Ward says that tact is the ability to shut your mouth before someone else wants to.

Tact is the ability to fleece the flock without making them flinch.

Husband (who's forgotten) to wife: "How do you expect me to remember your birthday when you never look any older?"

Tact is what a man needs when he chooses heredity as a subject of conversation.

Diplomat: one who thinks twice before saying nothing.

Tact is a matter of knowing how far to go too far.

TACTLESSNESS

Famous last words: "This cake is simply delicious, darling. Did you buy it yourself?"

TALENT

One machine can do the work of fifty ordinary men, but no machine can do the work of one extraordinary man.

Ever noticed that the world is full of people who know how the other fellow should use his talents and resources?

TALKING

If there's anything we can't stand, it's people who talk while we're interrupting.

Many things are opened by mistake—but none so frequently as one's mouth.

Think twice before you speak and then say it to yourself.

Repartee: what a person thinks of when he becomes a departee.

Lecture: something that can make you feel numb on one end and dumb on the other.

Bob Hawk says that an echo is the only thing that can keep a woman from having the last word.

Women find themselves at quite a disadvantage since men can now travel faster than sound.

Absence makes the tongues go faster.

Some men tell their wives everything that happens—others tell them a lot of things that never happen.

There's something unique about a whisper—it makes people believe what they wouldn't otherwise.

Franklin P. Jones says that the man who can make a woman listen usually does it by talking to someone else.

Many a wife is outspoken—but not by many.

A. A. Latimer says that whoever named it "small talk" was a poor judge of quantity.

Harold Coffin says that stereophonic sound is when you're trapped between two women who are telling about their operations.

Have you seen this sign in a barbershop window: "Four Barbers in Attendance—Panel Discussions"?

368

Heard in a coffee shop: "There's one sure thing about Malcolm. If there's nothing to be said, he'll always say it."

Our idea of a convincing talker is one who can keep both hands in his pockets while describing the fish that got away.

Did you hear about the girl who speaks four languages—and another one with her eyes?

Howard Haynes says that a chance remark is anything a man manages to say when two women are talking.

You might as well keep your mouth shut: If you talk about yourself you're a bore. If you talk about others you're a gossip.

We have a friend who lets her mind go blank, but forgets to turn off the sound.

Woman: a person who stands twenty minutes talking at the door because she hasn't time to come in.

We know a man who wears his thoughts on his tongue.

Kid was asked: "What were your father's last words before he died?" and the kid replied, "He didn't have any. Mother was with him to the end."

Some persons have eyes and see not and ears that hear not, but we've known few persons with tongues who talk not.

Any man who says women aren't good listeners should be careful what he says.

She developed an impediment in her speech—she stops to think.

Sign in an air-base office: "Be sure brain is engaged before putting mouth into gear."

The best way to save face is to stop shooting it off.

William Feather says that the only way to escape detailed, warmed-over recitals of an event is to fib and say you saw and you heard it all.

Roberta Yates once said, "He's a man of few words, but he keeps repeating them."

TALL TALES

A Floridan, visiting in California, picked up a melon and asked,

"Is this the largest apple you can grow out here?" and the native son replied, "Stop fingering that grape."

TARDINESS

When a man is always late for dinner, either his wife is a poor cook or his secretary is very pretty.

Boss (to stenographer): "Congratulations, Miss Jones—this is the earliest you've ever been late."

TAXES

Herb Shriner thinks Congress will do something about hidden taxes this year. "They won't do away with them," he says, "they'll just hide them better."

Jack Benny told Jayne Mansfield, "You look like a million bucks, and that's quite a lot—about $116,000 after taxes."

Ah, for those good old days when Uncle Sam lived within his income—and without most of ours.

Stephanie Martino explains that it's better to give than to receive and it's deductible.

Work hard, save your money, keep on hustling, and some day you may be able to pay your taxes in one installment.

Don McNeill tells of a special fountain pen for tax collectors—it writes under hot water.

It's getting harder to support the government in the style to which it has become accustomed.

Tax evader: an income-poop.

Income tax is the fine for reckless thriving.

Some of today's most imaginative fiction is seen on income-tax forms.

Bruce Williams says that a penny saved is the government's share of the nickel you earned.

If it's such a small world today, why does it take so much money to run it?

Income tax: something that could be a lot worse. Suppose we had to pay on what we think we're worth?

When the time comes for the meek to inherit the earth, the taxes will probably be so high they won't want it.

Death and taxes may be with us always, but death doesn't get any worse.

Taxes are the way the government has of artificially inducing the rainy day everybody has been looking for.

If you think you have found a tax loophole, make sure that you can get more than your head through it.

Panhandlers now wear a sign on their chest which says, "It's tax deductible."

You may think your taxes are staggering, L. S. McCandless says, but they never go down.

One thing that keeps a man from holding his own is the Bureau of Internal Revenue.

A New York doctor says that prehistoric man was neither stoop-shouldered nor bow-legged. Then came taxes.

The Internal Revenue Department apparently works on the theory that "Man wants but little here below."

It looks like eventually we will all make our living by collecting taxes from each other.

Quipped a hard-hit businessman, after paying his income tax: "All my success I owe to Uncle Sam."

Bureau of Internal Revenue: institution looking for men who have what it takes in order to take what they have.

We fought a war once over taxation without representation—look what it is costing us now with representation.

Everybody should pay their taxes with a smile. I tried, but they wanted cash.

A liquor tax is the only one which provides its own anesthetic.

Home-coming husband to wife: "I got a raise. Now we can afford last year's taxes!"

It is hard to believe that America was founded to avoid taxation.

Graduates shouldn't say "Good-bye" to logarithms and calculus. They'll need both when they figure their income tax.

Taxpayer: a person who has the government on the payroll.

A taxpayer is a person who doesn't have to pass a civil-service exam to work for the government.

From Indianapolis: A tax clerk was taken aback by a blank tax return which was accompanied by this note: "You were notified several times that I have been dead for four years. Please send no more of these blanks."

TAXIS

Taxi meter: a device for showing how fast you aren't getting there.

TEACHERS

"I don't really dislike school," the teacher said. "It's the principal of the thing."

A mother wrote to her youngster's teacher: "I kept Bob at home because of a cold. What a peaceful day you must have had."

A young woman took a job as private teacher but suddenly quit. Upon being asked why she said, "Had to. Backward child. Forward father."

The teacher in an overcrowded classroom started her morning attendance report: "Help! They're all here!"

My teacher is a former actress and very hammy. She takes bows every time I clap the erasers.

Did you hear about the young teacher who said to his girl friend, "Bet you wouldn't marry me, would you?" She not only called his bet, but she raised him five.

TEAMWORK

Bright young thing to oarsman after his crew had lost the race: "Never mind, dear. You were wonderful. You rowed faster than anyone in the boat!"

372

TEEN-AGERS

Distressed teen-ager: "Mom! Dad! What happened to my new record—the one I played all day yesterday?"

A teen-ager's aunt said she would like to buy him some records but wondered how to choose them, so he wrote: "Listen to the beat, and if you don't like it, send it to me."

If you have teen-agers in your household, you'll find it difficult to understand how farmers can possibly grow a surplus of food.

A teen-age girl returned from the movies and her mother asked, "How was it?" The girl replied, "Terrible. I could hardly sit through it twice."

Father to son: "Mind if I use the car tonight? I'm taking your mother out and I want to impress her."

Teen-ager, to doctor listening to her heart: "Does it sound broken?"

One teen-ager to another: "The trouble with Father is that he remembers what it is to be young."

Adolescence is when daughter knows best.

Some young people think curbing their emotions means parking by the roadside.

When Walt Disney was planning Disneyland he asked one of his teen-age daughters what he could add to the park which would interest girls of her age. "Boys," she answered.

Teen-age boy coming into Denver coffee shop: "Boy, oh boy, I got her home just in time! I'm starving."

Teen-age is the time between pigtails and cocktails.

Earl Wilson says you can usually tell when a high-school boy is serious about a girl by the way she calls him up every evening.

Adolescence: that period when children feel their parents should be told the facts of life.

Asked how old her daughter was, a woman replied: "She's just at the age when she responds to every remark with 'Oh, Mother.'"

Parents of a teen-age daughter are often miss-informed.

Teenagers: people who express a burning desire to be different by dressing exactly alike.

Some teen-agers regard home as a drive-in where pop pays for the hamburgers.

When she says she has a boyish figure—that's straight from the shoulder.

Mother to teen-age daughter, "Now don't sit down at that phone—dinner is going to be ready in less than an hour."

Going steady may be a matter of love, but for most youngsters, it's merely Saturday-night security.

Adolescence, mothers find, is the period in which their young suddenly feel a great responsibility about answering the telephone.

A disconsolate teen-ager told her parents, "Jim and I aren't going steady any more. I went out on a blind date and there he was."

A teen-ager, seeing his mother working in the yard, said, "You shouldn't be out in the hot sun mowing the lawn, Mom. Where's Dad?"

A girl's father was annoyed by the way his daughter's dates drove up to the house and honked loudly for her to come out. When a horn blared the next evening, daughter yelled out from the upstairs window, "Sorry, Jack, you'll have to come in. Father says no more curb service."

We asked our kid how he could demolish a large plate of cookies when we had just finished dinner and he replied, "Eating makes me hungry."

The nice thing about being a teen-ager these days is that you can pick up any magazine and have your suspicions about your parents confirmed.

A pre-teen, says Joseph Stone, is too old for toys and too young for boys.

A teen-ager answered the telephone and said, "Of all the crazy things! It's for you, Father!"

A teen-ager told her chum, "For Christmas I'd like to get Larry something for his car that he would never think to buy himself—but all I can think of is gasoline."

"Gee, Dad," stammered the young man, "I'm in love with a girl and—" and his parent interrupted, "Well, you couldn't have made a better choice."

374

TELEGRAMS

From the official British Post Office Guide: "Telegrams, other than government, must be written in plain language."

TELEPHONE

Nothing spoils the cheerfulness of a phone call like the question, "How many tickets will you take?"

Pity the poor student who had to call the Chinese laundry about a clean shirt. He tried and tried to get the telephone operator to give him the Wong number!

Sign in telephone booth at navy base: PLEASE LIMIT CALLS TO FOUR GIRLS.

One young fellow to chum: "I was in a phone booth talking to my girl, but someone wanted to use the phone so we had to get out."

The wife of an obstetrician overheard her seven-year-old answer the phone: "Yes, this is Doctor Harper's house. Sorry, Doctor Harper isn't here right now. How far apart are the pains?"

TELEVISION

An adult Western is one in which the hero kills just as many men as in a kids' Western, but he doesn't enjoy it.

Television has made a semicircle out of the family circle.

Nowadays a husband and wife either have to have minds that run in the same channel or two television sets.

The biggest drawback to educational television is that most children want to major in cowboys and Indians.

One thing you can say about typical TV cowboy shows: they stick to their guns!

The reason they sing most of the commercials is that they would sound even sillier without music.

June Havoc says that one thing's sure: on TV the jokes last longer than the comics.

Spectacular: "Let's make the show longer and more expensive and maybe they won't notice how lousy it is."

375

Television certainly helps you get acquainted with a lot of new people—mostly repairmen.

Have you heard about the new TV show for burlesque queens? It's called "Who Shed That?"

Feminine gowns on TV don't seem to be causing a great deal of back talk.

Jack Gould reviewed a new quiz show in the New York *Times*: "There were rewards for everybody but the audience."

Our idea of a good television mystery is one where it's hard to detect the sponsor.

TV spectacular: the bill you get from the repairman.

A mother rushed her little boy away from a TV program featuring scantily clad chorus girls. She told him: "Yes, it's bedtime for everybody! See, those ladies are already half undressed."

Television performers have one advantage—they can reach millions of people who can't reach them.

For a gal to get into TV, she has to know somebody or have some body.

Salesmen of second hand TV set to customer: "Now here's a good set formerly owned by an elderly lady who never stayed up past eight o'clock."

"Television is a kind of radio," Fred Allen said, "which lets people at home see what the studio audience is not laughing at."

A network newscaster announced, "The FBI is leaving no stern untoned . . . ."

What passes for entertainment on a lot of television drama programs is a crime.

TV and Hollywood have reached a stalemate: the former revamps old films and the latter refilms the old vamps.

A TV repairman spread his tools out on the floor of the home to which he had been summoned and asked the housewife, "What seems to be the trouble?" and she replied, "Well, for one thing, all the programs are lousy."

Herb Shriner, telling about a dentist who distracts his patients with TV: "He waits 'till the commercial comes on, then pulls the tooth—that way you don't feel any extra pain."

TV will never replace magazines. You can't fold a TV program, lie back on the couch, open the set in the middle, and spread it over you for a quick nap.

Comment on glamour gal in a TV show: "What an evening gown! You couldn't tell whether she was inside, trying to get out, or outside trying to get in."

In these days of TV, a person who wants to talk in the average living room has to go through channels.

Ever noticed how a baseball game on TV usually has several wild pitches—by the sponsor?

Where there's smoke, there's probably a television commercial.

Nowadays, whatever is not worth saying is sung as a TV commercial.

Suggestion for a new TV show: a panel show in which the panelists interview other panelists and try to guess which panel show they're on.

By the time parents decide a TV program is something the children shouldn't see, they're too interested in it themselves to cut it off.

TV has a lot of first-grade comedy in it—the trouble is that most of the audience has gone beyond the first grade.

Some of these movies on TV are so old that they show bandits driving up in front of the bank—and finding a parking place.

TV producer's phone call to his new psychiatrist: "I'm too busy this week, Doc, so I'm sending my first five lessons on tape."

A contestant on a quiz program, confronted with the question, "What is a blunderbuss?" replied, "A baby buggy."

TEMPER

Men are like steel—when they lose their temper they lose their worth.

Our neighbor says his wife is even-tempered—mad all the time.

Funny thing about temper. You can't get rid of it by losing it.

377

Keep your temper. Do not quarrel with an angry person, but give him a soft answer. It is commanded by the Holy Writ, and, furthermore, it makes him madder than anything else you could say.

Strike when the iron is hot—not when the head is hot.

Art Linkletter once asked a boy of seven how he would go about settling an argument with another boy and he replied, "I'd count ten and then hit him on the nose."

Thomas Hood observed that an irritable man is like a hedgehog rolled up the wrong way, tormenting himself with his own prickles.

TEMPTATION

Most people who fly from temptation usually leave a forwarding address.

The trouble with resisting temptation is that it may never come again.

The easiest way to resist temptation is publicly.

You will understand how Charlie McCarthy felt when he said, "I'm torn between vice and versa."

A woman flees from temptation, but a man just crawls away from it in the cheerful hope that it may overtake him!

TENNIS

Shorts on tennis courts are quite a menace to those who come to concentrate on tennis.

TESTIMONIALS

A manufacturer of patent medicines received this testimonial: "Since taking your tablets regularly, I am another woman. Needless to say, my husband is delighted."

When a nationally known concern which puts out various toilet articles recently conducted a contest to obtain a slogan for their toilet soap and perfume, one contestant suggested: "If you don't use our soap, for goodness sake use our perfume!"

378

TEXAS

Texas nursery rhyme: The butcher, the baker, the Cadillac maker. . . .

A ticket clerk in an airline terminal asked a Texan, "Where to?" and he replied, "Anywhere. I've got business all over."

A Texan at a Nassau beach ran over to a crowd and found that his wife was being revived. He asked what they were doing to her and the guard said, "We're going to give her artificial respiration." The Texan replied, "Artificial, hell. Give her the real thing. I can afford it."

Watching a recently departed oil-rich Texan buried in his air-conditioned Cadillac, according to his latest request, a near-rich relative commented, "Yep, that's what I call livin'."

Texas housewife to husband: "Will you get out the car, dear, and drive the children to the backyard so they can play."

Did you hear about the rich Texas woman who has two chinchilla wraps—one for each chin?

Cute little blonde talking to wealthy Texan: "How much did you say your name was?"

When a Texas class was told that the next day they would learn to draw, eighteen youngsters showed up with pistols.

"You don't mean to tell me that you have 365 days of sunshine in Texas every year?" and the native son replied, "I shore do, and that is a mighty conservative estimate."

Boasted the Texas cattleman to the visitor: "We don't brand them. We have them engraved."

The middle-aged Texan went to the psychiatrist and begged, "Doc, I shore need your help. I'm in a bad way. I been a Texan all my life and suddenly I just don't give a damn!"

A cattle woman brought her son and prospective daughter-in-law into one of the swankiest jewelers in Dallas to buy flat silver. She did all the talking, ordered the most expensive set in the store. "What initials?" the clerk inquired. "Initials, hell," boomed the woman, "I want our cattle brand on that silver."

THANKSGIVING

What should you be thankful for on Thanksgiving Day if you're trying to lose weight?

Cheer up! Every dog has to live with his fleas.

Things could be tougher. You can still read the other fellow's paper over his shoulder, park at a meter on what's left of his nickel, and get through the swinging door on his push.

In an essay on "Things I'm Thankful For," a little boy listed "My glasses," and explained, "They keep the boys from fighting me and the girls from kissing me."

THEATERS

A theater is a place where long-bodied people sit in front of us, talkative ones behind us, and the nomadic type on each side.

Turkey in the straw: a flop in summer theater.

A student working at a summer theater made a disastrous mistake. The chorus was making a quick change on a dark stage when someone yelled for "Tights." He thought they said "Lights."

THINKING

The narrower the mind, the broader the statement, Ted Cook observes.

Be careful of your thoughts—they may break into words any time.

The human tongue is only a few inches from the brain, but they seem miles apart.

You can't stop people from thinking—but you can start them.

Clyde Moore describes the fellow "who has a one-track mind and the traffic on it is very light."

There is nobody so irritating as somebody with less intelligence and more sense than we have.

A woman makes up her mind and face several times a day, and is seldom satisfied with the results of either.

The reason some people get lost in thought is that it is unfamiliar territory to them.

The average man is a fellow who thinks things over very carefully about ten minutes after he has already done it.

Instead of broadening their minds, some people who travel merely lengthen their conversations.

A man's mind is like a car. If it gets to knocking too much, he'd better have it overhauled, or change it.

Oscar Levant quipped: "That guy lives on the wrong side of a one-track mind."

THOUGHTFULNESS

Our idea of a thoughtful wife is one who has the pork chops ready when her husband comes home from a fishing trip.

Thoughtfulness is leaving the lawn mower and garden tools where your wife can find them easily.

THOUGHTS

At the age of twenty, we don't care what the world thinks of us, at thirty we worry about what it is thinking of us, at forty we discover that it wasn't thinking of us at all.

C. L. Edson says that many a train of thought is just a string of empties.

Too many people just aren't equipped to attend a meeting of the minds.

Men can live without air for a few minutes, without water for two weeks, without food for about two months—and without a new thought for years.

THRIFT

The hardest thing for a husband to do when he brings home the bacon is to salt a little of it away.

He is tighter than the top olive in the bottle.

Some men still have the first dollar they earned, but most of us can't hold onto the last one.

Be thrifty when you're young, and when you're old, you'll be able to enjoy and afford the things that only the young can enjoy.

Miser: a person who is always close but whom you can never touch.

In Edinburgh there's a prudent man who talks through his nose to save wear and tear on his teeth.

TIME

Sign on bulletin board: "Why is it that there is never enough time to do it right but there is always enough time to do it over?"

Time heals all things—except a leaky radiator.

Our neighbor down the street usually takes his wife to a night club—it's the only place still open by the time she gets dressed.

A contestant on a TV quiz program was asked to name a great time-saver and he replied, "Love at first sight."

Luke Neely says that time flies, all right, but during working hours it often seems to be bucking head winds.

About the only thing that comes to him who waits is whiskers.

Alarm clock: an invention used to awake adults who have no babies.

Calendar: what a public speaker goes by if he forgets his watch.

No one will ever steal the clock from our office. Everybody around keeps his eyes on it.

Quentin Walters says that time may be a great healer, but it is no beauty specialist.

Some phenomena still baffle science, such as how the Good Humor wagon manages to be in front of everybody's house at a quarter of six.

Daylight-saving time was started by an old Indian who cut off one end of his blanket and sewed it on the other to make it longer.

Husband, trying to get wife off to a party, shouted: "For the last time—are you ready to go?" and she yelled, "For heaven's sake, be quiet—I've been telling you for the last hour that I'll be ready in a minute."

Alarm clock: a device to scare the daylights into you.

382

Days are like suitcases. By careful arrangement, some people can pack much more into them than others.

The greatest reformer of them all is Father Time.

Blessed is the man who appreciates his own time too highly to waste the time of someone else.

People who have time to waste usually spend it with someone who doesn't.

Too many people waste half their time finding ways to waste the other half.

Woman to husband: "I told them you had plans for the rest of the day—I want you to help me a few minutes."

A mother was explaining to her daughter about how to tell time: "These are the hours, these are the minutes, and these are the seconds," she explained, pointing them out. Puzzled, the little girl asked, "Where are the jiffies?"

Thirty days has September, April, June, and Uncle Zeke who'll be out Saturday.

Perfect timing: being able to turn off the "hot" and "cold" shower faucets at the same time.

TIRES

Spare tire: the one you check the day after you have a flat.

TOASTMASTER

A toastmaster is a man who eats a meal he doesn't want to tell a lot of stories he doesn't remember to people who've already heard them.

A good toastmaster: a person who has a good memory and hopes other people don't.

TOASTS

Know how members of the Hay Fever Club toast each other? Like this: "There's looking at-choooo!"

TOLERANCE

Tolerance is allowing other people to do what you like.

Tolerance: that uncomfortable feeling that the other fellow may be right after all.

The most important evidence of tolerance is a golden wedding anniversary.

Tolerance is the patience shown by a wise man when he listens to an ignoramus.

TOURISTS

Overheard: "And the third day out the weather was so awful George had to be lashed to the bar!"

Just heard about an American tourist who couldn't pay his bill in a French sidewalk cafe—so they threw him in!

It seems that some of our American tourists abroad are trying to foster the belief that Yank and jerk are synonymous.

Tourist: person with a heavy tan on his left forearm.

A tourist is a fellow who travels hundreds of miles in order to get a snapshot of himself standing by his automobile.

TOWN

Fred Allen's description of a New England town: "The place was so dull that one day the tide went out—and never came back."

Hick town: one where, if you see a girl dining with a man old enough to be her father, he is.

TOYS

Sheldon White describes this toy: "Send six box tops—this lifelike toy a small boy can build with a little bother, a pint of glue, a clamp or two, his uncle or his father."

TRAFFIC

If you think a woman driving a car can snarl up traffic, you ought to see a man pushing a cart in a supermarket!

Policeman (to traffic violator): "How long have you been driving—if you'll permit the complete misuse of a word."

Wife to speeding husband: "Slow down and let the motorcycle policeman pass you. He may be trying to catch someone."

Popular expressions are sometimes misleading. They call it "the rush hour" around five o'clock when you sit in your car for half an hour waiting for the traffic to move twelve feet!

A red traffic light is the place where you catch up with a motorist who passed you at sixty-five miles an hour a few hundred yards down the highway.

The biggest problem for traffic planners: urban, suburban, and bourbon drivers.

These days there are too many people in too many cars in too much of a hurry going in too many different directions to nowhere for nothing.

TRAINS

Upper berth: where you rise to retire and get down to get up.

TRANQUILIZERS

W. Earl Hall points out that science has never drummed up quite as effective a tranquilizing agent as a sunny spring day.

A well-adjusted person is one whose intake of energy pills overbalances his use of tranquilizers just enough to leave him sufficient energy for his daily work.

You can overdo anything. Some doctors say that their patients are taking so many tranquilizers that they don't worry about paying their medical bills.

Dr. Frederick Yonkman, medical director of a pharmaceutical company, speaking of the headaches of naming new drugs: "It's a shame we can't call the new tranquilizer 'Dammitol.'"

TRAVEL

Short cut: a route on which you can't find anybody to ask where you are.

Warning: The sun never sets on the British possessions or the American tourist.

A futile trip seems to be the one made by a fellow who went to Scotland to get a liberal education.

Clifton Fadiman says: "To feel at home, stay home."

From the Newport, Pennsylvania, *News-Sun*: "Mr. Lunford returned home after visiting indifferent cities in Florida."

Don't boast of your abilities until you have successfully folded a batch of road maps.

The *Mayflower* was a small ship on which several million Pilgrims came to America in 1620.

Over a push button at roadside service station in Wyoming: "Buzz twice for night service—then keep your shirt on while I get my pants on."

Sign in Manila airport: "Please start kissing 'way ahead of time so planes can leave on schedule."

Seasickness is when you travel across the ocean by rail.

"Marry me, darling," he said, "and I'll make you the happiest woman in fifty states," and she replied, "No, thank you. None of this life in a trailer for me."

A smart-aleck tourist asked a native, "What's your speed limit here?" and the native replied, "Ain't got none. You fellows can't go through here too fast for us."

A certain Alaskan Chamber of Commerce will be delighted every summer if all roads lead to Nome.

Map: a piece of paper to help you get lost.

Arizona sign: "This is God's country. Don't drive like hell."

If at first you don't succeed in folding the road map, throw it away and get another at the next filling station.

Multimillion-dollar highway: a ribbon of concrete that can be snarled up in two minutes by a stalled jalopy in a quarter-inch snowstorm.

Traveler: one who returns with brag and baggage.

386

Did you hear about the guide who lost his way? He told the troup, "I'm the best guide in Maine, only I think we're in Canada now."

Conductor asked man, "Where's the boy's ticket?" and the man explained that his son was only three years old, to which the agent exclaimed, "Three! Why, look at him—that child is seven if he's a day," and the father answered, "He's still only three—can I help it if he worries?"

You've heard about the resort where the tourists were so thick that they were getting into each other's snapshots.

A custom official was examining a suitcase in which a socialite returning from Europe had hidden an undeclared bottle of perfume. As his hand roamed near the danger zone, the small daughter squealed, "Oh, mummy. He's getting warm, isn't he?"

Breath-taking scenery usually leaves tourists speechless only until they reach home and friends.

One couple to another: "We took one of those 'all-expense tours'—and that's just what it was."

A hitchhiker leaving Omaha used this technique with success: on his chest was a huge placard, "She Lives in San Francisco."

Situations-wanted ad in Chicago *Tribune*: "Young man desires traveling job. Uncle Sam, please do not answer; once was enough."

TREES

There's something feminine about a tree. It does a strip tease in the fall, goes with bare limbs all winter, gets a new outfit in the spring, and lives off the saps in the summer.

TRIBUTES

A bad, bad man had been shot in a saloon brawl in Cripple Creek in the old days. They buried him and then everyone stood around the grave expectantly, waiting for someone to say a few good words for the deceased. At last one old man said, "Ol' Jim used to shoot a mighty good hand of marbles when he was a kid."

TROUBLE

Trouble is about the only thing you can borrow without references.

387

One way to keep happy is to learn to enjoy trouble.

Never trouble trouble until trouble troubles you.

Dorothy Dix once received this note from a puzzled reader: "Of course my wife and I have spats like all happily married couples, and I once broke her ribs. But we have never had any disagreement of a serious nature."

You can always save yourself a lot of trouble by not borrowing any.

He's nursing a grouch. His wife is sick.

When you look for trouble, you don't need a search warrant.

When we can't make light of our troubles, we can keep them in the dark.

Leon Henderson says that the trouble with trouble is that it always starts out like fun.

In Lincoln, Nebraska, a man finally discovered why he kept breaking out in a rash. The doctor told him he was allergic to money.

If you could kick the person responsible for most of your troubles, you wouldn't be able to sit down for six months.

It's the little things that really trouble you; you can sit in comfort on a mountain but not on a tack.

TRUTH

Cal Tinney says that a truthful woman is one who won't lie about anything except her age, her weight, and her husband's salary.

Figures don't lie but girdles condense the truth.

The trouble with stretching the truth is that's apt to snap back.

Josh Billings reminds us that "As scarce as truth is, the supply is always greater than the demand."

Convention speaker: "These are not my own figures I am quoting. They are the figures of someone who knows what he is talking about."

"You seem to have plenty of intelligence for a man in your position," sneered a lawyer as he examined a witness. "If I wasn't under oath I'd return the compliment," was the reply.

Description of a bubbly woman whose veracity had come into

question: "Well, she doesn't exactly tell the truth all the time. There just isn't that much truth."

Any fool can tell the truth, but it requires a man of great sense to lie well. A good memory also comes in handy.

Our prehistoric ancestors told monstrous lies to each other about the wonders of far-off countries. Now we have chambers of commerce.

The truth never hurts unless it ought to.

UNDERSTANDING

Men's failure to understand women isn't so bad. It's women's ability to understand men that wrecks us.

There are two periods in a man's life when he doesn't understand women—before and after marriage.

UNEMPLOYMENT

Millions are idle, but it's comforting to know that most of them have jobs.

This is the only country in the world where a man cap hop into his car and drive to town to collect his unemployment insurance.

UNHAPPINESS

Unhappiness is not so much not getting what you want but not wanting what you get or knowing what you want.

Little kid, who had been hurt in fall, told his mother, "I didn't cry; I just clouded up."

VACATIONS

Relax! Take a vacation. There are several spots where you can get tanned and faded at the same time.

Sam Levenson says that some people save a lot of money on a vacation—they keep cool all summer by sponging.

When it comes to getting a sun tan, ignorance is blister.

Alternative to a vacation: Stay at home and tip every third person you see.

Why is it that the rainy days for which we save our money always come during our vacation?

Vacation: a sunburn at premium prices.

If a vacation does nothing else, Charles Ruffing observes, it lets you know how well off you were when you still had the money to take a vacation.

Vacation consists of two weeks of playing and fifty of paying.

The bigger the summer vacation, the harder the fall.

A husband who was painting his house said to a neighbor husband who was washing windows: "You're lucky, only getting a two-week vacation. I get three!"

Man, showing snapshot of himself with fish, to neighbor: "But my daughter caught the really big fish on our vacation—a young man twenty-two years old!"

Sad fact of summer life: Most vacation spots don't feature the same gals that were in the ads.

A vacation is a short period of time during which you go broke trying to make strangers believe you can't.

The worst thing about taking vacations in winter, John T. Mc-Cutcheon, Jr., muses, is July.

Summer is that season of the year when you ride bumper to bumper to the beach, where you sit the same way.

The sum of the parts can be greater than the whole—especially when it comes to repacking a vacation suitcase.

Vacation has been defined as a period during which people find out where to stay away from next year.

Anyone who says you can't take it with you never saw a car packed for a vacation trip.

We know a guy who figures his vacation has been a success if his self-winding watch runs down.

A salesman, held up in small Wyoming town by a bad snowstorm, wired his firm: "Stranded here due to storm. Wire instructions." Back came the reply: "Start summer vacation immediately."

About the only thing you can do on a shoestring these days is trip.

Good vacation advice: Every time you feel the need for exercise, lie down and rest until the feeling goes away.

Vacation folder: a trip tease.

Sun-tanned businessman to envious colleague: "It ought to be a wonderful tan. I figure it cost me $173.78 per square inch."

Sharron Fife says "The shortest distance between two points is the beginning to the end of a vacation."

August is a beautiful vacation month—except for those who went in July.

Scottish vacation: Stay at home and let your mind wander.

Vacation: After a couple of weeks of it you feel good enough to go back to work and so poor you have to.

Phil Baker used to tell of a butcher who closed up for a vacation— went on a meat loaf.

Vacations are great levelers. The person who takes one returns home just as broke as the person who stayed home because he couldn't afford to go.

Nobody knows where the plumber goes on weekends, but presumably he goes off fishing with the doctor, the locksmith, and the television repairman.

Vacationist to druggist: "Do you have anything that's good for mosquito bites on top of poison ivy over sunburn?"

VIEWPOINT

Firmness has two meanings. In reference to one's self it means decision—to one's neighbor, obstinacy.

VISION

Vision: what people think you have when you guess correctly.

VISITS

Some folks can stay longer in an hour than others can in a week.

VITALITY

Of course life doesn't begin at forty for the fellow who went like sixty when he was twenty.

VOCABULARY

We have always wondered what appeal crossword puzzles have to a man of few words.

Said the preacher as he slipped on the banana peel: "It's odd how old, forgotten words spring to mind, isn't it?"

The average woman's vocabulary is much smaller than that of a man, experts tell us. But it isn't the original stock that counts—it's the turnover!

VOTING

Maybe one reason so many people don't vote is that they vote the way they think.

WAGES

One circus elephant said to another, "I'm getting sick and tired of working for peanuts."

WAITERS

Vexed diner: "You say you're the same waiter who took my order? Somehow I expected a much older man."

WAITING

It's Ivern Boyett's idea that the only things that come to him who waits are birthdays and second notices.

WAR

War: a period that begins by paying off old scores and ends by paying off new debts.

War doesn't determine who is right—only who is left.

Rear Admiral Chester Nimitz once explained that a ship is always referred to as a "she" because it costs so much to keep one in paint and powder.

War paint: lipstick smear on a married man's collar.

Chemical warfare began a few thousand years ago when girls started using perfume to get their man.

WARNING

Notice in rural weekly: "Anyone found near my chicken house at night will be found there the next morning."

From a San Francisco newspaper: "In the event of an atomic attack, close your windows, lie down on the floor, and turn on the gas."

From a classified ad in a small Mississippi paper: "Positively no more baptizing in my pasture. Twice in the last two months my gate has been left open by Christian people, and before I chase my heifers all over the country again, all the sinners can go to hell."

WATCH

Watch: what an after-dinner speaker puts on the table as he arises and does not consult it any more.

WEALTH

Untold wealth is what is not reported on the income-tax return.

Poverty is a state of mind often induced by a neighbor's new car.

Millionaire: a man who travels between his air-conditioned home and air-conditioned office in an air-conditioned car, and then pays fifty dollars to go over to the steam room at the club and sweat.

Anybody, it seems, can become wealthy in America today by inventing something that can be used once and then thrown away.

It may be hard for a rich man to enter the kingdom of Heaven, but it's usually easy for him to get on the church board of trustees.

Nothing distributes the wealth like taxes and a large family.

WEATHER

A kid was asked to name the four seasons of the year and he said, "Marbles, baseball, football, and basketball."

Rheumatism was nature's first effort toward establishing a weather bureau.

It's easy to arrive in Florida and know the seasons—in the winter you see stuffed shirts and in the summer you see stuffed shorts.

Noah was another weather prophet whom nobody believed when he said it was going to rain.

A visitor asked a native if much snow falls in windy Cheyenne, and he replied, "No, but there's a heck of a lot goes through here."

"Mean" temperature is what the people of California think the people of Florida have—and vice versa.

Weatherman on telephone: "My corn hurts, too, madam, but we still say it will be clear and sunny."

The Portland *Oregonian* published the following forecast: "Tomorrow, snow, followed by little boys with sleds."

From a Montana newspaper: "Tomorrow we may expect strong northwest winds reaching a gal in exposed places."

Headline in Memphis newspaper: "HEAVY RAINS ASSURE CITY'S MILK SUPPLY."

Weather control is progressing so fast that we may soon read, "Rain postponed on account of football game."

Last summer was a real sizzler! The thermometer was up in Hades.

WEDDINGS

After the wedding, "They should be very happy. They're both so in love with him."

A wedding is proof that a man's will power is no match for a girl with wile power.

Sweet young thing to friend at wedding, "Her 'something borrowed' is my boy friend."

Bride to her groom after a big church wedding: "Wow, such excitement! Next time I'm going to have a quiet wedding at home."

Wedding story in Louisiana newspaper: "The bride wore a white sat in gown."

Usher, passing collection plate at wedding: "Yes, ma'am, it's unusual, but the father of the bride requested it."

Wedding story in Georgia paper: "The groom has been married previously on two occasions. He has also been through World War II."

Classified ad: "For sale, wedding dress, white chantilly lace over satin. Used once, successfully."

Statistics show increases in marriages. Life seems to be just a marry chase.

They're making wedding rings lighter and thinner these days. In the old days they were meant to last a lifetime.

Eldon Pederson says that the average girl walks on air as soon as she gets engaged, and waits until after the ceremony to put her foot down.

One sweet thing to another as they watch bride and groom leave the church: "She was the one who advised me to play hard-to-get with him."

Bride's father to groom: "My boy, you're the second happiest man in the world."

WEIGHT

One shouldn't do two things at the same time; that includes women who put on weight and slacks.

Nature is generous. When you begin to sit around, she provides more cushions.

Little girl showing bathroom scales to playmate: "All I know is, you stand on it and it makes you mad."

Diet is a short period of starvation preceding a gain of five pounds.

WIDOWS

And then there was the widow who told the bachelor: "Take it from me—don't get married."

The widow said her husband was a total loss—he died without insurance.

A widow is lucky because she knows all about men—and the only man who knows about her is dead.

WILL POWER

A woman was boasting to a friend that her husband had quit smoking. "My, that takes will power," said the friend, and the woman replied, "Indeed it does, and that's just what I've got."

Will of your own is more likely to help you succeed than the will of a rich relative.

In these days of low-cut gowns, tight-fitting waists, and sheer stockings, it takes will power for a man to look a woman in the eye.

WILLS

Where there's a will there's a delay.

WINTER

Winter is the season of the year when you keep the house as hot as it was in the summer when you complained about it.

WISDOM

Wisdom is knowing the difference between pulling your weight and throwing it around.

What you don't know takes a lot of explaining to the children.

WISHES

Next to being young and pretty, your best bet is to be old and rich.

WIT

Desmond McCarthy, describing some friends, said: "They were at their wits' end, and it hadn't taken them long to get there."

WIVES

A wife who says she can read her husband like a book rarely does. Instead of skipping what she doesn't like, she goes over and over it.

Every wife leads a double life—her husband's and her own.

Wife to husband: "Instead of buying me an expensive birthday present this year, why not give me something you've made yourself—for instance, money."

A wife is a person who can look in the top drawer of a dresser and find a man's handkerchief that isn't there.

The ideal wife is one who knows when her husband wants to be forced to do something against his will.

Let your wife know who's boss right from the start. There's no use kidding yourself.

The allowances husbands give can't compare with the allowances wives make.

My wife is asking for pin money—and the pin she wants has twelve diamonds in it.

A word to the wife is sufficient, provided that word is "yes."

About the time we can make both ends meet, my wife moves the ends.

The man of the hour is the one whose wife asked him to wait a minute.

Wife to husband with hangover: "I don't see why your head should hurt this morning. You certainly didn't use it last night."

There is nothing quite as satisfying to a woman as a double chin, provided it's on her husband's former girl friend.

What you can't explain to your wife is precisely what the other women understand without elaboration on your part.

Hollywood crack: "She's old enough to be his wife."

Arthur Godfrey says that the best way for a housewife to have a few minutes to herself at the end of the day is to start doing the dishes.

What the average woman wants is a great big strong man whom she can wrap around her finger.

"Help your wife," advises a home economics lecturer. "When she washes the dishes, wash the dishes with her; when she mops the floor, mop the floor with her."

A wife wants to know why they don't print newspapers on transparent paper, so wives can see their husbands at breakfast.

If your wife doesn't treat you as she should—be thankful!

If you want the little woman to burn up from curiosity, just clip a brief item from the morning paper before you hand it to her.

When a wife insists on wearing the pants, some other woman is usually wearing the fur coat.

The Devil was looking over his new arrivals and he noticed one man strutting like a peacock. He spoke to him, "You act like you owned the place," and he replied, "I do. My wife gave it to me."

One wife to another: "Does your husband still find you entertaining after a year's marriage?" and she replied, "Not if I can help it."

Affection: the sudden feeling that a wife gets for her husband when she wants a new fur coat.

WOLVES

Wolf: a male who devotes the best leers of his life to women.

Wolf: a man you can't trust too far or too near.

The average wolf is quite slap-happy by the time he becomes thirty-five.

WOMEN

Career girl: a gal who'd rather bring home the bacon than fry it.

About the only exercise some women get is running up bills.

Men never learn anything about women, but they have a lot of fun trying.

Historians say that women in the Middle Ages used cosmetics. And women in the middle ages still use them.

Women are unpredictable. You never know how they are going to manage to get their own way.

A glamorous woman is one who looks poured into the kind of dress other women look dumped into.

You've heard about the gentleman who asked "By whom?" when told that the wife was outspoken.

Backbone: what a woman shows a lot of nowadays in her choice of an evening gown.

Eve was the only woman without a past.

A bus driver is one man who isn't afraid to tell a woman where to get off.

One chorus girl to another: "He liked my company, and I just loved his—the Fidelity Trust."

The only trouble in being able to read women like a book is that you are liable to forget your place.

H. L. Mencken once said that when women kiss, "it always reminds me of prize fighters shaking hands."

Woman is about the only creature who, if there is anything she doesn't know, imagines it.

"Good heavens!" cried Whistler as he saw his mother on her knees scrubbing the floor. "Have you gone off your rocker?"

Woman was placed on earth, Charles Dwelley says, to give man a foretaste of both paradise and purgatory.

A woman doesn't really make a fool of a man—she merely gives him an opportunity to develop his natural capacities.

A publisher declares that women don't make good mystery writers. There speaks a man who has never been sent to the supermarket with his wife's shopping list.

Recent surveys show that four out of five women haters are women.

The first woman had to take a rib from a man—and women have been taking ribs ever since.

Jack Herbert observes that women are a lot like ships. If kept in good shape and painted occasionally, they will stay seaworthy.

If you give some women enough rope, they'll hang another clothesline in the bathroom.

Men really understand women—they just make believe they don't because it's cheaper that way.

A woman has two chances to man's one of becoming a success. If she can't get what she wants by being smart, she can usually get it by being dumb.

Ruth Renkel observes that most men have a way with women, but it's seldom their own.

Adrian Anderson says that a woman seldom throws a fit unless there's a man around to catch it.

Why is it that a woman can hurry through a department store aisle eighteen inches wide without brushing against the piled up glassware, then drive home and knock the doors off a twelve-foot garage.

About the time you can read a woman like a book, you'll need bifocals.

Hear about the woman who fastens things on people with snap judgments?

"In my home town," a young thing explained to a mother, "it is considered unlucky for a girl to wear cotton stockings." The mother asked "Why? What happens?" and the girl said, "Nothing."

Conductor: "You ladies can start looking through your purses—I'll be back in ten minutes to take tickets."

There are only two ways to handle women, but unfortunately nobody knows what they are.

The best way to approach a woman with a past is with a present.

Woman is a man's solace, but if it wasn't for her, he wouldn't need any solace.

Harold Coffman says that any man who can see through women is missing a lot.

The practice of putting women on pedestals began to die out when it was observed that they could give orders better from that position.

Now that the highest mountain peaks have been climbed, man has explored everything but the bottom of a woman's purse.

Any woman who takes "no" for an answer is probably making a survey.

A St. Paul department store featured a collection of exquisite plastic shoes. Above them was a large sign: "Shoes of Tomorrow." A little old lady stood there a long time, studying each shoe. Then she asked timidly, "Please sir, what time tomorrow?"

Only a woman could manage to make a man think she is fascinated by his talk about himself and at the same time plan her spring wardrobe.

The Kinsey Report proved just one thing—women like to talk.

High heels, according to Christopher Morley, were invented by a woman who had been kissed on the forehead.

Rex Mobley says that by the time a man understands women, he's no longer interested.

There are only two ways to handle women. Does anyone know what they are?

A woman is only as old as she looks—unless another woman is doing the looking.

Franklin P. Jones says that a woman never forgets her age once she decides on it.

Two men were gazing at Niagara Falls, and one remarked, "If you think that's something, you should see my wife when she cries for a new hat."

Women are funny. They are insulted if you look at them on the street—and disappointed if you don't.

The way to fight a woman, John Barrymore once said, is with your hat. Grab it and run.

If you don't think women are explosive, try dropping one.

WORDS

Sweetest words: "Your dentist has the flu and will have to cancel your appointment today."

When one word leads to another, it generally ends up in a quarrel, a speech, or a dictionary.

WORK

Better to wear out than to rust out.

Paul Garruth says that some men remind us of blisters—they never show up until the work is done.

Two can live as cheaply as one—if both work.

Hard work is an accumulation of things you didn't do when you should have.

If you think you work harder than the average worker, then you're an average worker.

A wife pushed her half-awake husband out of the front door and told the neighbor who had come after him, "He's all right once I get him into orbit."

A doctor examined a man and told him he needed more hard work, and the fellow replied, "But gosh, doc, I'm a piano mover." The doctor replied, "Well, after this, move two at a time."

Applicant to personnel director: "Of course I can give you references—my first husband, Rudy; my second husband, Lee; my third husband, George . . . ."

"Anyone can do any amount of work," Robert Benchley once said, "provided it isn't the work he is supposed to do."

One good thing about being a clock watcher is that you at least know what time it is.

White-collar worker: one who carries his lunch in a briefcase instead of a pail.

Some people get results—others get consequences.

A girl we know prefers the night shift because then she doesn't have to get up in the morning.

"I do most of my work sitting down," Robert Benchley said. "That's where I shine."

Mountain climber: a man who should never lose himself in his work.

Work is the only thing that keeps some men from a job.

The window cleaner is another fellow who has to sponge for a living.

Applicant: "I used to work from dark to dawn in a lingerie shop. I was a nightie watchman."

Overheard in government building coffee bar: "Gee, I'd better get back to the office or I'll be late for quitting time."

Boss to man who had asked for a raise: "You can't come in here and ask for a raise like that. You must work yourself up," and the fellow replied, "But I did—look, I'm trembling all over."

A chorus girl is the only person who gets anywhere by kicking constantly.

An easy chair is a place where you shouldn't be forever depositing your quarters if you want to bank dollars.

Carl Ellstam observes that there is nothing that brightens up your place of work like a beautiful clock on the wall that shows it's quitting time.

The old saying that "hard work never hurt anybody" is probably true today. No one is going to give it a chance.

A youngster defined work as follows: "Work is something other people think for you to do—play is what you think of yourself."

Department head to clerk: "I wouldn't wake you Mr. Jones, if it weren't something important. You're fired."

A person has to work himself to death these days to buy labor-saving devices.

The employment manager asked, "What kind of a position did you have in mind?" and the college graduate replied, "A sitting position, sir."

It has almost reached the point where if a person takes a day off he falls behind in his income-tax payments.

Be careful that you don't garden from daybreak to back-break.

Psychologists say people tend to be dissatisfied with their jobs when they can't see that their efforts achieve something. A dull job, in other words, is one that has no point.

No man goes before his time—unless the boss has left early.

The trouble with a husband who works like a horse is that all he wants to do evenings is to hit the hay.

Harry Oliver reminds us that "nobody ever drowned himself in sweat."

All work and no play, Raymond Duncan observes, makes Jack a dull boy and Jill a well-to-do widow.

The world is full of willing people. Some willing to work—and others willing to let them.

WORLD

In ancient days, common belief was that the world was flat. After centuries of attempting to debunk that theory, common belief is that it's flat on its back.

WORRY

Worry will make almost anybody thin except the people who worry because they are fat.

Blessed is the man who is too busy to worry in the daytime, and too tired to lie awake at night.

Worry: putting today's sun under tomorrow's cloud.

Don't forget that today is the tomorrow you worried about yesterday.

Worry is the interest we pay on trouble before it is due.

Don't worry if you feel despondent. The sun has a sinking spell every night, but it rises again right on time the next morning.

The reason why worry kills more people than work is that more people worry than work.

"Don't worry" is a better motto of ours if we add the word "others."

Brooding over your troubles will surely hatch a lot of them.

Before marriage a man will lie awake all night thinking about something a woman said; after marriage he'll fall asleep before she's finished saying it.

It is said that the fellow who worried yesterday about tomorrow isn't here today.

The fellow who never worries may not be smart enough to know what it's all about.

Doc Rockwell says that worrying about what's in outer space seems rather silly in view of the fact that few of us know what's in the glove compartment of our own automobile.

Ulcers are the direct result of mountain-climbing over molehills.

Don't tell me that worry doesn't do any good. I know better. The things I worry about don't happen.

One woman to another: "The doctor told Leslie he must take off a few pounds. I'm worrying him by telling him I want a mink coat."

Raisins are just grapes that worried too much and got wrinkles.

"If all our misfortunes were laid in one common heap," Socrates observed," whence every one must take an equal portion, most persons would be content to take their own and depart."

If you must worry, do it in advance; otherwise you will miss most of the chances.

Worry is stewing without doing.

WORTHLESSNESS

Useless: a glass eye at a keyhole.

WRECK

There's likely to be a wreck when a deluxe auto runs into a jalopy bank account.

WRITERS

Stanley Walker tells of the author whose works were so little known as to be almost confidential.

Dan Bennett says that if you think no evil, see no evil, and hear no evil, you'll never write a best-selling novel.

Returning from a vacation, a writer of detective stories found his apartment rifled by burglars. On his desk was a note written on his own typewriter: "Figure this one out in your spare time, brother."

The world never recognizes a poet until after his death—and then he is safe.

The dedication for Inez Puckett McEwen's *So This Is Ranching* reads: "Dedicated to my infant grandson, William Craig—the only gent on whom I've ever been able to pin anything."

An author dedicated his first book: "To my wife, without whose absence this book could not have been written."

Franklin P. Adams sent a copy of his book *Nods and Becks* to his former boss, the New York *Post* editor, with this inscription: "To Ted Thackery, who fired me with ambition."

A society woman gushed to Michael Arlen about how she wanted to be a writer and then asked the best way to start writing. "From left to right," he answered brusquely.

Rosemary and Stephen Vincent Benét dedicated *A Book of Americans* to their children thus: "To Stephanie, Thomas and Rachel, our other works in collaboration."

YOUTH

The young man who drives with one hand not only endangers life and limb, but he puts his liberty in jeopardy, too.

F. Robert Becker reminds us that one way to keep youth from slipping away is to hide the car keys.

You are young only once. After that you have to think up some other excuse.

The only way one can stay young in spirit, Sydney J. Harris says, is by fully accepting the fact of growing older.

A twelve-year-old lad recently told his mother that he might start "going steady." "With what?" was her devastating reply.

The younger generation is a group that is similar in many disrespects.

In this age of rock-and-roll it isn't surprising to see a sign in a Brooklyn drugstore: "Teen-age spoken here."

"I've found the secret of youth," Bob Hope declares, "I lie about my age."

The younger generation isn't so bad. It's just that they have more critics than models.

406

A man is always as young as he feels, but seldom as important.

You're only young once, but come to think of it, maybe that's enough.

We don't know what modern youth is coming to—but whatever it is, chances are he'll drive his car into it.

Spare the hot rod and save the child.

After you lose your membership in it, the younger generation seems pretty bad.

Students at a Detroit school christened one of their drinking fountains "Old Faceful."

A modern child is one who, when shown the statue of Venus de Milo, says, "She certainly must have used a harsh detergent."

Dance floor: where youth will be swerved.

Index

Boners, as types of humor: 18
Borden, Richard C.: 87
Borge, Victor: 39, 242, 262, 299
Bos, Carlos: 123
Bottom (the stooge): 7
Bowman, Blanche: 361
Boyett, Ivern: 392
Boyle, Hal: 225
Bradley, Schulley: 114
Bremer, Sylvia Strum: 242
Brody, Sidney: 300
Brook, Clive: 215
Brown, Joe E.: 119
Bruce, Lenny: 26, 121
Bryan, William Jennings: 6
Buchwald, Art: 41
Build-ups, examples of: 77
Bunyan, Paul: 115
Burack, A. S.: 60
Burns, Bob: 361
Burns, George: 89
Burns, Loyd: 219
Bush, Elsa May: 212
Buttram, Pat: 162

Caesar, Sid: 51, 110
Cantor, Eddie: 37, 101
Cartoon quips: 21
Carver, Ron: 58, 62, 86
Cerf, Bennett: 105
Chadwick, Hal: 226, 280, 291
Chaplin, Charlie: 120
Chase, Ilka: 215
Chevalier, Maurice: 138
Classifying humorous material: 26
Coffin, Harold: 251, 305, 368
Coffman, Harold: 400
Collie, G. Norman: 351
Collins, Frederick L.: 312
Collins, Tom: 94
Comedy writers: 26
Comedy Technique (by Robert
  Orben): 80
Comic records: 25
Como, Perry: 298
Conditioning of audience: 14

Connolly, Mike: 323
Considine, Bob: 356
Convention on-goers, as source of
  humor: 22
Conwell, Dr. Russell H.: 111
Cook, Joe: 7
Coolidge, Calvin: 81, 300
Coward, Noel: 9
Cowper, William: 31
Creative humor: 103
Crockett, Davy: 119
Crosby, Bing: 230, 310
Cullen, Bill: 308
Cummings, Bob: 202
Cummings, Parke: 229

Dana, Bill: 25
Darrow, Clarence: 146
Dawes, Charles G.: 133
Definitions, humorous: 58
Dialect, difficulty in using: 31
"Disappointment Theory" of humor: 4
Disney, Walt: 373
Dix, Dorothy: 279, 388
Donnelly, Jack: 156
Double meaning, in dialogue: 66
Droke, Maxwell: 89
Dumb jokes: 56
Duncan, Raymond: 167, 404
Dunne, Finley Peter: 119
Durante, Jimmie: 239, 249
Dwelley, Charles: 399

Eastman, Max: 6, 11, 15, 72
Eden, Sir Anthony: 211
Edison, Thomas A.: 25, 214
Edson, C. L.: 33
Eliot, Charles: 178
Ellstam, Carl: 403
Epitaph, humorous: 75
Evans, Bergen: 119
Exaggeration, as device in humor: 15,
  61

Fadiman, Clifton: 65, 160, 386
Feather, William: 333, 369

413

414

When It's Laughter You're After has been composed on the Linotype in ten-point and eleven-point sizes of Caledonia, a type face created in this century by W. A. Dwiggins, a dean of American type design. Dwiggins has transmitted some of his sly good humor into a lilting calligraphic letter which seems altogether appropriate for this book on American humor.

UNIVERSITY OF OKLAHOMA PRESS

NORMAN